DANIEL
CRAIG
ULTIMATE PROFESSIONAL

DANIEL
CRAIG
ULTIMATE PROFESSIONAL

DANIEL O'BRIEN

Reynolds & Hearn Ltd
London

Front Cover:
The Golden Compass press conference at Claridges Hotel,
London, 27 November 2007

Back Cover (clockwise from top left):
Infamous (2006); *Casino Royale* (2006); *The Golden Compass* (2007);
Layer Cake (2004); *The Invasion* (2007); *Sylvia* (2003); *The Mother* (2003)

First published in 2007 by
Reynolds & Hearn Ltd
61a Priory Road
Kew Gardens
Richmond
Surrey TW9 3DH

A CIP catalogue record for this book is available from the British Library.

ISBN 978 1 905287 85 7

Designed by Chris Bentley.

Printed and bound in Great Britain by MPG Ltd, Bodmin, Cornwall, UK.

CONTENTS

PROLOGUE

I always wanted to be an actor. I had the arrogance to believe I couldn't be anything else.
DANIEL CRAIG

Prior to assuming the mantle of James Bond in *Casino Royale*, Daniel Craig belonged to the well-populated ranks of the almost famous. He'd been around in the theatre, films and television for 15 years or so. Classically trained, having graduated from both the National Youth Theatre and the Guildhall School of Music and Drama, his reputation as a gifted, conscientious and above all dedicated actor had steadily grown.

He'd made an impression with *Our Friends in the North* (1996), an epic BBC drama that gave him his first big break. Stardom remained elusive, however, and Craig continued to work as a jobbing young actor, gainfully employed but still struggling to emerge from the herd. He got another break in *Love is the Devil: Study for a Portrait of Francis Bacon* (1998), cast as Bacon's violent, self-destructive lover. The film scored as an art-house success but not many people paid to see it – and Craig's hard work was overshadowed by Derek Jacobi's magisterial performance as Bacon.

He shone in *Some Voices* (2000), a study of mental illness, yet its target audience was inevitably limited. When Craig landed the starring role in a TV version of *Sword of Honour* (2001), many felt his time had come. In truth, he seemed miscast as an angst-ridden Catholic army officer and the production was a fumbled enterprise. By the time *Sword of Honour* aired, Craig had already taken the Hollywood dollar for *Lara Croft Tomb Raider* (2001), the film of the video game. Like many British actors before him, Craig had the chance to 'Go Hollywood', taking a series of well-paid if undemanding roles in big-budget mainstream films. This went against the grain of Craig's character and he shunned the easy route. The much-derided *Lara Croft* may have raised his US profile but Craig wisely passed on the sequel.

Craig's wariness of playing safe goes back to his Liverpool childhood. He was raised by his mother, an art teacher who nurtured his interest in theatre. But, having studied at the Guildhall, he found the acting profession insular and initially unwelcoming. Craig felt he was a victim of class prejudice, giving him a life-long aversion to the *Brideshead Revisited* school of acting. In some ways, he resembles the generation of working-class British actors who emerged in the 1960s and became international film stars: Albert Finney, Terence Stamp, Michael Caine and, of course, Sean Connery.

I first became aware of Craig when the BBC trailed *Our Friends in the North*. His craggy face and piercing eyes stood out in the highlights montage. No matter that the long wig he wore in the later episodes made him resemble the character who used to introduce *Monty Python's Flying Circus* with a cry of "It's..." To my enduring shame, Craig's name failed to stick with me at that time. He got lost in the crowd in the all-star *Elizabeth* (1998), a film stolen by Australian leads Cate Blanchett and Geoffrey Rush. I didn't pick up on Craig again until *Road to Perdition* (2002), his second major Hollywood movie. He played second fiddle to an uncomfortably cast Tom Hanks, a more assured Paul Newman and pretty boy Jude Law. While Craig had less screen-time than Law, his character – a sadistic-yet-spineless gangster's son – cut deeper. This was a talented actor with great screen presence, but a future blockbuster star? It didn't even occur to me.

After that, Craig won plaudits – and publicity – for filming sex scenes with the 60-something Anne Reid for *The Mother* (2003), but few people liked the movie. I also passed on *Sylvia* (2003), which sounded like another dreary biopic of a tiresome literary martyr (eg, *The Hours*), in which Craig played feminist hate figure Ted Hughes, a gifted if disagreeable gent. And with *Layer Cake* (2004) I was wary of yet another British gangster movie desperate to be the next *Lock, Stock and Two Smoking Barrels*. It also got some lousy reviews.

Then, for nearly two years, Craig was inextricably linked with rumours about the post-Pierce Brosnan James Bond franchise. I have to admit, I didn't see it coming. I had assumed that Brosnan's replacement would be tall, dark and conventionally handsome. I also expected the new Bond to be pitched somewhere between Brosnan and Sean Connery, by common consensus the two most successful 007s. Some had suggested that Clive Owen was the one and only choice. Others claimed that Bond owners Eon Productions wanted a bigger name, favouring Ewan McGregor. When Craig's name came up, I was more than a little surprised, and I wasn't the only one.

Craig certainly wasn't unknown, unlike Bond number two, George Lazenby. But as Bond candidates went, he seemed about as likely as Vinnie Jones or Robbie Williams. (Of course, Craig could at least act…) And when he was formally announced as The New James Bond, debuting in *Casino Royale* (2006), some fans denounced his casting as a terrible mistake. Craig proved them wrong, winning universal acclaim for his portrayal of a grittier Bond, inexperienced, insecure and troubled by killing.

Hailed as the best Bond since Connery, who publicly endorsed his fifth successor, Craig is in a unique position. He has claimed the world's most famous film icon as his own. But whether his enthusiasm endures over the sequels is another matter. James Bond offers an odd, ersatz form of stardom, as the character rather than the actor is the real selling point. Playing Bond doesn't guarantee more than a fleeting brush with fame, let alone a successful acting career.

Just ask George Lazenby. Even Connery, still the number one Bond for many fans, took over a decade to re-establish himself as a star in his own right.

It's said that Craig has become more relaxed in interviews since assuming the role of James Bond. Perhaps he had little choice in the matter. Obliged to face the world's media, he had to develop a thicker skin and a more press-friendly persona or be swallowed up. Plus he's become a lot more experienced fielding questions both professional and personal in a very short space of time. In interviews, he acknowledges his parents' split but remains vague about the details. He refers to his personal relationships – with his mother, father, stepfather, daughter and current partner – without inviting further questions. Interviewed in *Marie Claire*, he seemed downright hostile to the idea: "I'll talk about my work but if you want to talk about my personal life, forget it – it's nobody's fucking business." Craig seems happier discussing his political views, some way to the left of New Labour, and hatred of violence.

He also avoids the showbusiness circuit; as he puts it, "I don't believe in self-promotion, really, I can't be arsed." He has been described as a restless personality, in marked contrast to his con-trolled screen performances. His fingernails look chewed, he fidgets during interviews and converses at breakneck speed. He has a finely honed line in self-deprecating humour, beating potential detractors to the punch. And, like many actors from Brando onwards, Craig has publicly questioned the worth of his profession, equating acting with "showing off," "actorly" talk with bullshit, and telling *ES* magazine that "I don't want to be dressing in costumes and pansying around" – which, if taken seriously, would rule out numerous acting jobs. Interviewed by Liz Hoggard in *The Observer*, he put it bluntly: "At the back of every actor's mind there's the thought: 'Is this where I'm going to be for the next 20 years? Maybe there's an adult job out there for me, one that doesn't involve all of this shit.'"

Yet he discusses his craft with passion, intelligence and insight. And he denies being a Method actor, treating the suggestion as a joke:

I'm not the sort of person who takes my work home with me …
I'm not a Method actor. I get involved on every single level when
I'm doing a film. My job is acting, my job is making sure the
other actors are in a good situation, there's how the film looks,
how it feels. That's the job. That's the method – the method is,
it's a seven-day-a-week job. That's why I take long holidays.

Craig remains committed to the stage and recent theatrical successes include the Royal Court production of *A Number*, which cast him in three roles. But Craig's love for the theatre hasn't blinded him to the shortcomings of some of Britain's more revered theatrical institutions. He once remarked that the prestigious Royal Shakespeare Company needed "a great fucking boot up the arse." Is Craig now the man to supply that boot? Maybe so, but don't expect him to be treading the boards at the RSC any time in the near future.

An undisputed – if reluctant – star on his home ground, Craig is poised to become a major US player, if the cards continue to fall his way and if he really wants it. My guess, though, is that Hollywood feels ambivalent about Craig. He's got the looks, the star quality and now the box-office hit. Yet perhaps the face is a bit too craggy, the expression too sensitive, the suggestion of troubled depths at odds with the demands of mainstream stardom. But if he shows some commercial muscle independently of the Bond franchise, the world is his proverbial oyster.

Craig has worked long and hard to be recognised as an actor, and he will make damn sure that the Bond factor doesn't overwhelm his other achievements. Craig has always given committed performances – well, almost always – even if the overall TV show or movie left something to be desired. Having worked my way through Craig's back catalogue, I've been struck by his consistency and professionalism, often in the face of weak scripts and haphazard direction.

For the time being, James Bond is Daniel Craig. Daniel Craig, however, is a lot more than James Bond.

ONE

'COMMON AS MUCK'

D aniel Craig likes to keep his life story short and simple: "Grew up on the Wirral, left home at 16 or 17, came down to London, did the National Youth Theatre, managed to stay in London somehow, went to drama school, became an actor. There is some other stuff, but really that's it." While this mini-biography is commendably brief, it misses some of the finer details.

Daniel Wroughton Craig was born on Saturday 2 March 1968 in Chester, Cheshire, England. His parents lived at 41 Liverpool Road, though Craig fans intending to make a pilgrimage would probably not be welcomed by the current owners. His father, Tim Craig, had served as a merchant seaman before joining the construction industry as a steel erector. He later became landlord of the Ring O'Bells pub in Frodsham, Cheshire. Craig's mother, Carol Olivia, was a teacher who studied at Liverpool Art College. According to *The Sun*, the attendant midwife wrapped the new-born Daniel in a copy of rival paper *The Guardian* before giving him to Carol Craig. This seems unlikely, not to say unhygienic. Then again, Craig would become an avid *Guardian* reader in later life, though doubtless *The Sun* wished it otherwise.

Little has been made of Craig's unusual middle name. In an article dated 15 October 2005, *The Mirror* gave his father's full name as Tim Wrougton-Craig, though elsewhere he's referred to as plain Tim Craig. Wroughton is also a village in Wiltshire, just south of Swindon. The name dates back to the 14th century and literally means 'farm on the river Worf'. It also provides Craig with a kind of phantom acting antecedent in the form of Richard Wroughton, who lived between 1748 and 1822. Making his debut in Covent Garden aged 20, Wroughton became a mainstay at Drury Lane and even took the liberty of adapting Shakespeare's *Richard II* to better suit his star persona. His picture hangs in the National Portrait Gallery. Incidentally, Richard Wroughton was born Richard Rotten, unlike Johnny Rotten, who was born – and reverted to – John Lydon. So it goes. An actor called Rotten was asking for trouble, so the change of name is understandable. Not to mention fortunate for Daniel 'Rotten' Craig.

Craig's parents divorced early in his childhood. For whatever reason, he is vague about when this happened, citing four, five or six as his age at the time. Most sources give 1972 as the year, when Craig would have been either three or four. Carol took Daniel and his elder sister Lea to live in Liverpool with her parents, who ran the Deva Hotel in Chester. They subsequently moved to Hoylake, Wirral.

Craig dealt with his parents' divorce with a resilience often found in young children. While Carol was now officially a single mother, her offspring didn't become the dysfunctional tearaways of common prejudice. Young Daniel did little to warrant the 1970s equivalent of an ASBO, a friendly clip round the ear. He and some friends stole a few small items from the local corner shop. While the others made good their escape, Craig's attempt to shoplift some crisps resulted in immediate capture. He realised there and then that he wasn't cut out for the criminal life: "Nobody told me the plan so I was slow. I was a crap thief. I never did it again."

Carol soon remarried, to a painter named Max Blond, whom she met via Liverpool Art College. Blond proved both a good stepfather and a friend to Daniel and they remain on close terms. Craig also stayed in contact with his father, who took him to his first Bond movie, *Live and Let Die*, in 1973. The film marked Roger Moore's debut in the series, after Sean Connery's comeback-cum-swansong in *Diamonds are Forever* (1971). While Moore's suave public schoolboy was a long way from Craig's later interpretation of the role, the action set-pieces and voodoo hoodoo made for grand entertainment. Especially for a five-year-old boy in need of a little escapism. Craig also developed a lasting crush on leading lady Jane Seymour. Perhaps it was the way she shuffled her Tarot cards.

Father and son also shared a passion for rugby. Craig would become an accomplished teenage athlete, playing for Hoylake Rugby Club and Birkenhead Park Colts. Tim Craig took his son to watch rugby union matches, a tradition that continued for many years. Interviewed in April 2003, Craig mentioned that they were off to Dublin the following weekend for the last game of the Six Nations tournament. Journalist Gaby Wood characterised Craig as a secret rugby fan. If so, the secret had been revealed in a national newspaper, with Craig conceding that "It's not the coolest thing in the world to like." At least it differentiated him from the showbiz arrivistes who acquired a sudden passion for football to boost their 'lad' appeal. Craig is also a soccer fan, supporting Liverpool Football Club.

Tim Craig's social circle included several musicians, whom Daniel first got to know when his father ran the Ring O'Bells in Frodsham. One of Tim's closest friends was Tony Tyler, an editor on the *New Musical Express*. Growing up around Liverpool, Tyler had known Craig senior since they were seven years old. He became an informal godfather to Daniel and they kept in touch for the rest of Tyler's life.

Standing 6'5", Tyler was a colourful character, to say the least. As a teenager adrift in Hamburg, he played an all-night card game with John Lennon. Tyler then caught pneumonia and was sent home by the British Embassy. During a stint in the Royal Tank Regiment, he became the last British soldier to be injured by a musket ball (really). Moving to London, Tyler watched from backstage when Bob Dylan played with The Band at the Royal Albert Hall in 1966. An accomplished musician in his own right, Tyler played the organ on an Italian-language cover version of Procol Harum's 'A Whiter Shade of Pale'. It was a number one hit in Italy in the summer of 1967. He emigrated to San Francisco with his new American wife and worked as a piano salesman, though he never sold a single piano. Tyler's favourite authors included James Bond creator Ian Fleming. Stricken with terminal cancer in 2006, Tyler was disappointed that he wouldn't live to see Craig's debut as Bond in *Casino Royale.*

Carol Craig was heavily involved with the Liverpool Everyman Theatre. She knew the set designers via the art college and also met a number of rising young actors, including Bernard Hill and Julie Walters. The theatre's star writers included Alan Bleasdale and Willy Russell, whose plays reflected the Everyman's leftist image. Craig tagged along with sister Lea and found himself drawn to the world of acting.

Craig attended Frodsham Church of England Primary School, where he made his acting debut, aged six, in a production of Lionel Bart's *Oliver!* Interviewed by Charles Yates, headmaster Peter Mason recalled being impressed by the infant Craig. "Even at the ages of five and six it isn't very difficult to tell when someone has real ability and talent," Mason said. "We encouraged pupils to take part in prayers and to perform little plays in front of the parents. Both Daniel and his older sister Lea were very good. I could tell even then that Daniel was gifted."

Craig spent holidays with his grandparents Olwyn and Doris Williams, including a cruise around the Norwegian fjords. During this trip, the eight-year-old Craig put on a one-man show he'd devised himself. The result proved a hit with fellow passengers – or were they just being polite? – and Olwyn remained supportive of his grandson's acting ambitions. He died in 2005, aged 96, shortly before Craig was named as the new James Bond.

Tim Craig recalled one of his musician friends asking Daniel what he wanted to do when he grew up – "and without breaking stride he said, 'Be an actor.' I remember at the time blinking and doing a double-take because he said it with such certainty and he was so small." Carol Craig confirms that "Acting is all he ever wanted to do from being a boy."

When Craig was nine, his family moved to Hoylake, situated on the west coast of the Wirral, overlooking Liverpool Bay. Never a classroom star, Craig failed his 11-plus exam and was sent to Hilbre High School, a tough secondary modern in West Kirby, Wirral. He played in the rugby team, which won him a measure of respect and established the all-important 'hard man' credentials.

Craig continued to act, appearing in *Oliver!* (again), *Romeo and Juliet* and a Christmas production of *Cinderella*. His drama teacher, Brenda Davies, remembers, "He came to an audition for *Oliver!* with a friend but he wasn't due to audition for the part. He had a go and got the role. For me he was absolutely superb." Interviewed in *The Mirror*, Davies elaborated, "My jaw nearly hit the floor when he got up on stage. He had such timing and range and he had stage presence for a 13-year-old. I thought, 'What have we here?'"

In *Cinderella*, Craig played one of the Ugly Sisters, wearing heavy make-up, huge earrings and green Wellington boots. By all accounts, Craig was a big hit in the part. Interviewed in *The Mirror*, drama teacher Hilary Green remembered Craig with affection: "He was hilarious. He was always a bit special." Craig's Ugly Sister remains his first and to date only drag role. Former classmate Trudy Kilpatrick recalls Craig as both talented and ambitious: "You knew he was going to go on and do something. People looked up to him because he was a good actor and a few girls fancied him." Though maybe not in drag.

By the time Craig hit his mid-teens, he was clearly not destined for academic success. He later described himself as "failing miserably" at secondary school. Interviewed by Michael Parkinson in 2006, Craig explained, "It just wasn't going that way. I lost interest." To this day, he plays down his intellectual gifts: "I'm not very clever, you see." When Craig left Hilbre High School at 16, his prospects looked doubtful. In the mid-1980s, the rate of unemployment in Britain was at a record high, with Liverpool regarded as one of the worst blackspots. Craig enrolled on a foundation course but soon dropped out. He needed to find a new direction quickly, or join the ranks of the jobless and become just another statistic.

Carol Craig decided that her son's energies would be better

focused elsewhere. Years earlier, she'd won a place at London's Royal Academy of Dramatic Art, one of Britain's most prestigious drama schools. For various reasons, she had been unable to accept the offer, forsaking the chance to become a professional actor for a more stable career in teaching. The latter didn't seem a viable option for her son.

So in 1984, when Craig was 16, the National Youth Theatre came into his life. Carol applied to the NYT on his behalf and sent him to the company's Manchester auditions. Craig won a place at the NYT and waved goodbye to Hilbre High and the foundation course. By the age of 17, Craig was living in London and notching up an impressive list of acting roles with the NYT. As he later explained, "I went to London, because that was the place to go next for the opportunities. I just had a desire to do it … I went to drama school and things clicked. Luck and hard work, and it's been continuous since then." While Craig was diverted by "girls and pubs and parties," no one questioned his commitment to acting.

Craig's parents saw his National Youth Theatre debut in Shakespeare's *Troilus and Cressida*. Craig played Greek general Agamemnon who, as the play begins, has been leading the siege of Troy for seven long years. His first line, "Princes, / What grief hath set the jaundice on your cheeks?", was a challenge to any actor, requiring total conviction. Weary of the long conflict, Agamemnon survives to witness a hard-won victory: "If in his [Hector's] death the gods have us befriended / Great Troy is ours, and our sharp wars are ended." While Agamemnon wasn't a starring role, Craig had a great chance to test his acting muscle. By all accounts, he passed with flying colours. Artistic director Edward Wilson felt Craig showed exceptional promise.

Craig went on international tours with the NYT, visiting Valencia in Spain and Moscow in the then Soviet Union. In 1986, he appeared in a production of T S Eliot's *Murder in the Cathedral*. The role involved a lot of shouting and clenched-fist work. Judging from production photographs, Craig delivered the required menace with aplomb. He also looked good in medieval costume.

Short of cash, Craig worked part-time in restaurants as a waiter and kitchen-hand, time-honoured – if poorly paid – sidelines for struggling young actors. Interviewed by Michael Parkinson, he claimed that being broke never got him down: "When you're that age you don't notice it. It's the next pint or the next bread roll." Craig frequently crashed on friends' floors and is said to have spent more than one night on a park bench. He denies sleeping rough, telling Parkinson that these stories were exaggerated by the press. "I slept out a couple of nights," he said, "usually because I was too drunk to get home." It's even been claimed that Craig would rent flats, delay payment as long as possible and do a bunk before he could be prosecuted. For the record, Craig plays down the image of a starving artist: "I never had that hard a time. I've never considered myself to be in trouble. I did all the jobs I had to do – as long as I was earning money and feeding myself and paying the rent. Other people have it way harder and I feel very blessed."

While Craig had now committed himself to an acting career, progression from youth theatre hopeful to professional performer was neither easy nor guaranteed. When Craig's parents agreed to him dropping out of secondary school at 16, there were strict conditions attached. Interviewed in *The Mirror*, Carol Craig recalled, "I said if he wasn't going to university, he must promise to get into a top drama school – or go back to school."

Craig applied to several leading drama schools, including RADA, LAMDA and the Guildhall, initially without success. Craig particularly wanted to study at the Guildhall School of Music and Drama, based at London's Barbican Centre. After several unsuccessful auditions, he was finally accepted in 1988. For Carol, this showed that her son had made the right choice: "To be one of 25 selected out of tens of thousands proved he had talent."

Craig's fellow students included Ewan McGregor, Rhys Ifans, Alistair McGowan, later a successful impressionist, Damian Lewis and Joseph Fiennes. The three-year course was run by tutor Colin McCormack, an actor noted for his work with the Royal Court and the Royal Shakespeare Company. The Guildhall educated its students in the harsh realities of the acting profession. Craig recalls going to meetings with accountants from the actors' union Equity. The message was short and less than encouraging: "They'd say 90 per cent of you aren't going to work."

Craig's girlfriends at this time included budding model Marina Pepper, whom he met through fellow theatre students. According to Pepper, they lived together for a while. Pepper was later a Page Three Girl for *The Sun* before retiring from the glamour modelling business. When Craig was announced as the new James Bond in 2005, *The Sun* tracked Pepper down for an appropriate sound-bite: "I have gone seven times a night with 007." As kiss-and-tells go, it was brief and – some would say – flattering. Interviewed the same year, Craig seemed unsurprised that a few former acquaintances would cash in on their relationship with him. "If someone in my past decides they want to write about me, there's nothing I can do about it," he claimed. "It's their thing. It's what they're going through."

Craig graduated from the Guildhall in 1991, looking for his first professional break. In the early 1990s, most London-based actors sounded upper-middle-class to Craig. Keen to maximise his job opportunities, he worked hard to lose his Liverpool accent. Craig even grew his fringe long to blend in with fellow young hopefuls. As he told Gaby Wood, these ruses did little for his budding career: "When I left drama school it was Merchant Ivory or nothing." In Craig's case, it was usually nothing. "I think they figured out that I was common as muck."

TWO

NASTY PIECES OF WORK

I f the British acting establishment seemed initially unwelcoming, Craig got his first break from an unexpected source. He later remarked that the only roles available to British actors at the time were either fops or Nazis. Well, almost. Craig made his film debut as a Nazi admirer in *The Power of One*, a big-budget Hollywood movie. He won the role while still at drama school, which must have seemed like the best graduation present imaginable.

Produced for Warner Bros, this anti-apartheid drama was based on a novel by Bryce Courtenay, set in 1930s and 40s South Africa. The producer was Arnon Milchan, an interesting figure in US cinema who had been behind such films as *The King of Comedy* (1983), *Once Upon a Time in America* (1984), *Brazil* (1985), *Legend* (1985) and *Pretty Woman* (1990). The film was directed by John G Avildsen, whose credits included *Save the Tiger* (1973) and the original *Rocky* (1976). His biggest post-*Rocky* hit was *The Karate Kid* (1984); *The Power of One*'s screenwriter Robert Mark Kamen was another *Karate Kid* veteran. *The Power of One* itself starred Stephen Dorff, an American leading man who never made the big time. The supporting cast included Morgan Freeman and John Gielgud, who offered more gravitas than box-office appeal.

Starting at the end of May 1991, *The Power of One* was largely filmed in Zimbabwe. South Africa's apartheid system was still in force and the government had become increasingly twitchy about outside criticism of their faltering racist regime. Shooting a film that attacked white suppression of the black majority on authentic South African locations was out of the question. Zimbabwe seemed an acceptable – and safe – alternative, though President Robert Mugabe's regime had problems of its own. A few years on, of course, the post-apartheid South Africa would welcome filmmakers, whereas Zimbabwe became more or less a no-go zone for white foreigners. Avildsen also shot on location at Charterhouse School, at Godalming in Surrey. Craig had one big scene at this esteemed educational establishment, which didn't take pupils who'd failed their 11-plus exams.

Whatever his opinion of the script, Craig was well aware that, after slogging his guts out for countless NYT and Guildhall productions, he was finally getting paid for his hard work. "And it seemed a huge amount of money to me," he observed, "but it didn't last long, and why would it? I was 21 [23, in fact]. I went and spent it as quickly as I possibly could." Craig also got a free trip to Africa and the chance to work with John Gielgud, one of the giants of the British theatre. All Gielgud's scenes were shot at Charterhouse, back in England. This was just as well, as the 87-year-old actor had become a little too frail for long-distance travel. Craig had a scene with Gielgud but no dialogue, his character lurking in the background. Such are the frustrations of the professional actor. Craig would get to play a proper scene with Gielgud in *Elizabeth* (1998), the veteran actor's last film.

The Power of One opens in 1930 with the birth of PK, the son of liberal English parents who run an isolated farm. Orphaned at an early age, PK is sent to a hellish Afrikaner boarding school, where the English are despised as the scum of the earth. PK is mercilessly bullied by Jaapie Botha (Robbie Bulloch), a borderline psychotic who worships the Nazis. Spat on, pissed on and hung upside down, PK must watch helplessly as his beloved pet chicken is killed by Botha. Will the diminutive PK fight back and teach Botha a lesson? Not yet. This is a John Avildsen movie and the inevitable showdown is still two hours away. Released from the school after the hanging incident, PK is befriended by Geel Piet (Morgan Freeman), an all-wise philosopher and boxing coach. The obligatory training montage is soon underway. Years later, the 18-year-old PK (Stephen Dorff) has dedicated himself to giving the downtrodden black South Africans the education that could improve their lives. With a little boxing on the side.

The Power of One is often predictable and doesn't wear its good intentions lightly. Nominal star Stephen Dorff doesn't appear for the first hour and lacks both the screen time and charisma to carry the film. Telling an anti-apartheid fable through a white character may give the story more mainstream appeal but it also undermines the film's effectiveness. *The Power of One* certainly wasn't the inspirational classic that Warner Bros presumably hoped Avildsen would deliver.

So where is Daniel Craig in all this? Well, Jaapie Botha grows up to be Sergeant Botha (Craig), a brutal police officer. (Botha was also the surname of the then South African prime minister, but this is presumably coincidence.) Craig makes his entrance after 75 minutes, looking menacing in a beige uniform. Assigned to keep track of PK, a dangerous English liberal, Botha makes four brief appearances before Craig says a word. This doesn't exactly stretch his talents, though Craig delivers a good evil smirk during some night-time surveillance. Sergeant Botha isn't identified until his fourth scene, when PK spots a tell-tale Nazi tattoo on the former's arm.

Craig has a memorable first line: "Pisskop! I owe you something, you little bastard!" 'Pisskop' is Afrikaner for 'piss head', a cruel reminder of PK's childhood torment. Continuing as he started, Botha beats one of PK's black friends so severely that he loses the sight in one eye. Craig makes Botha a believable sadist, burning down a mixed-race boxing gym while PK watches aghast. He's also on hand when PK's white Afrikaner girlfriend receives a fatal truncheon blow to the head, though confused editing makes it unclear whether Botha is the culprit. During a police raid on a black township, Botha shoots an unarmed man in the back. By this point, Botha's evil credentials are so firmly established that his actions verge on the risible (how much nastier can he get?). It's a tribute to Craig that Botha never becomes a pantomime villain.

The character has little depth, though the script suggests that Botha is partly the product of a racist culture and a grim, loveless home life. This doesn't stop him from being a complete and utter bastard, underlined by the harsh Afrikaner accent that Craig captures so well. The showdown between PK and Botha is inevitable, good against evil. Cornering PK in the township, Botha makes it clear that the already racist rulebook has been thrown away: "I'll take you in when you're dead, you kaffir-loving shit!" (Kaffir is the Afrikaner equivalent of 'nigger'.) Craig outshines Dorff in the ensuing punch-up, delivering a head-butt with aplomb. The end result is 'Rocky versus Apartheid', with the outcome never in doubt. The only twist is that Botha is killed by PK's one-eyed friend. Craig gives Botha a suitably surprised look as a large piece of wood smashes into his head.

The Power of One opened in the US on 27 March 1992. The reviews were mostly dismissive, some critics condemning the film as an offensive trivialisation of an important subject. In Britain, *Empire* critic Angie Errigo was kinder than most: "Crude, patronising and mawkish, sure, but rescued by excellent performances, beautiful landscape photography, and hard-to-argue-with themes of natural justice, delivered with a punch." With the emphasis on the punch. Craig could take some kudos in having delivered one of the excellent performances, though he was too far down the cast list to get a name-check. Reviewing the film in *Time Out*, Colette Maude noted – somewhat inaccurately – that "The climax is a slugging match between PK and a former school bully which would make Rocky proud."

In this instance, the failure to mention Craig by name was probably no bad thing. Despite Warner's marketing muscle, *The Power of One* failed to find an audience. The film proved that Craig could ably play a violent racist pig. But did it net him many offers?

While Craig had done a good job, he wouldn't make another movie for three years. In the meantime, he secured a part at the bottom of the cast list in Euston Films' glitzy three-part adaptation of the Angus Wilson novel *Anglo-Saxon Attitudes*, which started filming in September 1991 before making its ITV debut in May the following year.

By contrast, Craig's personal life was blooming. He met Fiona Loudon, a Scottish actress and singer, and in 1992, at the age of 23, Craig became a married man. Their daughter Ella was born the same year. The marriage proved short-lived, Craig and Loudon divorcing in 1994. Cynics might speculate that the wedding only happened because Loudon became pregnant and both of them wanted to do the right thing. It's just as likely that they were too young to commit to the relationship. Craig had barely established himself as an actor and, presumably, the demands of marriage and fatherhood were too much for him at the time.

The child of divorced parents, he was now putting his young daughter through the same thing. Like his father before him, Craig stayed in regular contact, maintaining a strong relationship with Ella under difficult circumstances. Craig also remained on civil terms with his ex-wife. Loudon stayed in London, working as a music therapist, which made access a little easier. According to *The Independent*, Craig now refuses to mention Ella by name. Even so, her identity is hardly the best-kept secret.

Craig returned to the theatre in 1992 with a leading role in *No Remission*. This grim drama by Rod Williams was staged by the Midnight Theatre Company at the Lyric Theatre Hammersmith. The story unfolded in a prison cell inhabited by a murderer, a bank robber and a former soldier convicted of manslaughter. Craig played the soldier, an ex-paratrooper who ripped his victim open with his bare hands. This character maintains the calm, controlled demeanour of his military background, yet has fallen hopelessly in love with a young woman named Christabelle. When his cellmates reveal that the girl of his dreams is nothing more than a slut, his cool façade falls apart. *No Remission* was well reviewed, with Craig singled out for praise. *The Independent* noted that the young actor "contains his violence like an unexploded mine." The out-and-out villainy of *The Power of One* left little room for subtlety or depth. *No Remission* reminded audiences – and casting directors – that Craig was a gifted, versatile actor, not just another screen heavy.

On television, Craig secured a bit part in *Covington Cross* (1992). Produced for Thames TV, this offbeat medieval drama series featured Nigel Terry and Cherie Lunghi, who had both appeared in the Arthurian classic *Excalibur* (1981). *Covington Cross* was aimed largely at the US market, where 'medieval fayres' and joust tournaments were still popular (and parodied in *The Simpsons*). Executive producer Gil Grant wanted a *Bonanza* for the Middle Ages, endorsing family values and a conservative outlook in a historical context. The series was filmed on locations in Kent. Craig was cast in the pilot episode, which was shot in March 1992, and billed simply as 'walkway guard'. The role wasn't even big enough to warrant a name.

The US rights to *Covington Cross* were acquired by the mighty ABC network and the series premiered in America on 25 August 1992. Audiences didn't take to the Dark Ages soap opera and only seven of the 13 episodes were screened before the series was pulled. The pilot appeared in the UK the week after its US transmission, so at least Craig's brief walkway walk-on was seen in his native country. But, on both sides of the Atlantic, his first appearance in Ye Olde Englande played to negligible audiences.

Craig also landed a small role in the eighth series of *Boon*, starring Michael Elphick and Neil Morrissey. Elphick played Ken Boon, an ex-fireman turned private investigator cleaning up the mean streets of Birmingham. In its prime, *Boon* was a big hit for Central Independent Television. After seven series, the formula had become stale. Craig appeared in the first episode of the new run, 'MacGuffin's Transputer', broadcast on 8 September 1992. What's a transputer? It's a powerful microchip. Boon's eighth series would be its last and few lamented the show's cancellation.

Craig had a better role in the second season of the BBC series *Between the Lines*. This cop show starring Neil Pearson had an interesting premise, the main characters investigating corruption within the police force. Craig played Joe Rance in the episode 'New Order', which 'wrapped' in July 1992 but wasn't transmitted (as the first instalment of the second series) until 5 October 1993. Rance appears to be a dedicated neo-Nazi. In the first scene, he hangs a pig's head from the spire of a mosque, an insult requiring at least basic knowledge of Muslim tradition (pork is taboo). Rance certainly looks the part, with close-cropped hair, yellow shirt and braces. He later dons the full neo-Nazi 'uniform': bomber jacket, camouflage trousers and bovver boots. Craig's pale blue eyes are used to chilling effect, though his East End accent is perhaps overdone. In one scene, Rance does press-ups wearing only his white Y-fronts, allowing Craig to show that he was already in good shape (though still a long way from *Casino Royale* buff).

Between the Lines specialised in dramatic tricks and 'New Order' is no exception. In the first few minutes, it's suggested that Rance is in fact an undercover cop. When Detective Tony Clark (Pearson) smells a rat, he corners Rance for a covert heart-to-heart. Craig is convincing as both a racist thug – recalling *The Power of One* – and a dedicated policeman operating under great physical and mental strain. Smarter than the lead cops, he can't be intimidated into playing along with them. Clark believes that Rance has gone rogue, corrupted by the fascist brethren he was assigned to infiltrate. Rance certainly seems happy to beat people up to protect his cover. The script – and Craig – keep the audience guessing, right down to the last twist. It seems that Rance has been recruited by the security services for a new job at MI5. Would James Bond approve?

In August 1992, things looked up when Central Television hired Craig for *Sharpe's Eagle* (finally broadcast on 12 May 1993). Set during the Napoleonic era, the *Sharpe* TV films were based on a series of novels by Bernard Cornwell. Sharpe was played by the ruggedly dashing Sean Bean, who got an early break – and memorable death

– in *Caravaggio* (1986), and paid his Hollywood dues with *Patriot Games* (1992). Director Tom Clegg had a background in two-fisted TV action, working on *The Sweeney*, *Space:1999*, *Minder* and *The Professionals*. While Clegg's film credits – *Sweeney 2* (1978), *McVicar* (1980) – were disappointing, he provided a sure guiding hand for the *Sharpe* series. Scriptwriter Eoghan Harris was another *Sharpe* regular, condensing Cornwell's books without losing their appeal.

Set in 1809 Spain, much of *Sharpe's Eagle* was shot on location in the Ukraine, which offered appropriate terrain and lower labour costs. It's not one of the best in the series. The script seems over-written, the clichés falling thick and fast, and there's some chronic over-acting. Craig plays Lieutenant Berry, who sports long dark hair as black as his soul. Sidekick to the chief junior rogue, Berry proves the star attraction in the bad-guy stakes. Posh of accent and thuggish of manner, Berry watches soldiers running in the heat with open contempt: "Good God! Look at Dobbs dragging his feet." It's not the most punchy first line for a character, yet Craig infuses it with real feeling.

Berry despises the whole world, especially the poor working-class troops who don't have the money or connections to escape their lowly status. While Berry is written as a blackguard pure and simple, Craig makes something of the character. Berry treats his 'friend' and patron with a thinly veiled scorn that the latter is too stupid to notice. A sadist and misogynist, he wants to rape and horsewhip a defenceless Spanish Countess. Sex and violence are the same to a man devoid of empathy or humanity. Protected by his rank and uniform, Berry can indulge his brute appetites with little chance of reprisal.

It's inevitable that Berry will clash with the decent Captain Sharpe, a humble infantryman risen through the ranks due to his courage and leadership skills. They first knock heads – figuratively speaking – after 20 minutes, Berry backing down at sight of Sharpe's rifle. During a later bout of fisticuffs, Berry gets an early advantage, only to be cut short when others intervene. While dramatic necessity – and the ongoing franchise – dictate that Sharpe will emerge triumphant, Craig looks more than a match for Bean. Berry wounds Sharpe during a night-time mission, kicking him when he is down (how low can you go?). When Berry is knifed in the back by Sharpe's sidekick, the message is clear: this posh-talking scum isn't worthy to be killed by a true hero.

As a married man with a baby daughter to support, Craig was under pressure to favour well-paid jobs over quality scripts. He therefore agreed to a showy role in *The Young Indiana Jones Chronicles* (1993), co-produced by Amblin, Lucasfilm and Paramount. This TV series was a prequel to the popular *Indiana Jones* trilogy, devised by George Lucas and Steven Spielberg, which had kicked off with *Raiders of the Lost Ark* (1981). The concept was inspired by the prologue to *Indiana Jones and the Last Crusade* (1989), which featured the late River Phoenix as the teenage Jones. *Young Indiana Jones* starred Sean Patrick Flanery, as Phoenix wanted to concentrate on his film career. While series co-creator Lucas served as an executive producer, director Spielberg was busy elsewhere.

Craig was cast in the episode 'Palestine, October 1917', in which Indiana Jones helps British and Australian troops take the Turkish-occupied town of Beersheba during World War I. The Turks have placed explosives in the town's wells, a water supply of huge strategic importance. Can Jones infiltrate Beersheba, locate all the bombs and defuse them before the Australian Lighthorse Regiment storms the town walls? It's a long shot, but it just might work.

The director was Simon Wincer, an expatriate Australian who scored a big hit in the US with the TV Western serial *Lonesome Dove* (1989). Wincer's feature films included *Quigley Down Under* (1990), an offbeat 'Australian Western' starring Tom Selleck. The largely British supporting cast in 'Palestine, October 1917' featured Catherine Zeta Jones, marking time between her UK TV hit *The Darling Buds of May* (1991-3) and her Hollywood break in *The Mask of Zorro* (1998). Zeta Jones plays a Mata Hari-type spy who aids Jones on his mission (or does she?). The cast also included one-time

Doctor Who Colin Baker and actor-comedian Ben Miller. Craig played Captain Schiller, head of German intelligence in Beersheba.

'Palestine, October 1917' is scrappily assembled, with too much stock footage, including action highlights from director Wincer's *The Lighthorsemen* (1987), which covers the same historical events minus Indiana Jones. On this evidence, Sean Patrick Flanery is a charisma-free zone, making him a poor substitute for Harrison Ford. Jones' allies include T E Lawrence (Douglas Henshall), a real-life war hero immortalised in the film *Lawrence of Arabia* (1962). While Henshall gives a game performance, he's no match for Peter O'Toole. Catherine Zeta Jones is veiled much of the time, performing a PG-rated belly dance to excite the enemy soldiers but keep TV network bosses happy. The major plot twist involves Zeta Jones' character and she proves more fearsome than nominal arch villain Craig.

Schiller is a standard-issue bad guy, with no hint of depth. Sporting a twirlable moustache, Craig plays him as an arrogant swine who's not as sharp as he thinks he is. Craig's German accent is more believable than his dialogue, which includes the gem, "Eat lead, you swine!" Perhaps writer Frank Darabont felt that a World War I espionage tale was essentially a Western or even gangster movie in fancy dress. Craig does a fine line in impotent rage without losing a sense of menace. The effete Schiller has problems with the desert climate ("This heat is unbearable") yet strikes poses with relish. Grappling with Jones, Schiller puts the jackboot in before eating his own share of lead.

'Palestine, October 1917' finally received its US TV premiere on 14 August 1993. The episode was later released on video in an expanded version retitled 'Daredevils of the Desert'. If nothing else, this modest tale of junior-league espionage gave Craig his first taste of classic Hollywood escapism. True, it was a small-screen spin-off from a much bigger movie franchise, with neither George Lucas nor Steven Spielberg playing a hands-on role. While Lucas never called on Craig again, the Spielberg connection – however tenuous – would prove more rewarding.

Craig experienced a change of pace with the sitcom *Drop the Dead Donkey*, then in its third series. Made by Hat Trick productions for Channel 4, this popular show was set in the offices of a TV news company, with topical political gags added just before recording. Lines were often written on clipboards and bits of paper, as the cast had no time to learn them. Craig appeared in the episode 'George and His Daughter', first shown on 11 March 1993, and shared a scene with Neil Pearson, star of *Between the Lines*. The guest cast also included a pre-*EastEnders* Patsy Palmer, partially hidden behind glasses.

Shot on videotape, *Drop the Dead Donkey* was largely studio-bound. Episodes were recorded in front of an audience, whose laughter featured heavily in the final sound mix. This particular episode shows its age and the lack of subtlety grows wearing. There are some laughs, but the script is never as witty or biting as the show's reputation would suggest. Craig plays Fixx, a dodgy squatter who runs a gang of petty thieves, including the runaway teenage daughter of series regular George (Jeff Rawle). Dressed in a leather coat and combat trousers, he also sports a gold chain and gold earring. While Craig's rugged features and piercing eyes make Fixx appropriately menacing, he's verging on camp. Craig does his best with some weak dialogue but it's a losing battle. Fixx is written as a cliché and his brief screen time offers no opportunity for nuance.

A Cockney geezer, with accent to match, Fixx has a nasty streak. In his second scene, he also has a very bad shirt. Fixx proves to be all bluster without his sidekicks. The diminutive George (Jeff Rawle) vanquishes him armed only with a toasting fork: "You're a cowardly bully with all the charm of a parasitic infestation." The cowed Fixx is forced to stand on one leg and sing 'The Birdie Song'. It's a fair bet that Craig didn't include this scene in his showreel. Nevertheless, he deserves points for steely professionalism in the face of adversity.

Casting directors knew by now that Craig could do tough and menacing, with an accent if required. But the resulting parts offered him little chance to shine. *Covington Cross* was a literal non-starter,

Boon had passed its sell-by date and *Young Indiana Jones* wasn't likely to draw much US interest. *Drop the Dead Donkey* was still in its prime, but people watched it for the regular cast. Who noticed the one-off supporting actors? On top of which, Craig's episode gave no indication of his comedic skills, which might have broadened the roles on offer.

Having shown his acting chops in *Between the Lines*, Craig marked time with an episode of Yorkshire TV's more lightweight cop series *Heartbeat*, starring former EastEnder Nick Berry as a cheery rural policeman. Set in the 1960s, the series was pitched straight at the nostalgia market, accompanying the action with a selection of classic pop songs. Craig appeared in the third series episode 'A Chilly Reception', transmitted on 31 October 1993. He played Peter Begg, a prodigal grandson and unwelcome ex-boyfriend.

Next up was the BBC Screen Two film *Genghis Cohn*, which was shot in June 1993 and broadcast the following March. Director Elijah Moshinsky had recently made the BBC's Kingsley Amis adaptation *The Green Man*, where drunken womaniser Albert Finney defeats a paedophile ghost but loses his wife and mistress. Screenwriter Stanley Price had worked in films since the 1960s, scripting the 'swinging' caper movie *Arabesque* (1966). The cast for *Genghis Cohn* was headed by Anthony Sher, Robert Lindsay and Diana Rigg. The concept was outlandish, skirting the realms of bad taste. In the late 1950s, German policeman Schatz (Lindsay) – a former SS officer – is haunted by the ghost of Genghis Cohn (Sher), a Jewish comedian he murdered during the war. Despite game performances, neither script nor direction did full justice to the idea. Craig played Lieutenant Guth, who replaces the increasingly demented Schatz. Experienced in both German accents and brutish authority figures, he delivered the goods with practised ease.

While Craig's television work was mostly piecemeal, he continued to prosper in the theatre. He won a leading role, or roles, in the 1993 production of *Angels in America: A Gay Fantasia on National Themes* by US playwright Tony Kushner. Set in 1985 at the height of the conservative Reagan era, this epic state-of-the-nation drama had been a smash hit on Broadway. *Angels in America* consisted of two parts, 'Millennium Approaches' and 'Perestroika', running over seven hours. 'Millennium Approaches' received its UK premiere at the Royal National Theatre in 1992, directed by Declan Donnellan. The following year, the National Theatre staged the British premiere of 'Perestroika', alongside a revival of 'Millennium Approaches'. Donnellan directed once again and 'Perestroika' opened on 20 November.

Angels in America was a great showcase for Craig. It was also extremely demanding. Craig played four roles, notably Joe Pitt, a Republican Mormon from Utah. Pitt has moved to New York to work for lawyer Roy Cohn (Henry Goodman). A real-life figure, Cohn served as Senator Joseph McCarthy's right-hand man during the notorious anti-Communist 'witch hunts' of the 1950s. In *Angels in America*, Cohn gleefully recalls his role in having Julius and Ethel Rosenberg executed for passing secrets to the Russians. Pitt discovers that the ultra-conservative, ultra-patriotic Cohn is not all he seems. A vindictive hypocrite, Cohn has been brought down by a promiscuous, bisexual private life he would publicly condemn in others; Cohn died of AIDS in 1988.

Pitt has secrets of his own. A deeply conservative man, he is also gay, struggling to repress his sexuality by marrying childhood sweetheart Harper and praying to God for deliverance from his 'curse'. The marriage is a disaster, Harper seeking refuge in chemically induced stupor while Pitt takes long walks at night looking for male company. When he becomes involved with Louis Ironson (Jason Isaacs), a neurotic Jewish clerk whose ex-boyfriend is suffering from AIDS, Pitt is briefly liberated from his old life. This chance to be himself is fumbled, Pitt alienating Louis, Harper, Cohn and even his ultra-religious mother.

Craig captured the character's contradictions very well. Pitt starts off as a decent, if stifled man, trying to live a life he knows to be a lie. He loves Harper while acknowledging that he can never be in love with her. He admires Roy Cohn despite an increasing realisation that the man is a raging monster. When Louis appears on the scene, Pitt's initial bemusement turns into a longing for salvation. Ultimately, Pitt will be left behind by everyone, doomed by his inability to be honest with himself.

Deservedly acclaimed for *Angels in America*, Craig returned to the theatre in 1994 for *The Rover*. This Restoration comedy was written in 1678 by female playwright Aphra Behn. Staged by the Women's Playhouse Trust, the production also featured Dougray Scott, Andy Serkis and Cecilia Noble. The plot of *The Rover* has three roistering English mercenaries enjoying a night on the town in Naples at carnival time. As comedies go, Behn's play is too dark for some tastes, featuring pillage and attempted rape in addition to the expected ration of swashbuckling. Directed and designed by Jules Wright, the Women's Playhouse Trust production was certainly imaginative – the action was staged in a sand-filled arena, around which the actors travelled on bikes and rickshaws. Then, over a ten-day period, director Tony Coe reworked Wright's production, complete with 72 tons of sand, for the BBC's Open University Production Centre. This "support video for the second level course A210" brought Craig's talent to a wider – well, telly-watching OU student – audience.

Later in 1994, Craig accepted a supporting role in the BBC television film *Saint-Ex*, which began shooting in September. Directed by Anand Tucker from a script by Frank Cottrell Boyce, this drama-documentary centred on Frenchman Antoine de Saint-Exupéry, daring aviator and author of the children's classic *The Little Prince* (1943). The title role was played by Swiss actor Bruno Ganz, a memorable Jonathan Harker in *Nosferatu* (1978).

The stellar British supporting cast included Miranda Richardson, Janet McTeer, Ken Stott and Eleanor Bron. Craig played Guillaumet, de Saint-Exupéry's best friend and fellow flying ace. A charismatic, inspirational figure, Guillaumet survived a serious crash in the Andes mountain chain, only to be killed in World War II. Craig did well in the part, yet *Saint-Ex* spurned the conventional biopic format, alternating the dramatised scenes with documentary interviews and an attempt at visual poetry. *Saint-Ex* was belatedly premiered at the London Film Festival on 17 November 1996, drawing comparisons with *The English Patient*, also released in 1996, which could hardly work in its favour. The BBC then screened the film on 25 December as part of its *Bookmark* strand of literary documentaries, where it was inevitably overlooked in the packed Christmas schedule.

Having made his professional debut in a Hollywood film, Craig finally repeated the experience with *A Kid in King Arthur's Court* (1995). Produced for Disney, this offered a juvenile variant on Mark Twain's *A Connecticut Yankee in King Arthur's Court*, which had been filmed several times before. The kid was played by Thomas Ian Nicholas, already a TV veteran, and the supporting cast of slumming British actors featured Joss Ackland, Art Malik, Ron Moody and a young Kate Winslet. The film was shot on locations in the UK and Hungary, where labour costs were temptingly low for American producers.

Craig had few illusions about the worth of the project; director Michael Gottlieb had a shaky track record, including *Mannequin* (1987) and *Mr Nanny* (1993). So, money aside, *A Kid in King Arthur's Court* had little to tempt Craig. True, it was an American movie, offering his first big-screen role since *The Power of One*. Perhaps Craig was also drawn by the chance to play a good guy. Ever since wielding his rhino-whip as Sergeant 'Pisskop' Botha, he'd been veering towards typecasting as a brutish bad guy: *Young Indiana Jones*, *Drop the Dead Donkey*, *Sharpe's Eagle*, even *Between the Lines*.

Aimed squarely at the US market – both kids and exasperated parents – *A Kid in King Arthur's Court* wraps a positive message about self-confidence and assertiveness in a half-hearted medieval fantasy. The Olde Englande clichés are supplemented by the introduction of Big Macs, bubblegum and rollerblading in the halls of Camelot. Ackland's ageing King Arthur has really let himself go – thanks to poor costuming, he appears to be wearing a cheapo T-shirt under his royal robes. The only non-Caucasian actor is the Pakistan-born Art

Malik, who plays the lead villain. While no one would accuse the producers of having a hidden racist agenda, the effect is unsettling. Doubtless Malik, like Craig, was grateful for the work, but this wasn't progressive casting.

Back in medieval costume for the first time since *Covington Cross*, Craig at least had a character name this time around – Master Kane, the King's master at arms, who is charged with teaching the nerdish title character the fine art of combat. Sporting an ill-advised long fringe, Craig wears a leather jerkin and very tight breeches. This cut-rate medieval ensemble doesn't flatter him one bit. Craig gives an uneasy performance, with a so-so pseudo-posh accent. Forsaken by the script and director, he gets through his scenes with gritted teeth, suggesting a desperate longing to be elsewhere.

It doesn't help that Craig's character has very little to do. Master Kane gets his own subplot: a commoner in love with a princess (Kate Winslet). Can their romance triumph over adversity and social convention? Of course; it's a Disney film. While this sounds workable on paper, Craig is denied a real share in the action. His big scene comes towards the end, as Kane jousts with the evil Lord Belasco (Art Malik). Even here, Craig makes way for a stuntman once the visor goes down. Knocked off his horse, Kane loses consciousness while his beloved princess and the precocious kid save the day. Master Kane would be Craig's most ineffectual performance until Alex West in *Lara Croft Tomb Raider*.

A Kid in King Arthur's Court opened in US cinemas on 11 August 1995, during the school summer holidays. Trade journal *Variety* described it as "run-of-the-mill," and how right they were. The film didn't click with audiences and went straight to video in the UK, two years after its US premiere. Under the circumstances, neither Craig nor Winslet was too downhearted.

THREE

GRIM UP NORTH, AND ELSEWHERE

y the end of 1994, Craig's career hadn't really progressed since *Sharpe's Eagle*. He'd given a good account of himself in *Between the Lines*, but neither *Heartbeat* nor *A Kid in King Arthur's Court* were anything to write home about. There were hundreds of young British actors vying for the smallest bit parts in TV shows and movies, hoping that the next role could be the big break. Many were more conventionally handsome than Craig. Most were middle class and didn't fret that their accents would have casting directors slamming the door in their faces. As it happened, some BBC producers were casting a major role that didn't require pretty-boy good looks or a posh voice. Quite the opposite, in fact.

So it was that Craig won a starring role in the BBC's epic serial *Our Friends in the North*. Ten years in development, this state-of-the-nation drama was one of the corporation's most ambitious productions. The script was written by Peter Flannery, who'd struggled to interest the BBC in a story centred on working-class characters from Newcastle.

Craig played George 'Geordie' Peacock, a good man doomed by circumstance, ill fortune and his own short-sightedness. His co-stars were Gina McKee, Mark Strong and future Doctor Who Christopher Eccleston. At the time, Eccleston had the highest profile, with lead roles in the films *Let Him Have It* (1991) and *Shallow Grave* (1994);

he was also a regular in the hit crime series *Cracker* (1993-4). The supporting cast included Alun Armstrong, who had taken a bloody beating in the Newcastle-set gangster movie *Get Carter* (1971), and Peter Vaughan, a fine villain in *Straw Dogs* (1971) and the 1970s sitcom *Porridge*. The BBC also secured the services of Malcolm McDowell, who was cast as charming villain Benny Barratt.

McDowell's career was an interesting case-study for Craig. Born in 1943 in Leeds, he emerged during the late 1960s as one of Britain's most promising young actors. *If ....* (1968) made McDowell's name, but it was Stanley Kubrick's controversial *A Clockwork Orange* (1971) that turned him into probably the best-known British film star in the world, give or take Sean Connery's James Bond. This early success didn't last, however, partly due to the declining fortunes of the British film industry. Indeed, McDowell reached his nadir playing a Nazi in swastika underpants in *The Passage* (1978). From this point on, McDowell was largely typecast as a villain in such films as *Cat People* (1982) and *Blue Thunder* (1983). Hitting the booze'n'drugs with a vengeance, he did little of consequence for the next decade.

While McDowell was a wealthy man who worked in films on a regular basis, his career offered a classic example of dazzling early success followed by a long, long slide into mediocrity. It says something that McDowell was ready to leave his Los Angeles home for a co-starring role in a BBC TV serial. After a string of nothing roles (*Tank Girl* anyone?), he welcomed the chance to show that he could still cut it as a serious actor. Craig, by contrast – denied a shot at early stardom – had steadily built his theatre, film and television credits, alternating the big paydays with quality material. Perhaps this was the better route to take, for all the frustrations along the way. Craig never wanted to be in the position where all he had to show for ten years of acting work was a respectable bank balance.

Our Friends in the North was filmed over ten months, from November 1994 to September 1995. Early on, there were production problems and several key scenes had to be re-shot. Three directors were employed on the serial – Stuart Urban, Pedr James and Simon

Cellan Jones – which suggests creative clashes.

The first episode, '1964', was broadcast on 15 January 1996. This opening instalment focuses on Nicky Hutchinson (Eccleston), an idealistic undergraduate who returns from a summer in the US with dreams of changing the world. Nicky's attitudes are contrasted with those of his more down-to-earth friend Geordie, first seen sitting on a swing in his best (only?) suit. A self-styled ladies' man, Geordie dreams of pop stardom, and Craig ably conveys the character's wide-eyed fantasies of a world forever beyond his grasp. In reality, Geordie is trapped by an impending shotgun wedding, the result of a drunken one-night stand.

Witty and sharp-tongued, Geordie's confident exterior is a mask for a man in torment. His alcoholic father is a violent bully (a scarily believable performance by former comedian Willie Ross). Craig shows a man eaten up by sadness, desperation and – above all – the terror of taking after his father. Beaten by Gordon Peacock, Geordie finally fights back, felling his father with a head-butt. Far from being a moment of triumph, this retaliation sees Geordie at his most wretched. Hitch-hiking south, he heads for London in search of something – anything – better than the life he knew back home. He ends up sleeping rough on a park bench, an overnight stop Craig allegedly knew well from his student days. Geordie's bemused reactions to life in London make great use of Craig's subtly expressive face, an asset barely called upon in his previous TV and film roles. An uncomprehending witness to police corruption (one of the serial's main themes), Geordie bides his time waiting tables.

In episode two, '1966', Geordie falls in with Soho vice king Benny Barratt (McDowell). Affable and generous towards his loyal employees, Barratt becomes a father figure for Geordie. By episode three, '1967', London is swinging and Geordie cuts a sharp figure in a dinner jacket. He looks very much the businessman, with leather briefcase and handcuff accessory. Harsh reality rears its head when Geordie is obliged to turn on old friends. An affair with Barratt's mistress, also his prize whore, can only lead to heartbreak. In one devastating scene, Geordie briefs his girlfriend on her next client – a bent cop – while crying his eyes out. In this one scene alone, Craig proved he was now an actor of the first rank. His line "I shouldn't love you" becomes a cry from the soul.

Episode four, '1970', sees 1960s optimism dead and buried. Now sporting long hair – probably the best of the wigs on display – Geordie has no illusions left and no hope. He sticks with Barratt because he doesn't believe anything better exists for him. Reunited with Nicky, Geordie outlines his philosophy of life: "Things are this way because that's the way things are." Craig's piercing eyes have dulled and his features have set into numb resignation. Geordie's apathetic, apolitical outlook is contrasted with the activism of Nicky, now an anarchist journalist. Both will discover that they're treading a path to nowhere. Geordie talks back to corrupt policemen but remains a pawn. Leaving London, he links up with a single mother and her young daughter. Craig brings Geordie alive again, his warmth and tenderness coming to the fore. By this stage, the script's treatment of Geordie is becoming a little predictable. Just as things are looking up, he is brought back to earth with a painful thud. Unable to escape his past, Geordie is framed on obscenity charges when he returns to London.

By episode five, '1974', Geordie's only solace comes from fantasies of revenge against Barratt, who helped put him away for three years. Geordie's smile as he dreams of putting on a smart purple cravat is wiped away by the grim reality of his cell. Released from prison, Geordie seeks refuge in booze. Craig captures his slurred, drunken speech very well, evoking the spectre of Gordon Peacock, though the gurning expressions are perhaps overdone. Pulling himself together, Geordie attempts real-life vengeance on Barratt, only to be frustrated by the latter's arrest. Alone and aimless, he returns to Newcastle.

Episode six, '1979', sees Geordie on the pull with Tosker (Mark Strong) at the disco. As The Bee Gees belt out 'Stayin' Alive', he draws female interest but it's an empty conquest. Now a drug dealer for bent cops, Geordie sits alone in a squalid flat, lamenting his lost love.

Another quest for justice, or at least vengeance, leads nowhere. Craig does righteous anger very well, maintaining audience sympathy for Geordie despite his reduced screen-time and dubious occupation.

At this point, Flannery seems to be running out of things for Geordie to do. There's an element of repetition to his storylines, with correspondingly predictable outcomes. Geordie is absent altogether from episode seven, '1984', and makes only brief appearances in episode eight, '1987'. Now a bumbling, shouting derelict in London, Geordie fails to recognise a shocked Nicky. Mentally ill, he maintains a sense of humour but can't connect with the harsh Thatcher's Britain that has left him to rot. Having set his hostel mattress on fire, Geordie receives a life sentence for arson. Craig is heartbreaking as Geordie is shocked back into a terrible reality. A lost soul, Geordie joins an escape from a prison van, only to return a few minutes later. The tragedy of Geordie's life is that a gaol cell has become the only stability he knows.

Episode nine, '1995', sees Geordie back in Newcastle, a down-and-out with thick-lensed glasses. Failing physically and mentally, Geordie is a passive spectator in a world he no longer comprehends and perhaps never did. Craig plays him as hunched, beaten and lost, with just hints of the old humour and spirit. A scene where Geordie plays keyboards with an Animals tribute band is strangely moving. Invited into Tosker's home, he sleeps on the floor next to a deluxe four-poster bed. Geordie still tries to do the right thing, receiving a head-butt for his pains. It's the story of his life, with Craig expressing resignation rather than pain or anger as Geordie is knocked down once again. A crucial issue remains unresolved: is Geordie fated to follow in his deranged father's footsteps? While the script is non-committal, Craig's performance suggests that Geordie's innate decency will be his salvation.

Our Friends in the North brought Craig national recognition and a slew of job offers. Unfortunately, the latter were all for the same kind of role: rugged northerners with an eye for the ladies and a sensitive soul. While Craig owed a lot to Geordie Peacock, he didn't want to stay in his shadow. Wary of typecasting just as his career was taking off, Craig turned down all similar parts. The tabloid press also showed an interest in Craig, for a short time. He was offered coverage in various lifestyle magazines. Unwilling to trivialise his work as a serious actor, Craig declined to become part of the media circus. Ten years later, as the new James Bond, he would have little choice in the matter.

Craig's first television appearance after *Our Friends in the North* was in the US series *Tales from the Crypt*. Produced by Home Box Office (HBO), this collection of ghoulish stories was inspired by William M Gaines' infamous 1950s horror comics of the same name and was now in its seventh and last season. After season six, production had shifted from California to England, presumably for reasons of economy, with indigenous directors and character actors getting involved as a result.

Craig appeared in the episode 'Smoke Wrings'. The story was the 12th and last of the show's British-lensed season and was shot over a mere four days, ending on 28 February 1996. Although the series was based at Ealing Studios, 'Smoke Wrings' itself was shot on location at a multi-storey office block on the Great West Road between Chiswick and Isleworth. British director Mandie Fletcher was best known for the sitcoms *Blackadder II* (1985) and *Blackadder III* (1987), and the episode's multi-national cast included the Scottish Denis Lawson, the German Ute Lemper and the American Gayle Hunnicutt, whose son Nolan Hemmings had worked with Craig on *Sharpe's Eagle*. The end result was watchable, run-of-the-mill horror fare, more notable for its production gloss than any inspiration in the writing or direction. Craig is a weird young ex-con, Barry, who becomes a pawn in murderous power games at an ad agency, conspires with a not-all-he-seems derelict in the boiler room, unleashes a mind-altering device in the offices above and ends up defenestrating himself, with fatal consequences. For Craig, the show offered a welcome payday, brief US television exposure and not much more. Who watched *Tales from the Crypt* for the guest cast? 'Smoke Wrings' premiered in the US on

21 June 1996.

Craig also won a leading role in *Obsession*, a French-German co-production that started shooting in September 1995 but only reached German cinemas some two years later. The film was directed by German filmmaker Peter Sehr, who also wrote the script with his wife Marie Noelle. The director of photography was David Watkin, whose credits included *Help!* (1965), *The Charge of the Light Brigade* (1968), *The Devils* (1971), *The Three Musketeers* (1973), *Chariots of Fire* (1981), *Out of Africa* (1985) and *Hamlet* (1990). For Craig, Watkin's career evoked a glorious era of British cinema that ended long before he became a professional actor. *The Charge of the Light Brigade* was released the year Craig was born. *Chariots of Fire* hit cinemas when he turned 13. Now well past retirement age, Watkin continued to work on an intermittent basis. With the British film industry in a perpetual state of crisis, he and Craig found themselves embroiled in a continental co-production that stood little chance in the international market place.

The stars of *Obsession* were German actress Heike Makatsch and French actor Charles Berling, who had appeared in the arthouse hits *Nelly & Monsieur Arnaud* (1995) and *Ridicule* (1996). Craig took third billing, a reflection of his negligible status outside British theatre and television. The cast also included veteran US actors Seymour Cassel and Allen Garfield. *Obsession* was largely filmed on locations in Berlin and Munich, though the co-production deal obliged Sehr to shoot a certain amount of the film in France. While the story hardly required it, cast and crew therefore decamped to Paris and Dijon in the Côte d'Or.

Obsession focuses on Miriam (Makatsch), an organ scholar who plays trumpet in a pop group and at funerals. (This may be a reference to Makatsch's VJ past; she also contributes to the soundtrack.) Her boyfriend is Pierre (Berling), an earnest French research scientist. Their stable relationship is disrupted by John MacHale (Craig), a stonemason from Zimbabwe hired to do restoration work in Berlin. MacHale has another reason for visiting

Berlin, though, by the time the end credits roll, few viewers will care.

Sad to relate, *Obsession* is a dud in most departments, despite the talent involved. The film's main assets are the evocative tightrope imagery and an effective use of Felix Mendelssohn's 'Violin concerto, Opus 64'. The rest is one long fumble in the dark. There are interesting elements but little is made of them. Throughout *Obsession*, one question remains unanswered: what is this film about? Whatever the makers' intentions, *Obsession* soon turns into clunky melodrama, with unengaging characters who don't ring true. Most of the film is in English and scriptwriters Sehr and Noelle clearly had problems working in a second language. Even Craig is defeated by some of the weak dialogue. His co-stars, neither of them native English speakers, have no chance.

There are signs that Craig's role was reduced in post-production, including an unexplained cut on his forehead. Makatsch and Craig have chemistry, but the script gives them no chance to shine. Craig looks like a man in need of guidance that never comes. He does okay with the German dialogue and also plays the harmonica, or least mimes with conviction. This doesn't add much to the character, though it serves to link MacHale with Miriam on a musical level. The photography emphasises Craig's sandy eyebrows, normally an underplayed feature.

Craig is better served by the wardrobe department than the script or director. He cuts a striking figure in his long black coat and blue jeans. Dressed in a blue T-shirt and pale denims, Craig bears a passing resemblance to Steve McQueen in *The Great Escape* (1963). At this point in his career, however, he lacked McQueen's humour and lightness of touch. (There are rumours, hopefully unfounded, that Craig will play McQueen in a future biopic.) On the downside, Craig also wears an odd blue-grey 'mod' suit, which does him no favours.

Obsession's confused intentions are evident from the first scene. In the opening section, MacHale assists an elderly man (Cassel) suspected of shoplifting. Acting on impulse, he head-butts a security guard, then seems surprised when the police arrest him. Faced with a deportation order, MacHale goes on the run for a while – literally in one scene – living and working undercover. He is obsessed with an old film of a tightrope walker crossing the Niagara Falls. Convinced that the footage is somewhere in Berlin, he's eventually proved right, though the script declines to explain how or why. The lost film is connected to MacHale's family secret – his grandfather shot his grandmother out of jealousy – though this revelation lacks dramatic force, and the parallel modern-day love triangle is tedious. While Craig flashes his butt, even diehard fans may regard this as insufficient compensation.

When the action, such as it is, shifts to France, *Obsession* disintegrates. MacHale hangs around in wardrobes, his increasingly bonkers behaviour emphasised by close shots of Craig's intense blue eyes. Some scenes anticipate Craig's role in *The Mother*, though not in a good way. *Obsession* reaches its nadir with the following exchange:

```
PIERRE: What's going on?
MIRIAM: John is destroying his wardrobe.
PIERRE: What?
MIRIAM: Because I love him. And because he
loves me. And I treat him like shit.
```

A return trip to Berlin leads to a double revelation both daft and ineffective. We are left with a trio of self-absorbed characters who merit no interest or sympathy. On balance, *Obsession* is pretentious claptrap that thinks it has something to say about the human condition. It's a fair bet that Craig and his agent had something to say when they saw the final cut. *Obsession* wasn't released to UK cinemas and remains unavailable in Britain in any format.

The film may not have made it to Britain, but Heike Makatsch soon did. Born in Düsseldorf in 1971, she was the daughter of a teacher and a retired ice hockey player turned lawyer. She achieved fame as a presenter and VJ on a German music video channel called Viva. At just 23, Makatsch was earning over £100,000 a year, rather more than Craig had managed at that age. She drew the attention of Robbie Williams, who appeared on one of her talk shows during his Take That days. Williams gave Makatsch his mobile phone number, though she declines to say if she gave him a call.

At the time of *Obsession*, Makatsch had recently made her film debut in *Männerpension*, a successful romantic comedy. Cast as an aspiring singer afflicted by a lisp, she received favourable reviews for her performance. Makatsch quit television shortly afterwards to focus on her acting career. She was immediately taken with Craig – "I liked him straight away" – and they became a couple, sharing a home in north west London. Though Makatsch had relocated to England, her career was still based in Germany. For the time being, this seemed a viable arrangement.

Back in the UK, Craig now needed an eye-catching role that would banish the image of Geordie Peacock from viewers' minds. He therefore took a supporting part in Granada Television's *The Fortunes and Misfortunes of Moll Flanders*, based on the 1722 novel by Daniel Defoe. Directed by David Attwood, this two-part serial was scripted by Andrew Davies, who rose to prominence with the quirky BBC comedy-drama *A Very Peculiar Practice* (1986) and scored big hits for the BBC with *House of Cards* (1990), *Anglo-Saxon Attitudes* (in which Craig had featured in 1991) and *Pride and Prejudice* (1995).

Moll Flanders starred Alex Kingston, who had played small parts in *Covington Cross* and *Saint-Ex*. The cast also included Diana Rigg, who had appeared in *Genghis Cohn*. And cameraman Ivan Strasburg had shot *Sharpe's Eagle*, another action-packed period piece, though the action in *Moll Flanders* was of a different nature. Craig played charming rogue James 'Jemmy' Seagrave, the one great love of Moll Flanders' life. He filmed a passionate sex scene with Kingston which had to be toned down for network television. The more explicit material – 'too hot for TV' – was restored for the video and DVD releases.

Location filming took Craig close to Frodsham, Cheshire, where his father once ran the Ring O'Bells public house. The pub was still managed by Tim Craig's second wife, Shirley Lewis, whom he married in 1974. When they split, she stayed on at the Ring O'Bells and remained its landlady for the next three decades. Craig made a point of visiting the Ring O'Bells when he was in the area and dropped in with Alex Kingston.

Told as a gaol cell flashback, *The Fortunes and Misfortunes of Moll Flanders* is a curious combination of bawdy romp and social tract. The script emphasises the plight of women, especially the 'low-born', in a world where success and power are only achieved through money. The style tends towards the arch, Moll addressing the camera as she ponders her many predicaments. There's little in the way of subtlety and Kingston is too knowing – and too old – to convince as a virginal 18-year-old. Both victim and opportunist, Moll rides the wheel of fortune as foundling child, servant, mistress, wife (five times), widow (twice) and mother (of six). Along the way, she becomes an accomplished con artist and thief. Kingston is at her best during Moll's confession to a shocked Catholic priest, showing a comic touch barely hinted at in other scenes.

Craig has less screen time in *Moll Flanders* than his second billing would suggest. He makes his entrance after 45 minutes, appearing at Moll's carriage window. Looking dashing in a wide-brimmed hat with feather, Craig offers a winning smile, then vanishes without a word. Having caught Moll's attention, Jemmy Seagrave isn't seen again until the closing minutes of the first half. Adorned with a long dark brown wig, Craig utters his first line, "Delighted", as Seagrave is formally introduced to 'Lady Flanders'. He doesn't adopt a posh accent, a hint that the scheming Seagrave may not be the landed gentleman of reputation. Moll and Jemmy are kindred spirits, fortune hunters posing as aristocrats.

Craig has more to do in part two of *Moll Flanders*, contributing some good eye work when Moll balks at confessing her sins to the priest. He also adopts a suitably manly stance, given his costume, clenched hands on hips. Once Jemmy has become Moll's fourth husband, their respective charades must end. Craig shows the steely quality beneath Seagrave's surface charm. While Jemmy really falls for Moll, he talks business mid-smooch. Betrayed by his treacherous 'sister', Seagrave is poised to run her through until Moll intervenes. Craig and Kingston have good chemistry, conveying the tenderness and passion that bonds the couple even as their paths diverge. During the big sex scene, Craig pays close attention to Kingston's left breast, presumably because this suited the camera angle better.

When the money runs out, Jemmy turns outlaw. While Craig makes a passable dandy highwayman, he also captures the unhappiness beneath the bravura. Leaving Moll behind, Jemmy is generous to her after a fashion, offering stolen booty to atone for his absence from her life. When Craig disappears from the story, the audience misses him almost as much as Moll does. Even the brief all-girl action is insufficient compensation. A prison reunion is surprisingly poignant, while the more perfunctory happy ending has Moll and Jemmy transported to the Virginia colonies. A written coda informs us that they went on to acquire the wealth and status that had eluded them back home. There's a moral here, somewhere. Craig gives a strong performance in *Moll Flanders*, light-years away from Geordie Peacock in *Our Friends in the North*. It's just a shame that he's denied sufficient screen time for the relationship between Moll and Jemmy to gain much depth.

Moll Flanders appeared on ITV on 1 December 1996, nearly three weeks after making its US debut. The serial was a big ratings hit, helped no doubt by the well-publicised sex scenes. Its success on both sides of the Atlantic took Kingston to America and a co-starring role in the hit medical soap opera *ER*. Craig also received some attention, mostly from the tabloid press who'd pursued him after *Our Friends in the North*. He refused to play along and stopped doing interviews for a time.

A few weeks before *Moll Flanders* hit UK TV screens, Craig was seen in *Kiss and Tell* (1996). Produced for London Weekend Television, this run-of-the-mill crime drama was directed by David Richards from a script by Heidi Thomas. The plot centred on a troubled cop determined to prove that a missing woman was murdered, possibly by her husband. The cast also included David Bradley, who had given a moving performance as an idealistic-yet-doomed Labour MP in *Our Friends in the North*. This time out, Bradley played Craig's exasperated superior officer.

Cast as Detective Matt Kearney, Craig ably conveyed a man whose life is a step away from falling apart, both personally and professionally. He couldn't do much with the far-fetched plot, which has Kearney persuading his ex-girlfriend – a psychologist – to seduce the husband into making a confession. As Kearney eavesdrops on their intimate conversations, he becomes increasingly jealous. The twists and turns fail to grip and Craig's role is by its nature passive much of the time. While Craig had given an honourable performance, under the circumstances, he was clearly marking time once more. *Kiss and Tell* was first shown on 9 November 1996, with its US transmission following on 15 June the next year.

Back at the BBC, Craig played another troubled cop in *The Ice House* (1997), a daft murder mystery based on a novel by Minette Walters. Director Tim Fywell had a track record in thrillers, notably *A Fatal Inversion* (1992) from the book by Ruth Rendell, and the famous *Cracker* episode 'To Be a Somebody' (1994), featuring Robert Carlyle as a shaven-headed psychopath. Director of photography John Daly had worked on *Genghis Cohn* and *Our Friends in the North*. Craig received top billing for *The Ice House*, a reflection of his rising status in the industry, given that his character hardly dominates the proceedings and there are other big names in the cast, including Corin Redgrave and Frances Barber. The supporting actors included Willie Ross, who played Craig's father in *Our Friends in the North*.

Despite its pedigree, *The Ice House* suffers from a ludicrous script, with an unbelievable storyline and unconvincing characters. The premise involves three women, an isolated country manor and a body in the ice house. The plot unwinds with doses of implied lesbianism, male chauvinism, dark secrets and domestic violence.

Craig plays Detective Sergeant Andy McLoughlin, a Scottish cop with brooding features and a dour manner. Craig's Scots accent is okay despite early detours into Scouse. In his first scene, McLoughlin has an intense moment at the water cooler, suffering acute migraine and hand tremor. This policeman's lot is not a happy one. He also needs to brush up on his diplomacy towards minority groups. "I've nothing against dykes, Miss Cattrell," he says. "Just wouldn't stick my finger in one." This brash manner soon evaporates when McLoughlin pukes up at the sight and smell of a mouldering corpse. His wife has left him for another man and McLoughlin can't handle it, snogging a 'lesbian' suspect who taunts him over his obvious drink problem.

While *The Ice House* is mostly utter tosh, Craig's character becomes very interesting. The growing sympathy and attraction between McLoughlin and murder suspect Anne Cattrell (Kitty Aldridge) is intriguing and well acted. Outsmarted by Cattrell, McLoughlin responds with sexual aggression before realising that he likes her as a person and not just as a conquest to boost his flagging macho pride. McLoughlin is both a randy copper – with dialogue to match – and a lost soul. After saving Cattrell's life, he gradually shows a more sensitive side. Interviewing a victim of childhood rape, McLoughlin rediscovers the humanity that has been numbed by police routine, a failed marriage and alcohol. He learns a tough lesson in life's harsh realities but also finds redemption.

Alas, Craig's intriguing portrayal must give way to plot mechanics. The melodramatic denouement resembles *The Archers* gone loco and the final twist is predictable. As hinted early on, McLoughlin is happy to let natural justice prevail over legal niceties. The ending is romantic but also stupid. *The Ice House* was first shown on 5 April 1997. *Independent* writer Rowan Pelling was struck by "an intense young actor with deeply unsettling light-blue eyes and an almost feral degree of erotic appeal." Craig was clearly making an impression, even when constricted by the demands of a second-rate murder mystery.

Craig returned to the horror genre with a role in *The Hunger*, a TV series hosted by urbane 1960s icon Terence Stamp. The show was made by Scott Free Productions, a company headed by sibling directors Ridley and Tony Scott. The title derived from Tony Scott's cult 1983 vampire movie, best known for a lesbian love scene featuring Catherine Deneuve and Susan Sarandon. Craig appeared in the series' second instalment, 'Menage a Trois', first screened on 20 July 1997. The episode was directed by Jake Scott, son of Ridley, from a script based on a story by horror specialist F Paul Wilson. The biggest name in the cast was American actress Karen Black, whose more notable films included *Easy Rider* (1969) and *Nashville* (1975). Black's horror credits were also respectable: the TV movie *Trilogy of Terror* (1975) and the haunted house pic *Burnt Offerings* (1976).

But 'Menage a Trois' is nobody's finest (half) hour. The possession theme lacks originality and Jake Scott's background in music videos is evident in the pseudo-arty visuals. While the self-conscious direction – all flash cuts and jittery camerawork – calms down after a while, there's little style and zero substance.

The plot centres on an old dark house and a strange old lady in a wheelchair. This is Miss Gati (Black), who lives with Jerry Pritchard (Craig) and a succession of home helps. Craig is first seen perched on a stair, rolling a cigarette with practised ease. Jerry's job is a little vague, a handyman whose handiness is left unspecified. The new help is Steph Reynolds (Lena Headey), an attractive young nurse. The sexual tension between Jerry and Steph is well handled by the actors. Their sex scenes include a tasteful silhouetted liaison and a rough-and-ready kitchen table quickie. Steph soon asserts herself as the dominant partner, which seems to please Miss Gati no end. The predictable plot twist means a bad end for Jerry. Some sources claim that Craig also has a sex scene with the considerably older Karen Black, which would have been a useful dry run for The Mother. This isn't the case, though, given the tricksy lighting and editing, it's easy to see how the mistake was made.

The most interesting thing about 'Menage a Trois' is that Craig plays the dumb blond. This gender reversal depicts Jerry as a naïve opportunist exploited, abused and ultimately destroyed by female sexual predators. Far from offering a pseudo-feminist angle, the end results reeks of misogyny.

In the wake of *Our Friends in the North*, Craig's television career marked him as a talent to watch without conferring definite star status. *Tales from the Crypt* and *The Hunger* were negligible schlock-horror credits that offered brief US exposure but little chance of consequent job offers. *Kiss and Tell* and *The Ice House* were run-of-the-mill crime dramas shown in peak-time slots. While the latter proved a good vehicle for Craig, the conventions of the genre gave him limited room for manoeuvre. *Moll Flanders* scored a hit in most departments but Craig was not the main attraction, taking an emphatic second place to star Alex Kingston. Increasingly, it seemed that television – good, bad or indifferent – would not give Craig the big break he needed.

FOUR

RAGING IN THE DARK

C raig was appearing in major TV productions but had yet to emerge as an A-list leading man. It's been claimed that he'd already decided to focus on the cinema as a long-term goal. At this point, however, his tentative film career had gone very quiet. Supporting roles in two flop movies, and another that failed to escape from Germany, didn't make for much of a CV to tempt potential employers.

It was clear to Craig that Hollywood wouldn't come calling any time soon. This in itself didn't bother him overmuch. He knew from experience that American money didn't guarantee good scripts or strong roles. Craig wanted to play intriguing characters in high-quality projects that would reach a wide audience. In the meantime, he remained in demand for theatre work. In 1997, director Peter Hall offered him a leading role in the Old Vic production of *Hurlyburly*. Written by David Rabe, this off-Broadway hit examined the movie business and masculinity in a way that could be read as either pro-feminist or rampantly misogynist.

In *Hurlyburly*, Craig and Rupert Graves played Hollywood casting agents, both divorced, who get smashed out of their heads on booze and drugs. The unfortunate women in their lives are treated appallingly. As with *Angels in America*, Craig had to affect an American accent, which he did with some success. The cast also included Andy Serkis, from *The Rover*, and genuine American Elizabeth McGovern, best known for being raped by Robert De Niro in *Once Upon a Time in America*. One performance was interrupted by a bomb scare. Rather than cancel the show, the cast performed the last 20 minutes of *Hurlyburly* on a green outside the theatre. This demonstration of commitment and initiative impressed audiences and critics alike.

Craig then ventured back into Euro-filmmaking with *Love & Rage*, which was shot between November 1997 and January the following year. This bizarre Anglo-Irish-German period drama was co-produced and directed by Cathal Black, who had made an impressive debut with *Pigs* (1984), a dark comedy set in a Dublin slum, following it up with *Korea* (1995). The script, by Brian Lynch, was based on James Carney's book *The Playboy and the Yellow Lady*, which told a strange real-life story. Craig played James Lynchehaun, a charismatic psychopath who promoted himself as a Republican hero and inspired J M Synge's classic 1907 play *The Playboy of the Western World*.

Love & Rage starred Greta Scacchi, an Anglo-Italian actress who got early breaks in *Heat and Dust* (1983) and *White Mischief* (1987) prior to a brief taste of the Hollywood big-time in *Presumed Innocent* (1990), in which she was Harrison Ford's ill-fated mistress. While Scacchi looked stunning, she tended to be cast as cool, seductive and manipulative femme fatales who didn't generate much audience sympathy. (She has the distinction of having turned down the role in *Basic Instinct* that subsequently went to Sharon Stone.) Also in the cast was Stephen Dillane, who had appeared with Craig in the 1993 National Theatre production of *Angels in America*, and veteran Donal Donnelly, whose long career took in *I'm All Right Jack* (1959), *Waterloo* (1970) and *The Dead* (1987).

The film was partly shot on Achill Island, County Mayo, Ireland, where the actual events took place. The producers also shot some scenes on the less authentic Isle of Man, which offered tempting tax breaks to filmmakers. According to Eugene Finn, an expert on Irish cinema, the production was troubled, which might explain the shift in location and uneven end result. The action opens in 1903, then flashes back seven years to 1896. The accompanying voice-over hints at a dark tale indeed. The ensuing drama is both gloomy and whimsical, though the Irish clichés are kept to a minimum: soda bread, tin whistles, wolf hounds, fiddles and dancing. There's also a game called hit-the-barrel-man, which shouldn't be attempted at home.

Craig is first seen mounted on a dark horse, wearing a black wide-brimmed hat. Could this be in any way symbolic? Wealthy English divorcee Agnes MacDonnell (Scacchi) likes what she sees: "Now there's a superior specimen ... wild and animal-looking." During a horse race on the beach, Lynchehaun reveals himself as aggressive and competitive. He's also a cheat and a thug, leaving one opponent with a broken collarbone.

Agnes is spirited and independent. Her divorced status is a big deal in 19th century Catholic Ireland, as is her Englishness. A wealthy outsider, Agnes is also a snob, patronising her employees and acquaintances. Ready for some excitement, Agnes is captivated by Lynchehaun's rough charm and tendency to walk around bare-chested. Lynchehaun is an experienced poacher and a lousy pianist. He's also manipulative, playing people against each other. Within a short time, Lynchehaun is Agnes' tenant, then her agent, running her considerable estate.

Craig manages a passable Irish accent and his charisma goes some way to sustaining an ill-defined character. He also gives a fair rendition of the folk classic 'All Around My Hat'. The script is full of loose ends: why is Agnes so quick to believe the eavesdropping Lynchehaun, a cold seducer who gets in some practice with her maid? He also flirts with Dr Croly (Stephen Dillane), Agnes' one real friend, though the film remains vague about the nature of this male bonding. Having tried on some false whiskers in secret, Lynchehaun impersonates a doctor of theology to give a sermon in Agnes' local church. These strange games win Agnes over and the ensuing love affair leaves her breathless on the floor. While the 'artistically' shot sex scenes grow tedious, Craig can fake an orgasm with the best of them.

Lynchehaun is a bright-eyed predator, sexual and otherwise, but who is he and what does he want? Even with Agnes under his spell, Lynchehaun persists with the masquerade and role play, but to what purpose? He confesses to patricide but then claims to be fibbing – "Aren't I a good actor?" (Craig, a fine actor, plays a ham actor with some relish, though the drunk routine wears thin.) Lynchehaun seems to represent something, but what? Agnes' repressed sexual desires? The revenge of the Irish working class on their English overlords (and ladies)? Agnes' 'punishment' for defying social convention? The Devil himself? A Republican subplot leads nowhere until the closing scenes and Lynchehaun's boast, "I'm the very devil of a man," is too obvious to be taken at face value.

Writer Brian Lynch and director Cathal Black seem clueless about where the film is heading and what they want to achieve. The violence and sadism are unpleasant, if largely off screen, and the botched psycho-nutter finale is nothing more than a gender-reversal *Fatal Attraction* in period costume. A protracted Grand Guignol coda prompts only one question: what the hell is going on? Truth may be stranger than fiction but it doesn't always make for good drama, especially in these hands. While Craig emerges with honour intact, the film is a poor vehicle for his talent.

It's only fair to add that *Love & Rage* has its defenders, including Eugene Finn: "Black's most mature and his most flawed work, *Love and* [sic] *Rage* adventurously blends historical melodrama and high-gothic motifs to re-examine Ireland's colonial history." But, as with *Obsession*, *Love & Rage* didn't make it to UK cinemas or the home video market. The film was chosen to open the Dublin Film Festival in April 1999 but wasn't seen again until 2001, three years after its completion. So far, Craig's starring roles weren't getting him noticed in his native country.

Craig juggled his star turn in the virtually invisible *Love & Rage* with a supporting role in the widely seen *Elizabeth* (1998), the story of Queen Elizabeth I, the Virgin Queen. This rare British epic began shooting in September 1997 and was produced by Working Title for Channel 4 and PolyGram. Budgeted at $25million, *Elizabeth* was directed by Indian filmmaker Shekhar Kapur from a script by Michael Hirst.

Opening with a burning at the stake, *Elizabeth* is historical drama as conspiracy thriller, with a taut script, brisk pace and muscular direction to match. While some have noted its debt to *The Godfather* (1972), *Elizabeth* is much more than a gender-reversal copy in big dresses and doublet-and-hose. Elizabeth was played by Australian actress Cate Blanchett, whose film credits included *Oscar and Lucinda* (1997). The exceptional supporting cast featured fellow Australian Geoffrey Rush, an Academy Award winner for his performance in *Shine* (1996), as Sir Francis Walsingham, the Queen's trusted adviser and occasional hitman.

The British contingent was led by Richard Attenborough, John Gielgud (from *The Power of One*), Craig's fellow Guildhall graduate Joseph Fiennes, Christopher Eccleston from *Our Friends in the North*, and Terence Rigby, who had unsettled Craig's Geordie in the first instalment of the same series. The more offbeat casting included footballer Eric Cantona, TV quiz host Angus Deayton and the then-unknown Lily Allen. Compared to *Obsession* and *Love & Rage*, Craig had slid way down the cast list, from star to supporting player. Former co-star Eccleston took third billing, behind Blanchett and Rush. Craig was billed eleventh, just above Deayton, who only appeared in one scene.

Craig makes his entrance after an hour, hanging out at the Vatican with Pope John Gielgud. Craig plays militant Catholic priest John Ballard, a man with a mission to kill England's Protestant queen. Dressed in a dark habit, Craig cuts a shifty figure. In *The Power of One*, he'd shared a scene with Gielgud but no dialogue. Here they have a brief exchange, neatly sketching in the Pope's support for Elizabeth's murder. Ballard is issued with a Papal Bull which absolves the Queen's assassin of guilt and guarantees him a place in Heaven. This Catholic licence to kill is the 16th century equivalent of James Bond's

MI6 authorisation. Despite sharing the 'JB' initials, Ballard is no prototype 007. If anything, he resembles a Bond villain's sidekick, with a fanatical devotion to duty and no sense of humour.

While Craig has minimal screen-time in *Elizabeth*, his presence is well used. As Ballard alights from a boat, Craig is framed in a low-angle close-up that matches his blue eyes with the sky. The shot appears to have been faked in the studio, but it's a striking image nevertheless. Better informed than his co-conspirators, Ballard takes a rock and smashes the skull of one of Walsingham's spies. Craig claims to have improvised this brutal assassination technique during filming. Hopefully, he informed the other actor before the cameras rolled. While the actual skull-cracking is obscured, Craig's energetic rock-work lends the act conviction.

Dressed in a hooded black cloak, Ballard later advances on Elizabeth in unnerving slow motion. This figure of death is interrupted, however, leaving the Queen shaken and stirred but unharmed. The implication, of course, is that Ballard came close to killing Elizabeth with his own hands. This may be historically questionable but it makes for great drama. Ballard is captured by Walsingham while celebrating a forbidden Catholic mass. He's hung up and burned with a torch. While Ballard says nothing in the scene – apart from expressions of discomfort – it's clear from later events that he confessed. The Papal hitman may give it out but he can't take it.

Elizabeth opened in the UK on 2 October 1998. Reviews were positive, *Guardian* critic Richard Williams calling it "the very model of a successful historical drama – imposingly beautiful, persuasively resonant, unfailingly entertaining." Craig had appeared in an acclaimed, commercially successful movie, but had anyone really noticed him? His improvised rock-bashing moment deserved points for initiative, but the film belonged to Cate Blanchett, first and foremost, and Craig stood little chance of standing out in a cast that included Geoffrey Rush, Christopher Eccleston, Richard Attenborough, Kathy Burke, Edward Hardwicke and John Gielgud (in his last film role).

As things turned out, Craig didn't have to fret about being lost in the crowd, because he had a 'here's one I made earlier' ace up his sleeve in the form of *Love is the Devil: Study for a Portrait of Francis Bacon*. This far less conventional biopic had opened in UK cinemas just two weeks earlier – and in this one, Craig had a fully fledged leading role.

Produced by the BBC, with French and Japanese finance, *Love is the Devil* was written and directed by John Maybury. Maybury had worked as an editor and production designer for the late Derek Jarman, an outspoken gay filmmaker. Their collaborations included *Jubilee* (1978) and *The Last of England* (1988), which struck some viewers as a bold personal vision and others as unwatchable self-indulgence. Maybury later directed music videos for Cyndi Lauper, The Smiths, Boy George and Sinead O'Connor, among others. *Love is the Devil* had been in development since 1994, two years after Francis Bacon's death. While the budget was modest, Maybury commissioned a score from Japanese composer Ryuichi Sakamoto, who'd shared an Academy Award for *The Last Emperor* (1987).

Regarded as one of the greatest artists of the 20th century, Francis Bacon had an unmistakable style, rendering the human figure as a screaming grotesque or pustular slab of meat. During the 1960s and 70s, he had an unconventional relationship with George Dyer, a petty thief who first met the painter while breaking into his flat (so the legend goes). Bacon was played by Derek Jacobi, who had achieved stardom in the classic BBC serial *I, Claudius* (1976) and was at the time of filming best known for the TV series *Cadfael* (1994-8), a medieval murder mystery that proved more popular than *Covington Cross*. The supporting cast included Tilda Swinton, a Derek Jarman regular from *Caravaggio* (1986) to *Blue* (1993), the director's last film. She also starred in *Orlando* (1992), where Queen Elizabeth I was played by legendary 'Stately Homo' Quentin Crisp.

Pushing 30, Craig maintained a busy social life during the shoot. Jacobi recalls him indulging in all-night drinking sessions, arriving on set the next morning after just two hours' sleep. While Craig remained a consummate professional during working hours, his stamina was pushed to the limit.

Love is the Devil was a somewhat esoteric project, a stylised biopic of strictly limited audience appeal. None of this mattered to Craig. The role of George Dyer was the strongest he'd had since Geordie Peacock. The film wouldn't make much money but he would get noticed. Researching the part, Craig discovered that there wasn't much hard information on Dyer. His former criminal associates were tight-lipped about him and Dyer had been a marginal underworld figure who attracted little interest at the time.

Maybury's film is an art movie with guts. His striking, if self-conscious, direction emphasises the terrible beauty of violence and death. None of Bacon's paintings are seen in the film. It was assumed that the artist's estate denied permission for their use, or just asked for too much money. Whatever the reason, it's a shame that the portraits of Dyer weren't used. Maybury attempts to recreate Bacon's style on film, with murky shots of naked male bodies splashed with gore. Jacobi's uncanny portrayal of Bacon nearly steals the show. He also gets the best lines, such as "Champagne for my real friends! Real pain for my sham friends!"

To play Dyer, Craig had his hair and eyebrows dyed an unsettling shade of black. Dyer literally falls into Bacon's life during a botched break-in. Freaked out by the artwork and the artist, Dyer still proves an instant pick-up, becoming Bacon's lover and muse. Used to hanging out with East End criminals, Dyer is lost in Bacon's world, which focuses on a drinking club called The Colony, run by Muriel Belcher (Swinton). Sipping nervously on a glass of white wine, Dyer eyes Bacon's social set – painted queens, assertive dykes and self-styled bohemians – with both suspicion and incomprehension. Craig captures this confusion very well, Dyer getting aggressive at any perceived slight or insult.

Straight actors playing gay are invariably asked if they feel uneasy or uncomfortable filming love scenes with another man. Craig didn't find the role of Dyer difficult: "That was some of the easier stuff to do, because it was always clear and made a lot of sense. It's when things are unclear and when you don't know what you're doing – that's when things are difficult." Neither actor's sexuality – Jacobi is openly gay – had common ground with the dark romance of Bacon and Dyer. The latter carefully removes his expensive new clothes – including cufflinks – prior to a bout of sado-masochistic sex. Dyer winds a leather belt around his fist with loving precision. Only in the bedroom does he gain the upper hand over Bacon.

It's notable that the love scenes do not involve nudity, though Craig reveals all while reclining in a bath tub. He didn't regard nude scenes as a big deal, telling *The Daily Mirror*, "In today's world we expect female actresses to go naked so why not men?" When Ewan McGregor bared all – in *Trainspotting* (1996) and *Velvet Goldmine* (1998), among others – he received a lot of media attention. By comparison, Craig's full-frontal scenes in *Love is the Devil* and *Some Voices* caused little controversy, perhaps because they were serious dramas lacking the 'hip' appeal of the McGregor films.

Craig likes his characters to be "a bit weird" and Dyer certainly qualifies. Both amoral and innocent, he soon loses his bearings, seeking refuge in booze and pills. One memorable image has Dyer dozing on a casino couch while a vacuum cleaner glides by. When the action's over, he has nowhere to go. Dyer is even left out in the rain while Bacon cheats on him with a younger pick-up. Dyer's impotent rage is just one aspect of his self-destructive nature. Retreating to his old East End haunts, he drunkenly holds forth in a pub, buying champagne for everyone with Bacon's money. Torn between two worlds he can never fully embrace, Dyer eventually disintegrates. Bacon can be a mean, bitchy old queen but the film suggests that he genuinely cared for his neglected, patronised lover. Craig felt that the seven-year relationship between Bacon and Dyer must have had an element of true love.

Love is the Devil premiered at the Cannes Film Festival in May 1998, opening in the UK on 18 September. *Time Out* reviewer Gilbert Adair enthused, "The performances are terrific", singling out Jacobi for praise. Added *The Daily Mail*, "Craig is extraordinary." The film received little exposure in the US, though *Variety* critic David Rooney was impressed, calling it "unconventional, audacious and uncompromising in every sense." And nowhere more so than in Craig's uninhibited portrayal of Dyer.

In due course, Craig would work for John Maybury again in the 2004 movie *The Jacket*. In the meantime, he appeared alongside Heike Makatsch (plus the disembodied voice of Derek Jacobi) in Maybury's BBC documentary *TX: The Museum of Memory*, broadcast in June 1999 and described as a "visual meditation on memory, an avant-garde comedy employing elements of pop video, travelogue, state-of-the-art digital effects and a score by Daniel Goddard." Also in arts documentary vein, Craig would play 'the artist' in a December 2000 instalment of LWT's *The South Bank Show* devoted to artist Marc Quinn, in which the latter joined up with director Gerald Fox "to create a fictional art film which brings visual art alive." The presenter, as he had been ever since the show's inception in 1978, was Melvyn Bragg.

Craig had by now become a fixture in British movies, leaving television behind for the time being. In 1998 – in the run-up to the release of *Love is the Devil* and *Elizabeth*, and three years on from *A Kid in King Arthur's Court* – he was cast in his third Hollywood movie, *I Dreamed of Africa*. This Columbia production was based on the autobiography of Kuki Gallmann, a wealthy Italian who turned her life around after a car accident left her seriously injured. Leaving Venice for Kenya, Gallmann ran a farm with her young son and new husband. Published in 1991, Gallmann's book was a bestseller. The film rights were optioned by producer Stanley Jaffe, whose hits included *Kramer versus Kramer* (1979), *Fatal Attraction* (1987) and *The Accused* (1988). Gallmann, who served as a production consultant, had script approval and very little dramatic license was allowed.

Budgeted at $35 million, *I Dreamed of Africa* required a major US star to play Gallmann. Jaffe sold the project to Kim Basinger, who'd got an early break in the 'unofficial' James Bond movie *Never Say*

Never Again (1983), which featured Sean Connery's last appearance as 007. By 1998, she had unexpectedly become a hot property again in Hollywood, after winning the Best Supporting Actress Academy Award for *L.A. Confidential* (1997). Basinger's romantic interest was Swiss-born actor Vincent Perez and the supporting cast included Eva Marie Saint, who had co-starred in *On the Waterfront* (1954) and *North by Northwest* (1959), and Winston Ntshona, a Tony Award-winning actor who previously appeared in *The Power of One*.

I Dreamed of Africa was in production from late August to November 1998, shooting over 11 weeks. Most of the film was shot in South Africa because Kenya was too politically volatile to mount a major film production there. British director Hugh Hudson dispatched a second unit crew to Kenya to obtain the necessary shots, keeping his cast out of danger. Hudson had scored a sleeper hit with *Chariots of Fire* (1981) only to watch his career slide with the relative failure of *Greystoke: The Legend of Tarzan, Lord of the Apes* (1984) and the catastrophic failure of *Revolution* (1985). The year before making *I Dreamed of Africa*, he had reunited with *Chariots of Fire* producer David Puttnam for *My Life So Far*, a mediocre coming-of-age saga set in 1920s Scotland. With all due respect to Hudson, he probably wasn't the first choice for *I Dreamed of Africa*.

For Craig, the attractions of the project were strictly limited. It was a nothing part in a mediocre movie. The money was good, however, and he got to work in South Africa, which had been off-limits for *The Power of One*. He could also give his Afrikaner accent another airing, though toning it down this time around. Seventh billed, he plays Declan Fielding, Gallmann's ranch manager. His hair is darkened, leaving the actors playing the Gallmann family – Basinger, Saint and Liam Aiken – the only blondes on screen. Making his brief entrance after 25 minutes, Craig looks good in safari shorts and a blue T-shirt that matches his eyes. He also demonstrates a smooth over-arm bowling action, though cricket fans may not be impressed.

Aimed at no particular audience, *I Dreamed of Africa* is sunk by a weak, episodic script, lacklustre performances and a director whose mind seems to be elsewhere. There are intriguing elements in the narrative, however. Gallmann, a single parent with failure issues, starts a new life in Africa with a new husband, Paolo (Perez), whom she barely knows. Disillusion soon sets in, Gallmann contending with cattle disease and poachers while the restless Paolo goes on safari with fellow ex-pats. Any potential in this material is dissipated by the lack of narrative tension and character development. Taking place in the 1970s and 80s, the film is short on period detail, and the action is confined to soap-opera dramatics and extended travelogue.

In addition, Basinger is woefully miscast as an upper-class Italian, a real-life figure reduced to a one-note character. While Basinger foregoes make-up for the Kenya scenes, the film still smacks of an ill-conceived vanity project. The end result is a poor man's *Out of Africa*, with some eye-catching scenery and not much else. It's a measure of the film's failure that the double tragedy in Gallmann's life has no emotional impact whatsoever.

Craig has little to do in *I Dreamed of Africa*. Hudson's DVD director's commentary mentions him only once – "Daniel Craig, English actor, playing the manager" – which says it all. Yet Craig is the only Caucasian actor who manages to be believable in his role. Even the most minor touches have an authenticity lacking elsewhere, whether it's shaking hands, lighting a cigarette, riding a horse, or drinking from a canteen, spitting water and wiping his mouth. The film cries out for the relationship between Gallmann and Fielding to be developed. Her discontent with the absentee Paolo would make a growing interest in the considerate, good-looking Fielding both logical and dramatically interesting. Of course, the real-life Gallmann's veto over the script ruled out any radical departures from the facts. In the finished film, Gallmann and Fielding barely interact. *I Dreamed of Africa* was hamstrung by its enforced fidelity to the source material and, on its release in May 2000, flopped in US cinemas prior to going straight to video/DVD in the UK.

Craig then formed part of an impressive ensemble cast for *The Trench*, a British-French co-production. This World War I drama was

Daniel Craig at the GQ Men of the Year
Awards at the Royal Opera House, London,
6 September 2005

An early role for Craig
as Lieutenant Berry
in *Sharpe's Eagle* (1993)

Craig (as Matt Kearney) with Rosie Rowell (as Jude Sawyer) and Peter Howitt (as Graham Ives) in London Weekend Television's *Kiss and Tell*, 1996

Craig as Connor Rooney with Paul Newman as his father John in *Road to Perdition* (2002)

Daniel Craig and Gwyneth Paltrow on location in Cambridge during filming for *Sylvia* (2003)

Daniel Craig and Gwyneth Paltrow as poets Ted Hughes and Sylvia Plath in *Sylvia*

As Cecil Thomas in 'Addicted to the Stars', one of the segments of *Ten Minutes Older: The Cello* (2003)

Craig as carpenter Darren with Anne Reid as May in Roger Michell's *The Mother* (2003)

Craig filming the unused alternative ending of *Layer Cake* on location at Stoke Park Club

XXXX (Daniel Craig), Gene (Colm Meaney) and Morty (George Harris) meet the Duke in *Layer Cake* (2004)

The life of Joe Rose (Craig) is changed forever by a tragic ballooning accident in *Enduring Love* (2004)

Craig as Joe Rose with Samantha Morton as Claire in Roger Michell's *Enduring Love*

In the Fountain Room at Stoke Park Club, during filming on *Layer Cake*

written and directed by novelist William Boyd, whose film credits included the screenplay for *Chaplin* (1992). Craig's co-stars included James D'Arcy, who appeared in *The Ice House*, and Cillian Murphy, soon to become a rising star of British and Irish cinema. Starting production in November 1998, most of *The Trench* was filmed at Bray Studios, one-time home of the Hammer horror films.

The Trench is set in northern France in 1916, during the long, agonising wait for 'the big push' into German-held territory. This culminated in the infamous Battle of the Somme, one of the most disastrous engagements in the history of the British army. The film is filled with good intentions, but the end result feels overwritten and very familiar. The same ground – or trench – was covered more effectively in R C Sherriff's 1928 play *Journey's End*, memorably filmed in 1930 by James Whale. *Journey's End* is regularly revived on stage and it's hard to see what Boyd thought he could add to Sherriff's reflections on the insanity of war and the fears of ordinary men existing in nightmarish conditions. As a director, Boyd succeeds in building some tension, yet the predictable plot and thin characters make for uninvolving drama. It seems that Boyd lacked the film-making experience to bring this one-set drama alive. Much of *The Trench* feels like a filmed play, a serious mis-step for an original cinema project.

The second-billed Craig plays Sergeant Telford Winter, a career soldier dealing with raw recruits barely out of school. Winter's first line, "You be careful, Dennis", is polite but spoken with an undercurrent of menace. Hard-nosed and foul-mouthed, Winter works by the book. So far, so clichéd. In most scenes, Winter barks out orders and reprimands transgressors. While Craig plays these scenes with conviction, it's the stuff of a thousand other war movies. His relationship with the poetry-reading Lieutenant Ellis Harte (Julian Rhind-Tutt) is predictably awkward, though the actors give these scenes an edge lacking in the script. Craig plays Winter with a Wirral accent, emphasising the character's provincial, working-class origins, contrasted with his superior officer's upper-class, public school intonation. Winter is further humanised by the obligatory handing round of family photographs.

The most effective moment comes when the teetotal Winter offers a young soldier some of his wife's home-made jam. Craig beautifully conveys Winter's hurt when this gesture is spurned. Furiously spooning the jam into his mouth, Winter desperately seeks comfort from a literal taste of the home-life he knows he'll never see again. This one brief scene says more about humanity faced with the horror and darkness of impending death than anything else in *The Trench*. The climactic battle sequence falls flat by comparison, not least because the green Thames Valley location is an inadequate substitute for the mud-bath, barbed-wire hellhole of the Somme.

The Trench opened in the UK on 17 September 1999. Reviews were mixed, to say the least. *Time Out* critic Gilbert Adair accentuated the positive: "The claustrophobia contributes to an effective build-up of tension, and the film is actually very engrossing, partly due to the clarity, wit and assurance of Boyd's writing, partly to an excellent cast. Not original then, but in its own old-fashioned, unpretentious way, impressive and affecting." Adair did concede that the tight budget and Boyd's stolid visual style made the film's studio-bound nature very obvious. Writing in the *London Evening Standard*, veteran critic Alexander Walker was downright sneering: "The sort of small, compact, unambitious play you'd have expected to find on TV 20 years ago."

Alas, he was right. Craig and his fellow actors had done their damnedest to bring the film alive, but the material just wasn't there. *The Trench* did poorly at the box-office, reflecting the grim subject matter as much as the film's dramatic deficiencies. While William Boyd remains one of Britain's most respected novelists, he has yet to write and direct another film. He nevertheless had a keen appreciation of Craig's skills as an actor. Interviewed in *The Guardian*, he praised Craig's "amazing ability to express emotion of the most poignant kind as well as the most vehement kind. Not all leading men have that – they can do the tough stuff, but they can't always do both." He also called Craig "one of our best actors." Craig got on well with Boyd, forming a lasting friendship.

Craig next appeared in Film Four's *Hotel Splendide*, an unsuccessful blend of character study and offbeat romance that got under way in February 1999. This Anglo-French co-production starred Australian actress Toni Collette, whose success with *Muriel's Wedding* (1994) had taken her to Hollywood. Though not an A-list star, Collette had some impressive credits, including a co-starring role in *The Sixth Sense* (1999). The cast also included Stephen Tompkinson, from *Drop the Dead Donkey*, and Peter Vaughan, who gave a moving performance in *Our Friends in the North*.

It would be great to report that *Hotel Splendide* is an undiscovered masterpiece of black comedy. Great but completely untrue. While writer-director Terence Gross attempts to live up to his name, the film doesn't even score in the bad taste or scatological stakes. The title establishment is run by the odd, dysfunctional Blanche family on a remote island where the ferry only calls once a month. The deceased matriarch still exerts a forceful grip on her husband Morton (Peter Vaughan) and their grown-up children Ronald (Craig), Cora (Katrin Cartlidge) and Dezmond (Tompkinson). Both family and guests have been conditioned to believe that leaving the hotel would be fatal. Dezmond has dedicated himself to enforcing his late mother's bizarre – and stomach-churning – health regime. Reluctant chef Ronald is already showing signs of rebelliousness when his ex-girlfriend Cath (Colette) turns up, looking to rekindle their romance. She challenges Dezmond's culinary tyranny with her own brand of cooking, winning over the guests and, gradually, Ronald. Are we destined for a happy ending or will the increasingly weird Dezmond regain the upper hand?

At times, *Hotel Splendide* recalls former *Monty Python* animator Terry Gilliam on an off-day. (Think *Fear and Loathing in Las Vegas* or *The Brothers Grimm*.) While the actors seem game for a ripe slice of British eccentricity, the script and direction are mostly lacking. The bowel-related humour involves a heating system run on faeces; the working title was *Hotel Sordide*, which gives you some idea. Craig sports a wounded expression for much of the film, exercising in the freezing mud in his vest and baggy shorts. Fans hoping for a glimpse of the buff Craig physique will be sorely disappointed. Craig and Collette play well together, conveying a mutual passion slowly being rekindled in the most miserable surroundings imaginable. And Tompkinson shows a dark side barely hinted at in *Drop the Dead Donkey* or *Ballykissangel*.

Hotel Splendide went on limited release in the UK on 22 September 2000, turning up on TV on 26 March the following year. Writing in *Time Out*, Wally Hammond liked what he saw: "A one-off debut destined for the potential cult-movie drawer… it's played with undisguised gusto and feeling … Gross' surreal intelligence and sense of invention may well leave you moved and amused." This proved a minority view and *Hotel Splendide* has yet to acquire the anticipated cult status; in fact, most viewers will feel that it's the kind of movie that gives 'quirky' a bad name. Craig can take comfort in the knowledge that the film is now very hard to see – and seven years later, of course, he would check into a far more upmarket Hôtel Splendide in *Casino Royale*.

FIVE

HOLLYWOOD, GOOD AND BAD

Since *Our Friends in the North*, Craig had been dealing with varying levels of public recognition. Interviewed for *The Sunday Times* in 1999, he offered his thoughts on fame: "There may be a buzz generated about you, but you can't start soaking that in because you'll get stuffed. Things change very quickly in this business."

What kind of buzz was Craig generating as the millennium approached? *Our Friends in the North* and *Love is the Devil* had established his credentials on TV and film, but his career still lacked a powerful forward momentum. *Obsession* and *Love & Rage* were barely seen flops and *Elizabeth* was Cate Blanchett's triumph, with Craig lost in the all-star crowd. *The Trench* was an all-round disappointment. In Britain, he was a face people sort-of recognised, without being able to pin him to a particular role. And, having been wasted in *I Dreamed of Africa*, there was little evidence, on the international stage, that Craig had even registered as a talent to watch.

As the 21st century approached, Craig opted to return to television for a short-lived Channel 4 series called *Shockers*. This sequence of three psychological thrillers was well received at the time, and sired a further trio in 2001, but has since pretty much vanished from view. Craig starred in the second play in the 1999 batch, 'The Visitor', directed by Audrey Cooke from a script by Guy Burt. As the 50-minute drama begins, three housemates are expecting the cousin of their absent fellow tenant. When a charming man named Richard (Craig) turns up on the doorstep, they naturally assume he's their invited guest. Richard ingratiates himself into their lives with ease, though there are hints that his personality has a darker side. When it's discovered that Richard is not the tenant's cousin, he proves unwilling to leave.

'The Visitor' is a skilful piece of drama, steadily increasing the tension and claustrophobia. Craig gives an unsettling performance, suggesting great menace without actually saying or doing anything overtly sinister. It was screened on 26 October 1999 and there were some good reviews, one critic comparing it to a Harold Pinter play, with Richard turning into a cross between Iago, the villain from Shakespeare's *Othello*, and Vinnie Jones, football thug turned hard-man actor. Presumably the reviewer wasn't comparing Craig and Jones as actors. The latter's debut performance in *Lock, Stock and Two Smoking Barrels* (1998) was respectable enough, but he was light-years from Craig's level.

Marking time, Craig also appeared in a 12-minute short called *Occasional, Strong*, which made it to British cinemas on 12 December 2002, a good three years after it was produced. Writer/director Steve Green had made his name with music videos for the likes of Depeche Mode, and the story involved a getaway driver who misplaces his winning lottery ticket during a botched heist. When a street cleaner finds the ticket, he and his daughter are targeted by the gang. The action-packed first half of *Occasional, Strong* owes a then-fashionable debt to the aforementioned *Lock, Stock and Two Smoking Barrels*, but the second act heads off in a different, and less convincing, direction. The title, of course, refers to the terminology used by the British Board of Film Classification for categorising movies (the amount of violence, bad language, sex and so on).

Craig finally achieved top billing in a film with *Some Voices*, which began its six-week schedule on 12 September 1999. This sensitive study of schizophrenia was based on a play by Joe Penhall, first produced by the English Stage Company at the Royal Court Theatre in 1994. The main character, Ray, was played on stage by Ray Winstone, leading hard man of British TV and films. Penhall based Ray on a friend who suffered from schizophrenia, though Ray's condition isn't named in either the play or subsequent film version. Keen to break into movies, Penhall wrote the screenplay himself. Produced by Channel 4's Film Four division, *Some Voices* marked the feature film debut of director Simon Cellan Jones, who had worked on *Our Friends in the North*. Cellan Jones felt that Penhall's script was about survival in London, the archetypal Big City, a situation Craig knew at first hand.

Craig's brother was played by Liverpudlian actor David Morrissey, who had appeared in *Between the Lines* and the film *Hilary and Jackie* (1998). Craig's love interest was Kelly Macdonald, who'd co-starred with him in the 1997 Old Vic production of *Hurlyburly*. Macdonald's best-known film was *Trainspotting* (1996), where she played Diane, the school-age lover of anti-hero Renton (Ewan McGregor). The supporting cast included Ashley Walters, then a leading member of the controversial rap group So Solid Crew. Known for his 'gangsta' image – which culminated in a prison sentence for possession of a firearm – Walters played an assertive but non-threatening kitchen hand.

Craig sought professional advice while researching his mentally ill character. He consulted with a psychotherapist, who offered to take him on a tour of Maudsley Hospital in south London. Craig declined, feeling he'd be intruding on the real patients. He couldn't justify this disruption on the grounds of an 'authentic' portrayal or Method acting. Talking with the psychotherapist, Craig got a sense of how a schizophrenic related to both themselves and the outside world. He was especially interested in the common ground between schizophrenics and 'normal' people, the points of contact. Craig and Cellan Jones didn't want the character of Ray to become a showcase for 'great' acting, all mannerisms and nervous tics. Too often, when big-name actors played disabled characters – Dustin Hoffman in *Rain Man* (1988), Tom Cruise in *Born on the Fourth of July* (1989) – they seemed to have one eye set firmly on an Academy Award nomination.

Some Voices was filmed on location in Shepherd's Bush, west London. Cellan Jones recalls that Craig liked to be relaxed on set prior to a take, not 'switching on' until just before the cameras rolled. Craig and Macdonald had become good friends while appearing in *Hurlyburly*. (*Elizabeth*, in which she had a small role as the Queen's ill-fated lady-in-waiting, didn't give them any scenes together.) They were very comfortable with each other, which made the intimate scenes between their characters easier to shoot. Craig and Macdonald suffered for their art, filming scenes in an outdoor swimming pool in the middle of October.

According to Craig, Cellan Jones filmed on the London locations without an official permit. This could have caused problems with the authorities, especially as Craig was required to appear naked. Most actors in this situation are given the courtesy of a closed set. Craig's full-frontal nude scene was filmed in Goldhawk Road, not far from his home. Cellan Jones admits that he didn't tell Craig he wanted him fully naked until late in the day. Craig recalled the filming with an amused shudder: "Horrible! We agreed to do it when I was drunk at his house one night." Had Cellan Jones deliberately plied Craig with alcohol to get consent that wouldn't otherwise have been forthcoming? Probably not, but it made for a good anecdote. Craig certainly needed a drink on the day of filming, downing four large brandies. Both Craig and Cellan Jones claimed that passers-by showed only minimal interest. Under the circumstances, Craig didn't know whether to be relieved or insulted.

Some Voices is a charming, remarkably gentle film, despite the harrowing subject matter and occasional bursts of violence. Ray is first seen in a mental institution, adjusting a TV aerial to get a better picture. As the film progresses, it becomes clear that his own internal aerial gives him a seriously distorted view of the world. The television picture is briefly crystal clear, before Ray is distracted and drops the aerial on the floor. While Ray has his own moments of clarity, *Some Voices* isn't about recovery or cure, just the day-to-day realities – or otherwise – of mental illness.

Ray is an endearing figure, as good-natured and awkward as Geordie in *Our Friends in the North*. His dark hair with blond highlights suggests a man who wants to be different without making any bold statements. Vaguely aware of fashion, Ray wears the kind of Kangol hat popularised by Samuel L Jackson. Craig's believable west London accent gives the character an unaffected, down-to-earth quality. He also has a keen sense of humour. Initially careful with his despised medication, Ray is already showing signs of rebellion, drinking alcohol against his doctor's advice. Disorientated by the outside world, Ray sees great significance in the colours of disposable lighters, but has no grasp of the bigger picture. Craig felt that Ray lives only in the present and can't even see to the end of the week.

Ray has been released into the care of his older brother Pete (Morrissey), who runs a café offering greasy-spoon fare by day and international cuisine by night. The taciturn Pete clearly cares for Ray, without comprehending his brother's mental state. Ray apologises for missing Pete's wedding and divorce, encapsulating the failed relationship with an unselfconscious sense of the absurd.

Ray's life changes when he meets Laura (Kelly Macdonald), a pregnant young woman fleeing her aggressive boyfriend. Ignorant of Ray's condition, she is annoyed, mystified, then intrigued by his honesty and directness. Their subsequent romance is pleasingly quirky, if somewhat abrupt, with much frolicking in crop circles (perhaps the most dated aspect of the film). A love scene is charmingly awkward, Ray dependent on Laura's good-humoured guidance. Fixated on plastic lighters and spiral patterns, Ray shoplifts a St Catherine's Wheel firework (with more success than Craig enjoyed when he attempted to steal crisps as a child). While Laura is amused by this act of schoolboy bravado, Ray is transfixed by the spinning flame. In the long term, their relationship has nowhere to go. Faced with impending motherhood, Laura needs a sense of security that Ray can't offer.

Some Voices has a few flaws. The script doesn't always ring true and the more gimmicky bits of direction can't convey Ray's anguished mental state. While Penhall and Cellan Jones make strong contributions, *Some Voices* is Craig's film all the way. He generates sympathy for Ray rather than easy sentiment. Though articulate and charming, Ray is also difficult, demanding, reckless and selfish. He will even fake the side-effects of drugs to get what he wants. Happy with Laura, Ray abandons the medication that controls the symptoms of schizophrenia but numbs his senses, with predictable consequences. As the voices and hallucinations increase, Ray's spiral obsession takes over, prompting his attempt at full-frontal performance art. Craig conveys a sense of sad desperation, with Ray painfully aware of his disorder and lack of control. Seldom have Craig's piercing eyes been used to such haunting effect.

Some Voices premiered at the Cannes Film Festival on 15 May 2000, also receiving a showcase screening at the 54th Edinburgh International Film Festival. Keen to support the film, Craig attended the festival and made himself available to the press. Interviewed by BBC reporter James Mottram, he argued that the film was a character study of flawed, vulnerable humanity rather than a case study of mental illness:

> *I didn't want to do a zoo show. I didn't want to do a study of someone with mental illness. I just wanted to show someone who was trying to live their life. Compared to you or I, he's very sick, but he doesn't consider himself sick. This is his life. Any voices or fantasies, he lives with. Those are his everyday life things. The thing that worries him is socialising – the things that worry us all.*

Craig's committed, passionate performance in *Some Voices* went on to win the Best Actor prize at Edinburgh. The film then received a limited UK cinema release on 25 August. *Time Out* critic Trevor Johnston felt the performances were strong enough to carry the film without the added visual and audio trickery:

Morrissey skilfully registers abiding filial love tested by simmering exasperation; Macdonald's adept at lippy on top, vulnerable underneath; and Craig's vibrant yet haunted expressiveness tells us everything needful about this doomed sweetheart. It's thus over-egging it somewhat when the whirling camera effects and freaky sound mix overstates the point that our man really is not well.

In 2000, Craig returned to television with the lead role in *Sword of Honour*, based on a trilogy of novels by Evelyn Waugh. Produced by Talk Back for Channel 4, *Sword of Honour* was adapted by William Boyd, writer and director of *The Trench*. Having examined World War I, he now switched his attention to World War II. Boyd had already adapted Waugh's *Scoop* for a 1987 TV production.

The best-known TV adaptation of Waugh was *Brideshead Revisited* (1981), a huge hit on its original broadcast. Twenty years later, *Brideshead* was still the yardstick by which TV versions of Waugh were measured. This didn't sit well with Craig, who loathed the earlier series, with its posh accents, fey manners, foppish haircuts and questionable nostalgia for an era of rigid class divisions. *Sword of Honour* had to be something different. As Craig explained to journalist Mark Morris: "When I went to meet the director [Bill Anderson] I said 'If this is anything like *Brideshead*, fuck off. I can't be bothered with it.' He just went, 'No, we're not going to do that.'" While some might question Craig's diplomacy, the sentiment was undoubtedly heartfelt. Craig liked the depiction of hero Guy Crouchback as "a bit of a screw-up" who didn't invite easy sympathy.

Craig's co-stars included Katrin Cartlidge, who had appeared in *Saint-Ex* and *Hotel Splendide*, and Julian Rhind-Tutt, his superior officer in *The Trench*. Craig's father was played by veteran actor Leslie Phillips, famous for his fine line in smooth charmers with a touch of the cad.

Sword of Honour opens in Italy during the late 1930s. Craig looks suitably dapper as Crouchback, dressed in a grey doubled-breasted suit. His hair is dyed chestnut brown, which looks more natural – and less sinister – than some of Craig's darker dye jobs. Fluent in Italian, Crouchback is good-natured but naïve. He nearly gets himself shot trying to reason with Fascist cops as they arrest a Communist suspect. Crouchback sees only a woman in need of help, forgetting he's an unwelcome outsider in a volatile country run by a dictator. This is the character in a nutshell and he doesn't really change over the next three hours.

Crouchback is depicted as a modern crusader, more idealistic than his historical counterparts but just as doomed to failure. As Britain goes to war in 1939, he is desperate to enlist and serve his country. A great show is made of the fact that Crouchback is too old to be accepted by a regular regiment. Then in his early thirties, Craig looks too young and fit to be army reject material. In truth, he seems miscast on several levels. Crouchback is a devout, if troubled, Catholic and Craig simply doesn't convey the spiritual side of the character. He isn't helped by the script, which fumbles this crucial aspect of the books. The prolonged scenes with Crouchback's ex-wife grow tedious, partly because she's a boring, ill-defined character. What Craig does portray very well is a decent man trying to do the right thing in a world he doesn't understand. While Crouchback is miles apart from Geordie Peacock, they share this quality in common. Craig also looks at home during the action scenes, though Crouchback has little chance to shine on the battlefield.

Boyd saw *Sword of Honour* as a British version of Joseph Heller's novel *Catch-22*, which depicted World War II as both black comedy and surreal nightmare. But Boyd's script and Bill Anderson's direction never achieve the delicate balance between straight dramatics and absurdist humour. The 1970 film version of *Catch-22* struggled to capture the book's spirit and the TV *Sword of Honour* is no more successful with Waugh's literary style. Crouchback's adventures in Dakar, Egypt and Crete have a semi-comic tone that never quite works. The drama is weighed down by in-your-face direction and blatant symbolism. Despite Craig's miscasting, the scenes without him drag and the relentless misanthropy, and misogyny, grows tiresome.

Sword of Honour was shown in two parts, starting on 2 January 2001. *Guardian* critic Gareth McLean described Craig as being "magnetic as the man in search of meaning." While the reviews for Craig were mostly positive, *Sword of Honour* never established itself as a TV classic. If Craig hoped to topple *Brideshead Revisited* from its lofty perch, he was sorely disappointed.

In the summer of 2000, nearly a decade after *The Power of One*, Craig got his fourth Hollywood movie and first major Hollywood break. Unfortunately, it was in *Lara Croft Tomb Raider*. This big-budget fantasy was based on a popular British video game character, first seen in 1997. Well known for her skimpy outfits, big guns and implausibly large breasts, Lara Croft had become a star of the virtual shoot-em-up genre. Paramount decided the time was right to launch Lara Croft on the big screen. British director Simon West had scored a hit with the bullet-riddled action movie *Con Air* (1997), and the title role went to Angelina Jolie, a rising star after *Girl, Interrupted* (1999), for which she won an Oscar for Best Supporting Actress.

Craig was approached to play the part of Alex West, a former colleague of Lara's and possibly much more than that. It seems that Hollywood had started to notice Craig after *Love is the Devil*, strolling rather than stampeding to his door. Craig was a fan of the *Tomb Raider* video games, unlike the rest of the cast. He denied being a regular player, but expressed a preference for 'Tomb Raider II'. Also a fan of *Con Air*, he got on well with West during the initial interview, rating the director as both bright and funny.

Craig had no illusions about the movie, a slickly packaged Hollywood blockbuster that offered no great acting challenge. At the same time, he appreciated its potential value for his career. Craig remained committed to low-budget, character-based films that addressed serious issues. *Lara Croft* offered a major pay cheque and the chance to raise his profile in the US. Producers of smaller films would be able to raise money on his name. However *Lara Croft* turned out, this felt like the right move. As Craig put it, "It was shit-or-get-off-the-pot time."

Craig's character was originally called Alex Mars, but the name hadn't been cleared by Paramount's legal department. There was always the risk that a real-life Alexander Mars might sue the producers for impugning his good name. While this wasn't likely, there was a growing executive twitchiness in the air. Playing safe, Simon West decided to use his father's name, Alex West, on the grounds that it wasn't likely to land them in court. Craig's co-stars included Julian Rhind-Tutt, from *The Trench* and *Sword of Honour*, Noah Taylor, who had played the young Geoffrey Rush in *Shine*, Chris Barrie, best known for the cult sf sitcom *Red Dwarf* (1989-99), and Leslie Phillips, Craig's father in *Sword of Honour*. The cast also featured Jolie's father, Jon Voight, playing her screen father, Lord Richard Croft.

Budgeted at $80 million, *Lara Croft Tomb Raider* was in production from 31 July through to December. The locations included Iceland and Cambodia, with interiors done back at Pinewood Studios, near London. The Cambodian temple sequence was shot on the famous '007' stage at Pinewood. According to Simon West, this stage was so vast it had its own micro-climate.

During filming, Craig took time out to promote *Sword of Honour*. The plot of *Lara Croft Tomb Raider* remained off limits during interviews, not that Craig was keeping any big secrets. When the final cut proved lacking, the film was tweaked – without credit – by executive producer Stuart Baird, an experienced editor and director. His action credits already included *Executive Decision* (1995), and the last-minute *Tomb Raider* fix earned Baird kudos at Paramount and the chance to direct the execrable *Star Trek: Nemesis* (2002).

Similarly, *Lara Croft Tomb Raider* is noisy, soulless and dull. The story is a load of guff involving the Triangle of Light, control of time (yawn) and a shadowy organisation called Illuminati ('People of Light'). The tomb raiders are tomb vandals much of the time, which isn't a good advert for the archaeological profession. Director West seems to have lost his action movie mojo. The humour and style Craig admired in *Con Air* are nowhere to be found. The result is an expensive live-action recreation of a video game, shackled to a boring plot and lacklustre execution. The makers should have watched *Raiders of the Lost Ark* again, or even *Young Indiana Jones*.

As Lara Croft, Angelina Jolie fires guns, takes a shower, speaks with an odd 'British' accent, bungee jumps in silk pyjamas and shows off her breasts (enhanced with a padded bra). This could have added up to a memorable – if decidedly sexist – action heroine and Jolie seems up to the task. Alas, the script and direction let both her and the audience down. The writers 'humanise' Croft by giving her extreme father issues (something Jolie has experienced in real life).

Craig is fifth billed in *Tomb Raider*. This misleadingly suggests that his character actually has something to do. He must have realised early on that Alex West was a non-starter. Craig's performance is unusually muted and it has to be said that the US accent he employs is not among his best. He certainly looks good in an open-neck black shirt and grey suit. Stripping down to a white vest and khaki shorts, he shows off an impressive set of muscles. And then what? Not much. A mercenary tomb raider, Alex West has sold out to the bad guys, led by Manfred Powell (Iain Glen). West joins the battle against aggressive CGI stone monkeys, firing off a few shots before Lara takes over. (In one scene, West wields a Walther P99 pistol, James Bond's trademark weapon. An omen of things to come, or just a half-arsed homage that only hardcore 007 fans would spot?) For the most part, West is overshadowed by Powell, who gets a climactic one-on-one with Lara (of the punch-up variety). West wanted the sexual tension to be between Lara and Powell, leaving Alex West – and Craig – on the sidelines.

West is a figure from Lara's past, yet the script never clarifies the nature of their relationship. The implication is that they were more than friends and colleagues. Why so coy? Craig gets a shower scene, showing a strong, if damp, profile. He then walks around naked with a gun, though careful camera angles and a strategically placed table keep his groin obscured. When Lara enters the room, her dialogue – "Always a pleasure" – suggests she's seen it all before. At least Craig got to appear nude with Angelina Jolie, who stays fully clothed in this scene, having taken a shower earlier in the film. For the record, Jolie praised Craig as the best kisser she'd encountered on a film set.

In a scene cut from the release print, Lara interrupts West at a poker game, his fellow players all pulling guns as she approaches. Their brief conversation about trust and friendship is nothing major, and it's easy to see why West felt the scene could go. West also dropped Craig's shower scene from the preview version, feeling it didn't move the story along. When test audiences asked to see more of Alex West, the scene was reinstated. This could be taken as a tribute to Craig's charisma and talent. It's also likely that the preview audience wondered what on earth his character was doing in the film.

During the grand finale, West gets a switchblade in the chest and plunges into icy waters. Saved by Lara's time-reversal trick, he gets the hell out and is never seen again. While the producers hoped Craig would return for the sequel, he wisely let West remain missing in action. Alex West is a redundant love – or whatever – interest and could easily have been dropped from the film. His only purpose in the final cut is to establish Lara's heterosexual credentials. As with *The Hunger*, Craig had been relegated to the dumb blond role. If Lara Croft is a female James Bond, Craig is playing the equivalent of a Bond Girl. A Croft Boy, perhaps. While Craig avoids criticising the *Lara Croft* movie, it's no secret that he found his role unremarkable. This is one film Craig fans may want to miss. Unless they're really keen on the shower scene.

Lara Croft Tomb Raider premiered in the US on 11 June 2001, going on general release four days later. The film opened in Britain on 6 July, after a few snips to remove 'glamorous' knife play and a head-butt. Would the teenage boys fixated on Lara Croft stop playing with their joysticks long enough to check out the movie? While the critics jeered, *Lara Croft* was a hit, taking $274 million worldwide. Box-office aside, Craig's return to Hollywood film-making had proved less than glorious. His low profile in *Lara Croft Tomb Raider* would eventually prove an advantage, as people easily forgot that he was in the film.

By the time *Lara Croft* opened, Craig had completed work on a far more distinguished US film, *Road to Perdition*. This period gangster movie was co-produced by Twentieth Century Fox, the Zanuck Company and Steven Spielberg's DreamWorks outfit. The script was based on a graphic novel by Max Allan Collins and Richard Piers Rayner, who drew both on real events and the Japanese 'Lone Wolf and Cub' manga series.

Road to Perdition starred Tom Hanks, who had achieved stardom in the hit fantasy *Big* (1988). British director Sam Mendes had a background in the theatre and had made his film debut with the downbeat urban fable *American Beauty* (1999), which won several Academy Awards. The high-calibre supporting cast was led by screen legend Paul Newman, star of *The Hustler* (1961), *Hud* (1963), *Cool Hand Luke* (1967) and *Butch Cassidy and the Sundance Kid* (1969). Hanks' ill-fated wife was played by Jennifer Jason Leigh, who first came to notice in *Last Exit to Brooklyn* (1989). The British contingent included Jude Law, a rising star after his appearances in *The Talented Mr Ripley* (1999) and Spielberg's *A.I.: Artificial Intelligence* (2001). And Craig was reunited with child actor Liam Aiken, who played Kim Basinger's young son in *I Dreamed of Africa*. Second time out, their screen relationship would be less harmonious.

Though Craig hadn't worked with Mendes, he'd met the director socially on several occasions. Mendes was busy with pre-production for *Road to Perdition* when he caught Craig's performance in *Sword of Honour*. As Craig recalls, Mendes just happened to be watching television during a brief stopover in London. Mendes contacted Craig and arranged to meet the next day. Craig was accordingly cast as Paul Newman's son, partly on account of his eyes. Next to Frank Sinatra, Newman had the most famous blue eyes in showbusiness. According to Mendes, Craig's piercing blues were felt to be a close match. Craig's character, Connor Rooney, was based on a real-life gangster, Connor Looney. The name change made sense, as DreamWorks wanted *Road to Perdition* to be taken seriously, despite its comic-book origins.

Budgeted at $80 million, *Road to Perdition* began filming on 5 March 2001, mostly on locations in Illinois. Craig didn't socialise with screen father Paul Newman, hardly a surprise given the latter's advanced years (76). He related to Newman as a fellow actor and worked well with him on set. Craig was wary of being dazzled by Newman's icon status; "I couldn't go down that road otherwise I'd lose my shit," he pointed out. He admired Newman's continued passion for acting after five decades in the business. Despite his vast experience, Newman still became nervous before a take, determined to do his best.

Set in 1931, *Road to Perdition* is a tale of family loyalties and organised crime that tempers the pulp fiction plot with a self-conscious display of artistry. As Connor Rooney, Craig gives a forceful portrayal of twisted, gutless humanity, though his accent varies and the effect is a bit too actor-ish in some scenes. As with the overall film, Craig seems over-anxious to prove he's not just another ruthless gangster, but something deeper and more universal. Connor is first seen reclining on a couch in semi-darkness. Interrupted by a small boy, Connor seems direct but friendly: "Call me Uncle Connor." Craig achieves a skilful balance in this scene, Connor becoming unsettling despite his polite conversation.

Interviewed on set, Craig described Connor as "a pretty nasty piece of work" with a big chip on his shoulder. The nature of this chip is soon apparent. John Rooney is a widower, Connor his only son. Connor feels challenged by Michael Sullivan (Hanks), his father's trusted lieutenant and surrogate son. Sullivan is everything Connor can never be: loyal, conscientious and a dedicated family man. (The fact that Sullivan is also a gangster and cold-blooded killer is rather glossed over; after all, we're talking wholesome Tom Hanks here.) When John Rooney and Sullivan play a piano duet, Connor watches from the sidelines with an uneasy smile. While Connor joins in the Irish dancing, he's clearly seething inside, telling Sullivan's youngest son (Liam Aiken), "It's all so fucking hysterical."

John Rooney despises his son's weakness, but won't disown his only living flesh and blood. In a later scene, the furious Rooney senior beats Connor, then embraces him. The sobbing Connor takes the blows without protest, Craig playing the errant son as a small child punished for being naughty. In *Our Friends in the North*, Geordie Peacock eventually hits back against his abusive father. Connor's retaliation is more subtle, ripping off his father with a financial scam. It comes as no surprise that John Rooney knows about this treachery and lets others pay for Connor's sins.

When Connor disobeys his father's orders, he sets in motion a bloody vendetta that will eventually destroy the Rooneys and their entire organisation. At the same time, he senses a new power over Sullivan, whose eldest son has witnessed a multiple killing that could compromise them all. Leaving the crime scene, Connor offers a casual wave, Craig investing this simple gesture with sinister implications. Intimidated and humiliated by his father, Connor 'rectifies' his mistake with another act of violence. The scene where he shoots Sullivan's wife and youngest son – in the back – recalls the depredations of Sergeant Botha in *The Power of One*. Unlike Botha, Connor kills without finesse, clumsily covering his face with a handkerchief and stumbling down the stairs as he exits the Sullivan house.

In the second half of the film, Craig makes way for Jude Law's Harlan Maguire, a crime photographer and hitman. Having played his part in the narrative, Connor Rooney is reduced to a passive figure, hanging around in hotel rooms griping about his lack of freedom. Craig does what he can with these scenes, but Connor is just waiting for Sullivan's eventual visit. Connor is protected by Frank Nitti (Stanley Tucci), Al Capone's right-hand man. Nitti's polite, ice-cold demeanour contrasts with Connor's adolescent petulance. As Nitti explains with elegant contempt, "You're a big baby who doesn't know his thumb from his dick." Craig doesn't speak or even move in his last scene, where Connor faces an undignified bathtub execution. Despite this tailing off, Craig felt Connor Rooney was a fully developed role, a rarity in mainstream Hollywood cinema. As he told Steve Rose: "There's no excuse for what he does but you can see the reasons, and that's not a bad guy as far as I'm concerned, that's a character."

Road to Perdition opened in the US on 12 July 2002, followed by a UK release on 20 September. The cinematography and production design drew more praise than the script. *Guardian* critic Peter Bradshaw noted that "the actors don't have much room to breathe" but made an exception for Craig, "excellent as the cowardly, idle Connor Rooney." Though not a smash hit, the film took $161 million worldwide. Craig had finally appeared in a big Hollywood movie of which he could be justly proud.

SIX

MIDDLE-CLASS ANGST

While Craig was hardly a household name, the media were becoming more interested in his career and personal life. Among the fan fraternity, an entire, purple-prosed website had been dedicated to him, as Craig was well aware. "I don't look at it any more," he told interviewer Matthew Sweet in September 2002, "because I said in the press about a month ago that I thought it was a bit scary. And then I looked at it again – like you do – and there was me quoted: 'This website is a bit scary.'" For Sweet himself, the site was valuable for the opportunity it gave to "listen to a fabulously naff sound file of the collected advert voiceovers of Daniel Craig."

> You can hear him speak movingly and passionately about the pension schemes offered by Scottish Widows. You can hear him ballyhoo the heroic qualities of the Sandra Bullock picture In Love and War [1996], exactly the kind of gloopy film project he'd now thumb his nose at. Best of all, you can hear a radio commercial in which he pretends to be a Scouse drayman standing in a discount lager warehouse off a ring road on the outskirts of Liverpool.

In addition, *Sun* reporter Charles Yates talked to Tim Craig, who proved effusive: "I am proud of what he's done but I'm very critical of his acting too. If I don't think it's great I'll tell him straight." He gave due credit to ex-wife Carol as "the real driving force" behind their son's early acting ambitions. He touched, too, on the father-son relationship: "I am also proud because he is my mate. I taught him to drink. There's not many things nicer than standing at the bar with someone you love and who loves you that much." Daniel, it seemed, had a marked fondness for lager and Guinness, usually accompanied by one of his trademark roll-up cigarettes.

Tim stressed that his son was still an actor first and foremost, rather than a budding movie star. Daniel had turned down the chance to reprise his role as Alex West in *Lara Croft Tomb Raider – The Cradle of Life* (2003) and Tim approved the decision: "He is his own man and he's not driven by money. I know he has turned down serious cash to do other roles. He tells me that he's turned the parts down because he could never see himself standing up there and saying the words."

Craig also seemed to feel that he wasn't yet ready for the big paydays. In conversation with Sweet, he admitted that

> *In the past I've turned things down that, financially, would have been very nice. I know what I'm like with money, and I also know what I'm like with boredom. And I know that being on a long film would just bring out the worst in me. I don't want to do work that's about getting a house in Portugal. Money's obviously an issue and it's nice to have it, but I've tried to go for the jobs which are the most interesting available.*

On the same principle, he avoided displays of movie star ostentation, such as the obligatory luxury car. In 2003, he was still the proud owner of a clapped-out Saab.

Among the lucrative offers Craig turned down was a chance to star in a TV series based on the *Biggles* books. Captain W E Johns' Boy's Own adventures of a World War I flying ace had been enormously popular in their day but now seemed hopelessly old-fashioned. Previous attempts to adapt the books had either foundered in pre-production or proved disastrous. The projected TV series has yet to appear, suggesting that Craig wasn't the only actor to give *Biggles* a miss.

In 2002, Craig reinforced his commitment to serious work with an appearance in *Ten Minutes Older: The Cello*, a German-British-American co-production consisting of eight episodes. The concept behind this compendium piece was intriguing, if prone to pitfalls: eight leading European filmmakers were given carte blanche to express their feelings on the theme of time. Craig starred in the segment 'Addicted to the Stars', written and directed by Michael Radford, whose credits included *Nineteen Eighty-Four* (1984), *White Mischief* (1987) and the Oscar-winning Italian film *Il Postino* (1994). 'Addicted to the Stars' also featured Roland Gift, one-time lead singer with The Fine Young Cannibals, and was a ten-minute science fiction parable set in the year 2146.

The film opens with Radford's signature, a somewhat ostentatious gesture. The nifty special effects reflect the influence of *2001: A Space Odyssey* (1968), while the black and white flashbacks are a clichéd way of minimising narrative confusion. People still smoke in public in this version of the future – including dubious nuns – which now seems a less than accurate prediction. Craig plays astronaut Cecil Thomas, who has been on a trip through hyperspace alongside his trusty co-pilot (Gift). While Thomas has aged only ten minutes, the world has moved on 80 years, and the young son he left behind is now dying of old age. While the close-ups make good use of Craig's eyes, there are few demands on him as an actor. Craig captures Thomas' bewilderment with a future world he will only know for a short time. Both disconcerted and amused, he declines the sexual advances of a chirpy, artificial woman (android or clone?). A carefully framed shower scene reveals a non-futuristic tattoo on Craig's arm.

Leaving his son a gift of space rock, Thomas returns to space, as there's nothing left for him on earth. He places a photograph of his son, as the boy he remembers, on the surface of a distant planet.

Poignant in concept, this final gesture lacks sufficient dramatic weight to be effective. 'Addicted to the Stars' is carefully made, well acted and atmospheric, but too brief and sketchy to really engage the interest, let alone the emotions. The film doesn't even explain why Thomas is addicted to the stars. Is the lure of the bright lights too much for him to resist? Did Radford intend a parallel with the lives of celebrities, including film stars, who leave their old lives behind – and sometimes their families – in search of something more rarefied and glorious? Who knows?

Ten Minutes Older: The Cello was released to a handful of UK cinemas on 12 December 2003. *Time Out* critic Tony Rayns was unimpressed by 'Addicted to the Stars', calling it "a facile sci-fi paradox." For those interested, there's a companion piece, *Ten Minutes Older: The Trumpet* (2002), which some rate as the superior film.

Craig found a more substantial role in *Copenhagen*, which started shooting on 3 March 2002 and was produced for the new digital channel BBC Four (which had been launched the day before). This intriguing three-hander was based on a Michael Frayn play which premiered at the National Theatre in 1998, transferring to Broadway's Royale Theatre two years later.

Copenhagen centres on two Nobel prize-winning nuclear physicists, the German Werner Heisenberg – famous for his uncertainty principle – and the Danish Niels Bohr, a one-time friend, colleague and mentor. In 1941, they fell out following an argument about the atom bomb. Could this rift be connected to Heisenberg's position as head of Nazi Germany's atomic energy programme? Maybe. Frayn's play has their ghosts discussing this mysterious conversation, joined by the shade of Bohr's wife Margrethe. Craig was cast as Heisenberg, who had been played in the NT production by Matthew Marsh. Craig described Heisenberg as "a very bright, intelligent scientist" who may have been a corrupt Nazi stooge, a gibbering madman or an ice-cold genius who believed that morality had no place in science.

Copenhagen was filmed on authentic locations in Copenhagen and the UK, and Craig's co-stars were Stephen Rea and Francesca Annis. The director (and adaptor) was Howard Davies, who had a long association with the National Theatre and had made one feature film, *The Secret Rapture* (1993), plus the TV drama *Armadillo* (2001), scripted by William Boyd from his novel. Craig was Davies' first choice for the role of Heisenberg. Davies had been struck by Craig's performance in *Angels in America* and felt he'd gone from strength to strength as an actor, noting that "Danny was somebody just about to break through in his career."

Copenhagen is an effective piece of small-screen drama. Working from a cut-down version of Frayn's text, the cast give restrained, emotionally powerful performances as the realms of physics, politics and personal relationships are dissected and disputed in a chilly-blue afterlife. Craig's Heisenberg is an intriguing figure, ambiguous about his reasons for visiting Bohr in Nazi-occupied Denmark. Was he seeking to justify his work on Hitler's atomic energy project, looking for information on the Allies' rival programme or attempting to explain that he had actually impeded the Nazis' progress?

Davies felt Craig was "absolutely terrific" in the role. Critic Gary Kramer, however, rated Craig's performance as only a qualified success:

> *Craig handles the temperament of his character well, and as an actor he understands the cadence of speech, rhythms of the language, dialogue and pacing well ... He has a confidence his character has. (I think this is his strength as a performer – you believe him even when he may be lying.) That said: Do I buy him as a physicist? Not entirely. He spouts physical and quantum mechanics that I just don't get.*

Copenhagen was a flagship production for BBC Four, where it was first shown on 26 September 2002. Despite heavy promotion, it proved a ratings flop, drawing only 18,000 viewers.

In publicising *Copenhagen*, Craig compared Heisenberg's nuclear research project with the debate over WMDs (Weapons of Mass Destruction) that was current in Britain at the time. After 11 September 2001, US President George W Bush initiated plans to invade Iraq, which the US regarded as a sponsor of international terrorism. British Prime Minister Tony Blair gave Bush his full support, ostensibly on the grounds that Iraqi dictator Saddam Hussein had WMDs he could launch at the UK within 45 minutes. Like many people, Craig was sceptical of these claims, which rested on a questionable interpretation of flimsy evidence.

As the conflict developed, Craig took a keen, almost obsessive interest in the ongoing Iraq war, scrutinising the print and TV media on a regular basis. In interviews, he spoke out against US imperialism and the British government's unquestioning collusion. In Craig's view, foreign secretary Jack Straw had given a misleading reading of Hans Blix's UN report on Iraq's alleged programme of WMDs (Weapons of Mass Destruction). Craig's criticism of the US and UK governments drew little comment from the press. In the early 1970s, Hollywood star Jane Fonda's attack on the Vietnam war was hugely controversial, prompting many to question her future in the industry. Craig had yet to achieve this level of celebrity, which gave him greater freedom to speak his mind but less chance of reaching a wide audience. Moreover, many people agreed with his views on the war, which left him preaching largely to the converted.

To date, Craig's on-screen romances had been few and far between. His film lovers included Kate Winslet in *A Kid in King Arthur's Court* (chaste), Heike Makatsch in *Obsession* (perpetual frustration), Greta Scacchi in *Love & Rage* (dark and nasty), Derek Jacobi in *Love is the Devil* (sado-masochistic), Kelly Macdonald in *Some Voices* (sweet yet doomed) and Toni Colette in *Hotel Splendide* (plain crazy). In *Lara Croft Tomb Raider*, the knowing exchanges between Craig and Angelina Jolie suggested their characters were intimate, though the film fought mysteriously shy of saying yea or nay. In *The Mother*, Craig ventured into the realm of generation-gap romance, taking a lover 33 years his senior.

This BBC Films production started in June 2002 and was scripted by respected novelist and screenwriter Hanif Kureishi. Director Roger Michell had worked with Kureishi on the BBC serial *The Buddha of Suburbia* (1993) before scoring a blockbuster hit with *Notting Hill* (1999). The producers of *The Mother* applied to the Film Council for funding, only to be rejected. As Michell recalls, the Council regarded Kureishi's script as "too weak" to merit a share of lottery money. The £1.5 million budget was eventually met by the BBC, which was keen to expand its film division.

Craig's romantic interest was Anne Reid, well known to older TV audiences for *Coronation Street* (1961-71), in which she played Valerie Barlow, and to younger ones for the sitcom *Dinnerladies* (1998-2000); she also provided the voice of Wendolene in the Wallace & Gromit classic *A Close Shave* (1995). Reid signed for *The Mother* prior to Craig and the producers promised her she'd meet the male lead before he was cast. As Reid didn't know Craig's work, she borrowed a videotape of *Some Voices*. After watching the film for three minutes, Reid felt he was the right choice.

Whatever Reid's feelings, Craig was initially reluctant to appear in *The Mother*. He found Kureishi's script cold and the characters unsympathetic. Craig felt he couldn't connect with this world or these people. His agent had already advised him against the project, as the low budget meant Craig's salary would be negligible. Michell eventually talked Craig round. As an actor looking for challenging roles, he finally found the central concept of *The Mother* too provocative to resist. Set in affluent north London, it's essentially a two-hander between May (Reid) and Darren (Craig). May and husband Toots (Peter Vaughan, from *Our Friends in the North* and *Hotel Splendide*) are visiting their grown-up son and daughter when his frail health gives out, leaving her a widow. Neglected by her children, May finds sympathy and comfort with Darren, a middle-class drop-out unconcerned with social convention.

At its best, *The Mother* is a potent drama about the fear of loneliness and fading away. Much of the credit should go to Anne Reid, who gives an uninhibited, tour de force performance as May. Obliged to play the roles of wife, mother, grandmother and now widow, May refuses to withdraw gracefully into the twilight. Frustrated for much of her life, she wants to be a person again, with her own desires and needs. As *Time Out* critic Tom Charity noted, "Reid is wonderful, subtly revealing a difficult, longtime repressed woman coming out of her shell under the attentive curiosity of the younger man."

Sporting a beard for the first time in a film, Craig looks suitably physical, clad in figure-flattering T-shirt and jeans. First seen toting a ladder, Darren is an old friend of May's son and the current lover of her daughter. Working as a builder and carpenter, he seems to be drifting through life and not caring too much about anything. At first, May regards Darren as rough and uneducated, certainly not a suitable partner for her daughter (never mind that he's already married). She soon realises that he's the only friend she has in London. Reid and Craig give their growing relationship authenticity and heart. The much-touted sex scenes have an unexpected tenderness. Craig suggests a man plagued by neurosis and self-loathing whose kindness towards May is as much a distraction from his own problems as a display of true feeling. Craig was a canny piece of casting in more ways than one. His craggy features and grey-streaked beard make him look older than his mid-thirties. Perhaps the filmmakers were concerned that the age gap would be a turn-off to viewers.

As a showcase for two outstanding performances, *The Mother* is worth 112 minutes of anyone's time. As a film per se, it's a badly flawed piece of work. The much-derided Film Council were right in spotting that the script is weak in places, failing to bring the supporting characters alive. The plotting is overly schematic, not to say crude, especially the 'chance' discovery of May's sexually explicit sketches (would she really leave them just lying around?). And a subplot involving the way dysfunctional children blame their parents for perceived failures is handled in perfunctory fashion.

The flawed screenplay also undermines Craig's committed performance. Darren starts out as a sympathetic, if screwed-up, man, a college drop-out with an easy charm but few prospects in terms of gainful employment. He comments that there are several large men who would like to beat him up, suggesting that casual sexual liaisons are nothing new. The script is vague on Darren's home life. More than once, we hear about his estranged wife and the disabled son he adores, though these characters never appear in the film. As the story progresses, it's hard to believe that Darren harbours strong feelings for anything or anyone.

Towards the end, Darren is depicted as an amoral parasite who uses and abuses anyone foolish enough to show him kindness or generosity. At the same time, he is used by other people, including May, who craves the sexual attentions of a handsome, virile younger man. When Darren appeals to May for oral sex, like a slobbering dog begging for a treat, both characters seem degraded by their appetites and dependency. *The Mother* reaches its nadir with an out-of-nowhere scene where a coked-up Darren turns on May, demanding hard cash rather than the proffered ticket out of his empty existence. These are no longer credible characters, merely mouthpieces for a Hanif Kureishi rant.

Perhaps Craig should have trusted his initial reaction to the script. If ever a movie cried out for a rewrite, it's *The Mother*. The film is tainted by a contempt for all humanity, or at least the north London upper-middle classes who haven't achieved Kureishi's level of success. It's notable that May's daughter, a failed writer, is by far the most unsympathetic and unbelievable character. In this respect, *The Mother* is little more than a protracted sneer at a bunch of screwed-up losers.

Well received at the Cannes Film Festival, *The Mother* opened in the UK on 14 November 2003. Writing in *Screen International*, Allan Hunter praised it as "one of the most emotionally adventurous and ably executed British films of the year." The film also got raves in *The*

Times ("superbly acted taboo-busting drama"), *The Sunday Times* ("the performances from Reid and Craig are perfectly pitched and totally convincing") and *The Evening Standard* ("one of the most poignant and controversial British movies of the year"). *Guardian* critic Peter Bradshaw was more impressed by the actors than the script: "Anne Reid and Daniel Craig are two first-rate performers who submit to their pairing with professionalism and dedication. They deserved a better film than this." Despite some positive reviews, *The Mother* was never going to be a big hit. It wasn't released in the US until May 2004.

After completing *The Mother*, Craig made a return to the theatre in a two-hander called *A Number*. This new play by Caryl Churchill was staged at the Royal Court's Jerwood Theatre Downstairs in London's Sloane Square. The plot concerned genetics and human cloning, no longer regarded as the stuff of science fiction fantasy. The director was Stephen Daldry, whose film credits included *Billy Elliot* (2000) and *The Hours* (2002). Though the play ran little more than an hour, Craig's role was extremely demanding. He played three characters, the 'original' person and his two clones. One is an idealistic teacher, another a borderline sociopath.

By early September 2002, rehearsals were in full swing. Craig's co-star was Michael Gambon, one of Britain's most respected character actors. Craig greatly admired Gambon and relished the opportunity to work with him on stage; as he admitted to Steve Rose, "I would have cut off my left leg to do it. You can't turn things like that down." For his part, Gambon maintained that "I've never worked with a young actor so smoothly."

> *He's so intelligent and sharp and clever. And I'm not just saying that, he's just perfect. He can do anything. We rehearse for hours and hours on end and we try and reach conclusions, and he's very intelligent and sharp and has got it all off pat. He can just sum it all up. I'm an old carthorse, really. A bit lazy. So it's very nice to have Daniel around.*

The press night was a big success, *Observer* critic Susannah Clapp praising "the subtle, stealthy Daniel Craig, who registers difference by a clench of the jaw here, a drop of a vowel there." In *The Daily Telegraph*, Charles Spencer asserted that "Daniel Craig gives a virtuosic display as three of his [Gambon's] identical sons, brilliantly suggesting just how differently each of them has turned out."

Having opened on Monday 23 September, Craig gave his last performance in *A Number* on 16 November. He was among the nominees for Best Actor at the prestigious Evening Standard Theatre Awards, announced on the 24th of the same month. He lost out to Simon Russell Beale, who took the award for his performances as Vanya in *Uncle Vanya* and Malvolio in *Twelfth Night*, both staged by *Road to Perdition* director Sam Mendes. The other nominee was Tom Georgeson, whom Craig had worked with in the 'New Order' episode of *Between the Lines*. *A Number* was named Best Play.

By the time *The Mother* opened in cinemas, Craig had long since completed another BBC film. *Sylvia*, directed by Christine Jeffs, was a biopic of American poet Sylvia Plath. While Plath remained a respected writer, her work was often overshadowed by her stormy marriage to fellow poet Ted Hughes and her subsequent suicide in 1963. Over the years, a number of Plath biopics had been mooted only to fall through. For legal reasons, any film about Plath was problematic until Hughes' death in 1998. It didn't help that the subject matter was depressing and – arguably – not very cinematic. When Hollywood star Gwyneth Paltrow committed to the film, however, funding became available.

The role of Ted Hughes was originally offered to Colin Firth, who had found fame as Mr Darcy in TV's *Pride and Prejudice* (1995). While Firth bore no resemblance to Ted Hughes, he was one of Britain's few bankable leading men. The combination of Paltrow and Firth could give *Sylvia* a box-office appeal absent from the material ('The Stars of *Shakespeare in Love* Together Again!'). Firth's negotiations with the producers faltered when he declined to shoot a screen test. Many lead actors see this kind of audition as beneath them, something only newcomers or bit players should go through. Whatever Firth's reasons for refusing to test, his decision cost him the part.

Sylvia producer Alison Owen had worked on *Elizabeth* and knew Craig could do charismatic and brooding with the best of them. Unlike Firth, Craig was agreeable to a screen test and promptly won the role. Carol Craig had given her son a copy of Hughes' *Crow* for his tenth birthday. Impressed by what he read, the young Craig later attended a poetry reading by Hughes at a girls' grammar school in Liverpool. The experience proved memorable, though not for the reasons Hughes intended. As Craig explained to Gaby Wood, "He didn't read poetry particularly well. It was just this monotone crap." Years later, Craig worked out why Hughes' accent sounded so odd. Born in Yorkshire, Hughes studied at Cambridge University, where he attempted to lose his native accent by flattening it out: "It's his interpretation of what a posh accent should sound like, but not too posh because he's from the north. It's bizarre – and heartbreaking."

While the late Poet Laureate was much admired for his work, many despised him for his treatment of Plath, arguing that he drove her to suicide. Hughes' grave was the target of abusive graffiti, 'pig' and worse scrawled on the headstone. Craig talked to Elizabeth Sigmund, a friend of Plath to whom the writer dedicated *The Bell Jar* (1963), her autobiographical novel. He wanted to know what Plath and Hughes were like as a couple. Sigmund replied that they were inseparable. In Craig's view, the film was telling a genuine love story, tainted by tragedy.

The supporting cast included Blythe Danner, Paltrow's mother, Michael Gambon, Craig's co-star from *A Number*, and Julian Firth, who had appeared in *The Young Indiana Jones* episode 'Palestine, October 1917'. *Sylvia* was in production from late October 2002 to February 2003. Craig joined the film in mid-November, after finishing his run in *A Number*. For budgetary reasons, the US scenes were shot in New Zealand, Christine Jeffs' native country.

A tragic story, *Sylvia* was itself tainted by tragedy. Paltrow's father, director Bruce Paltrow, died shortly before the start of filming. Craig greatly admired his co-star's stoicism and professionalism under the circumstances. Frieda Hughes, Plath's daughter, refused to co-operate with the film, or permit the use of her mother's poetry where she controlled the rights. The producers were able to use extracts from 13 of Plath's poems, undermining Hughes' boycott of *Sylvia*. She later wrote a poem criticising the film for perpetuating the image of a "Sylvia Suicide Doll". On a more mundane level, Craig's tattoo had to be disguised with make-up for a bedroom scene. Even this ruse failed, the tattoo remaining visible in some shots.

Sylvia opens in 1956 Cambridge, where Plath and Hughes meet for the first time. While both Paltrow and Craig look too old for fresh-faced undergraduates, they perform with enthusiasm. Hughes stands brooding at a party, while others dance around him. He has instant chemistry with Plath, who falls head over heels for his poetry and then the man himself, "my black marauder." Their intense debates on the nature of poetry are interesting – sort of – without coming alive on screen. Hughes' rapid-fire quotation from Shakespeare's *Henry IV Part I* is more a tribute to Craig's acting prowess than an insight into his character. After some tastefully lit lovemaking and light-hearted punting on the river Cam, Plath and Hughes are married. Alas, happy ever after isn't going to be an option.

Perhaps *Sylvia* faced an impossible task, chronicling the life and times of a literary martyr in a form accessible to both Plath devotees and newcomers. The end result hangs heavy in the air, depressing and predictable. The costumes tone with the sets to a distracting degree, a sure sign that the drama isn't gripping. There's little sense of a time factor, which should be present given Plath's brief life-span. Nor are the stars done many favours by the script. In some scenes, Paltrow and Craig are out-acted by Jared Harris, cast as poet and critic Al Alvarez, who's allowed to create a person rather than a Flawed Icon. Made with obvious care, *Sylvia* falls way short of the tragic romance so clearly intended.

From the start, Plath is depicted as childlike, playful, obsessive and unstable. It's clear she never recovered from the death of her father, though the reasons for her extreme reaction are barely hinted at. Does Hughes represent a much-needed father figure? Again, the film is vague on details. Paltrow, who'd just lost her own father, invests Plath with a desperate, haunted quality, yet the unfocused script leaves the character a faint shadow.

Craig's Ted Hughes has charm, charisma and humour to spare. Critic Joe Queenan noted Craig's "verve and dash" as Hughes, comparing him with the young Richard Burton. Craig's hair is darkened, leaving Paltrow the only blonde star on show. The side parting is doubtless historically accurate, but it does Craig few favours. His accent is variable, which may be true to the real Hughes but still seems odd as a piece of acting. On the upside, Craig recites poetry with more flair than Hughes ever mustered.

Settling in Plath's native Boston, Massachusetts, Hughes looks uncomfortably out of place at first. He's soon a hit with the local literary crowd, giving poetry readings to packed houses. Hughes encourages Plath, pushing her to write from her own feelings and experiences. Supporting Hughes financially with a teaching job, Plath sees him drifting away from her into the embrace of other women. Craig felt people were too quick to pass judgment on Hughes, assigning him the role of heartless adulterer. He told Gaby Wood, "I genuinely believe that even if he did have affairs, it was part of a relationship – he wasn't a serial polygamist. He was in love with Sylvia, and he was always in love with Sylvia."

Hughes' first alleged affair is with one of Plath's students. While Plath is convinced of the relationship, Hughes angrily denies it: "If I do start fucking the students, you'll be the first to know." Does the gentleman protest too much? The issue is never clarified, though Craig's performance suggests a man who loves to be the centre of attention, especially from attractive young women. Relocated to London, Plath accuses Hughes of sleeping with a BBC producer. Again, Hughes dismisses the allegations, though his actions hint at a man with something to hide. The relationship deteriorates into physical violence on both sides. Plath has seriously lost it by the halfway mark, becoming withdrawn and paranoid. The best scene is an excruciating dinner party depicting a marriage gone to Hell. This sequence has an authenticity and resonance the film struggles to achieve elsewhere. Hughes' third affair, with a mutual acquaintance, is the first shown as indisputably true. Even here, the film suggests he was driven to it by his failing relationship with Plath.

At one stage, the film was to be called 'Ted and Sylvia'. The loss of Hughes from the title reflects the character's subordinate status in the movie. Craig is largely off screen for the last third of the film, which badly misses his commanding presence. When Plath finally seals the kitchen and turns on the gas oven, many viewers will be relieved. Hughes' response to Plath's suicide is reduced to a written coda. While Craig believes that Hughes loved Plath, the film hedges its bets, remaining ambiguous about Hughes' guilt, or otherwise, and ambivalent in its attitude towards him.

Sylvia was released in Britain in January 2004. *Mirror* critic David Edwards asserted that "this film is so dire it reduces its titular heroine to little more than a comedy figure ... Gwyneth Paltrow plays Plath as a self-obsessed misery guts with all the emotional maturity of a sulking adolescent." He conceded, however, that Hughes' "gruff Yorkshire real-man credentials are conveyed in a taciturn performance of few words and many meaningful looks from Daniel Craig." Reviewing *Sylvia* in *Time Out*, Jessica Winter felt the film was an interesting effort dissipated by "all the ankle-spraining lawn divots of the biopic: clumpy composite characters, the collapsed chronology and the expository ventriloquism." Winter gave credit to Paltrow's performance, "a fascinating double bind of Plath's sunny all-American exterior and her stormcloud inner voices," and felt that Craig's Hughes "radiates the fabled enormous erotic puissance, and the film rather admirably leaves him as a stone-bust enigma."

In the US, the film had opened, as a limited release, the previous October, qualifying it for Academy Award consideration in 2004. The US reviews were mixed, critics feeling that the film's unremitting gloom was an insurmountable problem. And, despite the heavy-duty literary pedigree – and the presence of Oscar winner Gwyneth Paltrow – the Academy didn't bite.

SEVEN
TRAPS FOR THE UNWARY

aving played an equivocal Poet Laureate in *Sylvia*, Craig returned to the world of organised crime in *Layer Cake*. Unlike *Road to Perdition*, this 'hip' caper movie made light of the criminal underworld, despite the odd severed head. *Layer Cake* was based on a novel by J J Connolly, who also wrote the script. Made in July and August 2003, the film marked the directing debut of Matthew Vaughn, who had made his name producing the Guy Ritchie hits *Lock, Stock and Two Smoking Barrels* (1998) and *Snatch* (2000). Ritchie was supposed to direct *Layer Cake* after completing *Swept Away* (2002), an ill-conceived vanity project for his wife Madonna. But by the time the rights to Connolly's book had been secured and the screenplay completed, Ritchie was busy with *Revolver* (2005), another stain on his CV.

Snatch had been financed by Hollywood major Sony Columbia. When the *Lock, Stock...* follow-up proved another success, the studio agreed to back *Layer Cake*. At this point, Ritchie was still on board to direct. After Ritchie left the project, Vaughn decided to take over as director, despite his lack of experience. While Vaughn's novice status didn't bother Sony Columbia overmuch, he had to deliver a leading man from the studio's wish list.

For his star, Vaughn wanted the British answer to both Steve McQueen and Clint Eastwood, something of a tall order. Sony Columbia were very keen on Craig, who had appeared in the studio's safari flop *I Dreamed of Africa*. While many actors would be flattered by the McQueen/Eastwood comparison, Craig was initially reluctant to work with the first-time director. He worried that *Layer Cake* would turn into 'Lock, Stock 3', a road he had no wish to take. According to Vaughn, Craig already had a reputation for turning scripts down. At their first meeting, he assured the wary star that *Layer Cake* would avoid the brutal – if comic-book – violence seen in *Lock, Stock...* and *Snatch*. (Vaughn proved true to his word, delivering a '15' rated movie.) Vaughn also convinced Craig that he was right for the main character, a drug dealer looking to leave the business after one last job.

Craig's decision to take on *Layer Cake* was more canny than Vaughn realised. While the British gangster movie revival was fading fast, Craig needed a change of pace. His upcoming releases, *The Mother* and *Sylvia*, were pushing his career in a niche direction that could limit his future casting. At the start of his career, he risked being typecast as a brutish villain. A decade later, Craig was becoming the poster boy for the emotionally stifled, sexually fraught British upper-middle classes. It was a role he played well, with an outsider's keen observation, yet the films hadn't fared brilliantly with either critics or audiences. In terms of economics, Craig had yet to carry a major commercial hit. As he freely admitted, "My choices of movies don't tend to make money, but I get to make interesting films." *Layer Cake* could change this, especially if it repeated *Lock, Stock...* and *Snatch*'s success in the United States.

Layer Cake was edited by Jon Harris, who had worked on *Snatch* and *Occasional, Strong*. Craig's co-stars included Tom Hardy, Burn Gorman and Colm Meaney, while the romantic interest was provided by actress-model Sienna Miller, a newcomer to movies. Miller's screen boyfriend – until Craig's character comes along – was Ben Whishaw, from *The Trench*. Vaughn also recruited *Lock, Stock...* actors Dexter Fletcher and Jason Flemyng (the latter had briefly worked with Craig on the 'Menage a Trois' episode of *The Hunger*) and the older generation was represented by Kenneth Cranham and Michael Gambon, from both *A Number* and *Sylvia*. The cast also featured

Jamie Foreman, son of gangster Freddie Foreman, who thrived in 1960s London alongside the notorious Kray twins.

Budgeted at £4 million, *Layer Cake* started shooting on 30 June 2003 on location in the UK and Amsterdam. While Craig didn't appear in the Netherlands scenes, he got to shoot at the exclusive Stoke Park Club, used for the famous golf sequence in *Goldfinger* (1964). The London exteriors included Guy Ritchie's house, one of his few contributions to the film. Craig's interrupted love scene with Sienna Miller was filmed at the St Martin's Lane hotel. Craig got on well with Miller, which inevitably prompted rumours of an off-screen romance. According to press reports, they continued the hotel liaison after hours, though both Craig and Miller denied this.

Craig disliked doing his character's opening voice-over. Sitting in a recording studio denied him the context and motivation he needed to bring the character alive. After extensive re-writing and re-editing, Craig pronounced himself happy with the result. *Layer Cake* was also a physically arduous shoot for Craig. Filming over July in one of the hottest summers on record, he had to work in a studio with no air conditioning. As the temperature soared past the 100-degree mark, Craig and co-star Colm Meaney could only work in 20-second bursts. One of the worst days came when his character was beaten up by Meaney, playing a businessman who hasn't forgotten his gangster roots. The cameras rolled for over two and a half hours while Craig was kicked and punched. He later noted that "Colm Meaney knows how to do it," presumably in reference to the latter's experience with action movies, rather than any real-life pugilistic skills.

Interviewed during location filming by *Empire* journalist Will Lawrence, Craig offered his thoughts on the unnamed anti-hero:

> *I suppose my character is cool. God knows how I managed to pull that off! He thinks he can control the situation, but fuck it, he's a coke dealer. By its nature it's a world of criminals and you're going to come unstuck at some stage. And that is the moral: if you're in there, you're in. For God's sake don't pity him.*

Was Craig genuinely worried about glamorising the drugs trade? There had long been a theory that crime films turned the protagonists into heroes, whatever their on-screen fate. In the event, *Layer Cake* would make little impression on the movie-going public's collective consciousness.

Also interviewed by Will Lawrence, Vaughn promoted *Layer Cake* as Craig's breakthrough movie:

> *I know he's done a lot of work but a lot of people haven't discovered it yet and I think – I hope – this will be the movie where people will think he's a really good actor and cool, in the true sense of the word. He's not just trying to be cool, he's got his own sense of style.*

But had all been sweetness and light between Craig and Vaughn? In September 2004, the pair promoted the upcoming release of *Layer Cake* with a Q&A session at the National Film Theatre on London's South Bank. Superficially, their conversation tended towards 'mutual appreciation society' proportions. But, though Craig had nothing but praise for Vaughn and the movie, his body language told another story. Looking uncomfortable throughout the talk, he fidgeted in his swivel chair, played with the cap of his plastic water bottle, fiddled with his ear and laughed uneasily. Never a relaxed interviewee, Craig did everything but get up and run.

Promoting the film in the US the following summer, Craig hinted that he'd acted as an unofficial producer on it, which might imply that Vaughn and his credited co-producers weren't up to the job without Craig's assistance. Or that Craig only signed for the film on the understanding that he exercised a certain level of control. Perhaps he was just helping out for the good of the project. It's easy to read too much into the statement, yet Craig chose to utter it at a press conference he knew would be widely reported. And on the DVD commentary, Vaughn speaks of "Mr Craig" with more respect than affection.

Layer Cake deserves points for ambition and effort, but not a whole lot for achievement. A big fan of Hollywood movies, Vaughn wanted to emulate such noted visual stylists as Brian De Palma (*Carrie, Dressed to Kill, Scarface, The Untouchables*) and Michael Mann (*Manhunter, Heat, Collateral, Miami Vice*), but perhaps he should have paid more attention to the basics of storytelling. Vaughn's flash, 'high style' approach is just fancy packaging for an empty product. The direction is often uncertain, with static scenes and little sense of pace or tension.

It's arguable that matching a first-time director with a novice screenwriter was asking for trouble. The opening voice-over goes for smart-ass and worldly-wise, with a smattering of expletives. There's a spurious dig at the inconsistency and hypocrisy of social and legal attitudes to drugs. Some of the dialogue is atrocious, leaving a strong cast up the proverbial creek without the essential paddle. Seldom have so many good actors given such caricatured performances. Only Gambon seems at home as a jovial but dangerous senior gangster.

Craig plays XXXX, a cocaine dealer with a foolproof retirement plan, or so he believes. A smart operator, XXXX doesn't see his profession as anything out of the ordinary, claiming that "I'm a businessman whose commodity happens to be cocaine." Handling his product in a dust mask and rubber gloves, he is anti-guns and violence. XXXX's departure from the drug scene is delayed when his employer asks him to track down the missing daughter of an old pal. Before anyone can yell 'blatant plot device', XXXX is in a shitload of trouble with stolen ecstasy pills and some very angry Serbian gangsters.

Craig certainly looks cool, modelling the Steve McQueen look previously evident in *Obsession*: blond hair, blue eyes, ruggedly handsome features, grey T-shirt, leather jacket. What's missing is the McQueen spirit. Craig often looks subdued and uneasy, which sort of works for the character – to a point – but gives the film a passive centre. In one scene, he's upstaged by a voice on a mobile phone.

XXXX gets the hots for gangster's moll Tammy (Sienna Miller), a plot development that leads nowhere much until the closing seconds of the film. While Miller is okay, her already minimal role was further reduced in post-production; as things stand, her character could have been cut from the film with no loss. And, as the going gets tough, XXXX decides to tool up, despite his dislike of guns (shared by Craig). He plays 007 with a World War II German luger, but is easily nabbed by thugs for hire. As the twists and double-crosses mount up, he turns into a balaclava-wearing avenger – emphasising those blue eyes – with unlikely ease. Just as XXXX seems to be toughening up, he's beaten to a bloody pulp by the middle-aged Gene (Meaney). In years to come, some would cite *Layer Cake* as Craig's extended screen test for the role of James Bond. On this showing, he deserved to flunk.

The film opened in the UK on 1 October 2004. According to *Time Out* critic Dave Calhoun, "Craig, Gambon and Cranham add some welcome gravitas to an otherwise tired genre. Peel away the suits, the wit, the drugs, the chases and the twists, and you're not left with much else to chew on. But what else do you need from a slick crime thriller with overtones of *The Long Good Friday*?" The comparison with John MacKenzie's 1980 movie is telling. *The Long Good Friday* put Bob Hoskins on the map, with a blistering performance as an East End gang boss who finds his territory under siege from the IRA (including a young Pierce Brosnan, 15 years before his debut as James Bond). The film quickly became regarded as a British gangster movie classic, on a par with *Performance* (1970) and *Get Carter* (1971). Would *Layer Cake* go on to take its place amid this distinguished company? Frankly, no.

More immediately relevant to Craig was the film's box-office performance. *Layer Cake* took £4.3 million in the UK, equalling its production cost on home ground. Four years earlier, *Snatch* grossed over £12 million in the same territory. Had Guy Ritchie's departure hurt *Layer Cake*'s chances? Probably not, as his own directing career had faltered badly. Craig was hardly a household name, so he couldn't be blamed for failing to draw the crowds. In truth, the film was released too late in the day. Since *Snatch*, a surfeit of British gangster movies – some watchable, most terrible – had killed the public appetite for the genre. It didn't help matters that *Layer Cake* failed to provide even the most basic excitement or thrills.

Layer Cake wasn't released in the US until May 2005. Promoting the film in New York, Craig made some interesting, if cryptic, comments to the assembled journalists. Daniel Robert Epstein was covering the press conference for the Underground Online website. According to Epstein's report, Craig suggested that "The movie business is based on criminals. Some of them are in movies and some of them make movies."

Was this just a throwaway remark or was Craig making a serious point? He wasn't pressed to explain himself more fully, which was probably for the best. Craig was on marginally safer ground discussing the illegal drugs trade. In his view, its importance to the global economy was an open secret: "We are kidding ourselves if we don't think of the drug business as a legitimate business. It's what funds governments and it's too much money to ignore." Provocative maybe, but hardly groundbreaking stuff, and Craig was careful not to mention any particular regimes that might be profiting from the drugs trade.

If the UK box-office for *Layer Cake* had been below expectation, the US gross was little short of disastrous, the film making just $2.3 million. *Snatch* had taken over $30 million, helped by the presence of Hollywood superstar Brad Pitt. Craig's US breakthrough would have to wait a little longer, it seemed. Vaughn, by contrast, signed on to make *X-Men: The Last Stand* (2006), only to drop out for family reasons prior to directing *Stardust* (2007), a lavish fantasy aimed at the *Harry Potter* fanbase.

On 15 September 2003, little more than a fortnight after *Layer Cake* finished production, work began on *Enduring Love*, a Film Four presentation in which Craig took the leading role. This intense drama was based on a 1997 novel by Ian McEwan, who served as an associate producer. The film version reunited Craig with director

Roger Michell, who worked on *The Mother*. McEwan's book was adapted by Joe Penhall, who scripted *Some Voices*. This time out, the UK Film Council, which declined to support *The Mother*, felt the screenplay was of an acceptable standard and agreed to co-finance the film.

Enduring Love co-starred Rhys Ifans, Craig's fellow Guildhall student, who had appeared in Michell's *Notting Hill*. Craig's love interest was Samantha Morton, whose film credits included Lynne Ramsay's *Morvern Callar* (2002) and Steven Spielberg's *Minority Report* (2002). The heavyweight supporting cast included Bill Nighy, Helen McCrory, who appeared in *Hotel Splendide*, and Corin Redgrave, who played Craig's superior officer in *The Ice House*. Relative newcomers included Ben Whishaw, from both *The Trench* and *Layer Cake*.

According to Michell, Craig and Ifans played their characters' fraught relationship for laughs between takes, relieving the tension. The climactic scene called for Craig to kiss Ifans on the mouth. Despite his experience playing gay characters – *Angels in America*, *Love is the Devil* – Craig didn't find this intense moment easy to shoot, telling *Empire* reporter Will Lawrence that "We couldn't look each other in the eye ... you should have seen the fucking state we were in!" Ifans later claimed that Craig had used his tongue, something Craig hotly denied.

Enduring Love has an extraordinary opening scene that merits classic status on its own. In this dreamlike sequence, Joe (Craig) and girlfriend Claire (Morton) find their summer's day picnic disrupted by a runaway hot-air balloon. A bizarre accident leads to a fatality and Joe, though unharmed, finds his comfortable world falling apart. It comes as no surprise that this scene ate up one third of the film's modest budget. The shifts in mood and tone are skilfully handled, going from romantic to surreal to horrific. The whole sequence has an eerie beauty rarely seen in British cinema. The only drawback to this tour de force beginning is making the rest of the film deliver on its promise. Expanded from McEwan's novel, *Enduring Love* faces an uphill struggle that eventually overwhelms the film.

Looking both manly and intellectual in T-shirt and glasses, Craig is convincing as an upper-middle-class academic. His charisma and physicality undercut the 'nerd' clichés, rendering Joe a plausible figure. Craig even brings off the movie lecturer's standard-issue jacket and jeans. All dressed up and raring to go, Craig then has to contend with a lumpen script. After the accident, Joe becomes preoccupied with ideas of duty, faith and guilt. Could he have done more to prevent the unnecessary death? While Claire's response is a clear "No," Joe just can't let it go. He visits the dead man's widow, finding her torn apart by her late husband's possible infidelity. His birthday dinner with Claire goes horribly wrong, their relationship reduced to meaningless ritual. Joe's growing obsession is sidetracked by Jed (Ifans), a strange young man who also witnessed the tragedy.

Taller than Craig, the gangly Ifans makes a good physical contrast to his co-star. Is Jed a religious fanatic? A lunatic? He turns out to be a stalker, at which point the film loses its bearings as much as the runaway balloon did. Attempting to combine character study and thriller, *Enduring Love* ends up working as neither. A lecturer in sociology, Joe's insights into human nature give him no clue as to how he should deal with Jed. Confused and angry, Joe resorts to baseball bat aggro, a handy dry run for Craig's later stint as James Bond (compare this scene with the bathroom punch-up in *Casino Royale*).

Jed accuses Joe of being in denial about the bond between them. Joe's heated responses to Jed's soft-spoken approaches make him seem the crazier of the two. Is Joe experiencing a breakdown or a revelation, confronting the lies in his own life and relationships? The film tosses these ideas away for a psycho-nutter showdown, complete with kitchen knife. The climactic moment where Joe and Jed kiss suggests an extreme fear of homosexuality. For the record, Michell downplays any gay element to their relationship. The film seems to be saying something about the nature of love. On this evidence, it really is the Devil. Craig had been here before and to better effect.

Enduring Love premiered at the London Film Festival on 26 October 2004, going on limited release a month later. The film opened in the US on 29 October, to make the 2005 Academy Awards deadline. As with *Sylvia*, this ploy didn't net any nominations. While *Enduring Love* drew mixed reviews, critics were impressed by Craig's intelligent, focused performance.

After *Enduring Love*, Craig agreed to play a small role in *Sorstalanság* (English title: *Fateless*), a Hungarian-German-British-Israeli co-production based on a 1975 novel by Imre Kertész. As a Hungarian-Jewish teenager during World War II, Kertész had been incarcerated by the Germans in a series of concentration camps. While *Fateless* wasn't an autobiography, much of the material came from Kertész's own experiences. He adapted his book into a screenplay and the film was entrusted to first-time director Lajos Koltai, a former cameraman whose credits included *Mephisto* (1981) and *Ten Minutes Older: The Cello* (not the 'Addicted to the Stars' segment). Starting production in December 2003 and budgeted at $12 million, *Fateless* was the most expensive Hungarian film to date.

Fateless tells the story of Gyura Köves (Marcell Nagy), a Jewish teenager whose comfortable middle-class life in Hungary is shattered by the German occupation. Köves endures vilification, imprisonment and transportation to the concentration camps at Auschwitz, Buchenwald and Zeitz. *Fateless* is undeniably powerful, though the muted colour tones and detached style do not invite ready viewer involvement.

Nearly two hours pass before Craig appears as a US Army sergeant. Zeitz concentration camp has been liberated and Köves faces the choice of either going home or starting a new life elsewhere. Sitting in a jeep, the sergeant greets Köves with a cheery "How you doin'?" After all the subtitled dialogue, it's almost strange to hear two characters speak in English. Craig delivers another plausible American accent as the compassionate sergeant offers Köves cigarettes, advice and food. Like Köves, he's a Jew, anticipating Craig's role in *Munich*. While Craig's two scenes last barely four minutes, he builds a good rapport with young star Marcell Nagy. *Fateless* went on limited release in the UK on 5 May 2006. Some viewers were surprised by Craig's belated appearance amid the unfamiliar Hungarian faces. If his cameo draws more people to check out *Fateless*, so much the better.

Craig's next film was a German-American-Scottish co-production called *The Jacket*. This Warner Bros release reunited Craig with John Maybury, his director on *Love is the Devil*. The film was co-produced by director Steven Soderbergh and superstar George Clooney. Soderbergh was a big fan of *Love is the Devil*, approaching Maybury with a view to collaboration. This time out, Craig didn't have the starring role, a traumatised Gulf War veteran. The lead was first offered to Mark Wahlberg, after which the producers approached Adrien Brody, the youngest ever winner of the Best Actor Academy Award for his performance in *The Pianist* (2002). Subsequent films included *The Village* (2004), where Brody gave an excruciating performance as the resident idiot. While writer-director M Night Shyamalan deserved much of the blame, Brody needed a better movie fast.

Brody's leading lady was British actress Keira Knightley, a rising star after *Pirates of the Caribbean: The Curse of the Black Pearl* and *Love Actually* (both 2003). Brody wasn't regarded as a sufficient box-office draw in his own right and Knightley's casting was a condition of *The Jacket* being financed. The supporting cast included veteran singer-actor Kris Kristofferson, Steve Mackintosh, who'd appeared in *The Mother*, and Jennifer Jason Leigh, whom Craig had murdered in *Road to Perdition*. Anne Lambton, from *Love is the Devil*, was cast as Nurse Harding but, after completing a few scenes, was stricken with pancreatitis and had to leave the production. She was replaced by Mackenzie Phillips, a former child actress best known for *American Graffiti* (1973). *The Jacket* started shooting on 19 January 2004 on locations in Scotland and Canada.

The action begins during the first Gulf War, when serviceman Jack Starks (Brody) is shot in the head. While Starks recovers physically, his mind seems badly damaged. Suffering blackouts, he finds himself arrested, charged and convicted for killing a cop. Sent to a mental institution, Starks is subjected to experimental sensory deprivation therapy that resembles a form of torture. Plagued by nightmarish visions, he struggles to recover his memory while retaining his sanity.

The film resembles an uneasy cross between *Jacob's Ladder* (1990) and *One Flew Over the Cuckoo's Nest* (1975). The tricksy direction and editing pile on the flashbacks and hallucinations without clarifying which is which. The convoluted screenplay offers a succession of unanswered questions. Did Starks really shoot the cop? Is the mental hospital all in his mind? Is the year 1992 or 2007? Who is the mysterious young woman who may be Starks' one chance of salvation? Does it really matter? *The Jacket* is a whacked-out psyche-delic mess, though moments linger in the mind.

Maybury wanted a good actor to play the film's one bona-fide lunatic. He'd been friends with Craig since *Love is the Devil* and knew what he could bring to the role. As it was essentially an extended cameo, Craig's participation wasn't heavily publicised and he didn't feature in the film's theatrical trailer. Cast as fellow inmate Rudy Mackenzie, Craig bears an uncanny resemblance to Tommy Lee Jones, with his dyed black hair and manic acting style. An incompetent would-be wife-killer, Mackenzie is largely a sounding board for Starks, who really needs someone he can talk to. Whatever Maybury's concerns, *The Jacket* makes few demands on Craig's acting ability or his previous experience playing mentally ill characters. While Craig's portrayal of Mackenzie is far broader than his more nuanced performance in *Some Voices*, it's exactly what *The Jacket* requires. His scenes, though brief, are among the film's high points.

The Jacket was released in the US on 4 March 2005, opening in the UK on 13 May. Budgeted at $29 million, the film took only $20 million worldwide; even Keira Knightley couldn't draw the crowds. The film's commercial failure made little difference to Craig's career. As a supporting player, he carried off his scenes with aplomb. It did, however, raise the question of when Craig would get his next starring role in a film. Had the disappointment of *Layer Cake* dampened his enthusiasm for another shot at the big time? Perhaps producers felt he didn't have what it took to play leading roles outside the niche market of *The Mother, Sylvia* and *Enduring Love*. No one expected these films to make much money, so Craig's lack of box-office appeal wasn't a major issue. And Craig's next few assignments seemed to confirm that his big break was still some way off.

In September 2004, Craig returned to televison to star in the BBC production *Archangel*, based on the bestselling 1998 novel by Robert Harris. This political thriller had initially been touted as Hollywood blockbuster material. At one point, the film rights were owned by Mel Gibson's Icon Productions, with Gibson intending to play hero Fluke Kelso. For whatever reason – possibly the story's backdrop of Communist Russia – Gibson decided against making the film and allowed his option to lapse.

Directed by Jon Jones, *Archangel* was scripted by Dick Clement and Ian La Frenais, best known for their hit sitcoms *The Likely Lads* (1964-6), *Porridge* (1974-7) and *Auf Wiedersehen Pet* (1983-2004). Budgeted at £3 million, the film had an 11-week schedule, winding up on 5 December 2004, and was shot on authentic locations in Russia and Latvia. Filming in Riga proved particularly arduous, with temperatures dropping to minus 30 degrees and rivers freezing over; author Robert Harris spent time on set, braving the biting cold. *Archangel* was an ambitious project, running 130 minutes over three instalments. The producers needed a big name for the lead and Craig seemed the perfect choice. He had a wealth of major TV and film credits, yet didn't carry the price tag that an established 'star' could command. And Craig's appearance in *Copenhagen* suggested he hadn't forsaken television for the big screen, provided the script was good enough.

Archangel presented Craig with a potential dilemma. He was being offered the lead in a tautly scripted dramatisation of a blockbuster novel. There was no reason to think it wouldn't be good. Against this, Craig's career had been largely film-based since the late 1990s. After meeting a bad end in *The Hunger* (1997), he had appeared in only three more TV shows, excepting a couple of arts documentaries. With 18 films on his CV, a return to television – even for a prestige production – could be seen as a backward step. But, given that the closest Craig had got to a mainstream starring role was *Layer Cake* (a mediocre film in almost all departments), the leading role in a major TV drama serial held undeniable attractions.

The plot of *Archangel* centres on the search for the lost diary of infamous Soviet dictator Josef Stalin. Interviewed by James Rampton, Craig argued that this theme was especially relevant to the contemporary political situation:

> *There is a hard-line element in Russia who believe that a return to Communism is the way forward. That is a lot to do with the way we live now and with threats of global terrorism and fear. Some people believe that the only way to deal with it is with an iron fist … [and] that is why [Russian President Vladimir] Putin is so popular – because he is so strong.*

After a prologue set on the night of Stalin's death in 1953, *Archangel* cuts to the present day as Dr Fluke Kelso (Craig) gives a lecture that neatly fills in the late dictator's background. Kelso comes across as brisk, professional and cynical. He's also a womaniser, albeit with a variable track record. An encounter with a former Red Guard leads Kelso to believe he's on the trail of Stalin's lost notebook.

Archangel isn't big on in-depth characterisation. The main protagonists are adequately drawn and the performances are generally strong, Craig speaking his Russian dialogue with conviction. Kelso is an academic stuck in a rut. It has been six years since his last book and the former Golden Boy of Soviet historians has lost much of his lustre. Kelso doesn't carry much domestic baggage. His wife (ex-wife?) and kids are never seen and have no bearing on the narrative. Craig is very good at playing a smooth charmer who finds himself out of his depth. While some of the tricks may seem basic –

the blinking of the eyes, the hesitancy of speech, the nervous smiles – Craig brings the role to life, creating a believable, sympathetic character. In one scene, Kelso is forced to dance with a cocky male journalist by a rural psycho with major father issues. The homoerotic undertones are played down in favour of a darkly humorous nightmare.

For much of the story, Kelso is a passive figure, used and abused by various factions. Stuck in a remote, snowbound cabin with an amoral TV hack and a gun-toting nutter, he becomes a helpless puppet. His return to 'civilisation' is no less painful. Soundly thrashed by Communist heavies, Kelso is a helpless witness to history in the making. On the upside, he stands to make a small fortune from book deals and lecture tours.

Archangel is good, story-driven television, a welcome throwback to 1960s Cold War thrillers. The plot moves at a fast pace and the chill blue tones emphasise that, yes, it's really cold in Russia. When Kelso falls into an icy river, Craig has the viewers' sympathy, even with a wetsuit underneath his costume. There are minor flaws. Part Two is weighed down by lengthy flashbacks, as the aged Stalin acquires a mistress hand-picked for her genetic good health. Some of the local extras lack conviction during a protest scene. The ending is both predictable and lacking in impact. But, overall, *Archangel* is a satisfying old-style mystery in which Russia is depicted as a country unable to deal with its past, the ghost of Stalin still unexorcised. Conversely, western academics and journalists are shown as ruthless opportunists, plundering Soviet archives to further their careers and reputations. It seems that lecturers can be as treacherous and back-stabbing as politicians or the secret police, if less inclined to torture and murder.

Archangel was first shown on 19 March 2005. *The Mirror's* 'Shelleyvision' gave the show and Craig the thumbs-up: "Totally ludicrous, thoroughly enjoyable and as good an audition for James Bond as you're likely to see." What could they mean?

EIGHT

COLD BLOOD

B y the time of *Archangel*'s BBC1 debut, Craig was facing one of his biggest acting challenges to date in *Infamous*, which began filming on 14 February 2005 on locations in Texas and New York, budgeted at a modest $13 million.

This unsettling drama told the real-life story of novelist Truman Capote and the creation of his 1966 non-fiction classic *In Cold Blood*. On 15 November 1959, in Holcomb, Kansas, a farmer, Herb Clutter, his wife and two of their children were killed by intruders. The victims had been bound, gagged and shot at close range. While the motive appeared to be robbery, the needless slaughter both appalled and fascinated Capote. Commissioned by the *New Yorker* magazine, he traveled to Holcomb to cover the case, accompanied by childhood friend and aspiring novelist Nelle Harper Lee. The murderers were still at large and Capote planned to write about the dead family, their friends and neighbours and the town of Holcomb rather than the police investigation.

On 30 December, while Capote and Lee were still interviewing local people, the police arrested two men, Dick Hickock and Perry Smith, who confessed to the crime. Convicted and sentenced to hang, they sat on Death Row for five years as four appeals were heard and rejected. Capote formed a close, often uncomfortable relationship with Smith. The planned magazine article was expanded into a book, which could not be completed until the killers' fates were known. While Smith questioned Capote's motives – rightly, many would argue – their unusual friendship persisted until Smith's execution in April 1965. *In Cold Blood* was a huge bestseller and a film version appeared in 1967.

Infamous was written and directed by Douglas McGrath, best known for the Jane Austen adaptation *Emma* (1996), starring Gwyneth Paltrow. The role of Capote went to British actor Toby Jones, who had appeared with Craig in *Hotel Splendide*. Cast as a lowly kitchen hand, Jones had little dialogue but caught the attention with his distinctive, highly expressive face. McGrath assembled a stellar supporting cast, led by *Emma* and *Sylvia* star Paltrow, Juliet Stevenson, Isabella Rossellini and Sigourney Weaver. The role of Harper Lee went to Samantha Morton, Craig's co-star from *Enduring Love*, but Morton was pushed out in favour of Hollywood star Sandra Bullock, whose flagging career had been revived by *Crash* (2004).

The pivotal role of Perry Smith was offered first to Mark Wahlberg, who committed to the film but had to withdraw. McGrath then approached Mark Ruffalo, who accepted the part and was scheduled to join the *Infamous* production once he finished shooting *All the King's Men*. When the latter over-ran, Ruffalo realised he wouldn't be available for his agreed start date on *Infamous*. Two weeks before McGrath began shooting, Ruffalo resigned from the film. Short of time and options, McGrath offered the role to Craig.

A fan of Craig's work, McGrath hadn't considered him for the part of Perry Smith because he wasn't American. Craig's CV included a number of American characters, on stage – *Angels in America*, *Hurlyburly* – and film – *Lara Croft Tomb Raider*, *Road to Perdition*, *The Jacket*, *Fateless* – so it's surprising that McGrath didn't appear to know any these. Craig had done a variety of American accents, mostly successful, though he sometimes reverted to English when shouting.

A fan of both Capote and *In Cold Blood*, Craig was delighted to be involved in *Infamous*. McGrath cited Craig as ideal casting, third choice or not: "I knew Daniel was right because he is very persuasive violently, very persuasive as a vulnerable person, but he is also totally magnetic. As Perry, you think is he dumb, or much smarter than I thought, which keeps you on a knife edge." McGrath also felt that Craig's relatively unknown status in the US would benefit the film. A few months later, of course, Craig was cast as the new James Bond.

The blond, blue-eyed Craig bore little physical resemblance to Perry Smith, the son of a Cherokee mother and Irish father. According to Capote biographer Gerald Clarke, Smith had black hair, sad eyes and pixie-like features. Capote described Smith as having "a changeling's face," switching from meek to brutish in the blink of an eye. McGrath asked Craig to dye his hair black and wear contact lenses to darken his eyes. Craig was normally reluctant to use contact lenses, as he found them uncomfortable, but he agreed that they were essential for *Infamous* and an acceptably soft type was employed. While Craig was willing to alter his appearance, he couldn't do much to reduce his height. Smith's legs had been deformed by a motorbike crash and he stood only 5'4", seven inches shorter than Craig.

From the start, the production was overshadowed by a rival film, *Capote*, which covered the same events as *Infamous*. Starring Philip Seymour Hoffman, with Latino actor Clifton Collins Jr as Smith, *Capote* wrapped on 1 December 2004, long before the first scene of *Infamous* was shot. It was inevitable that *Infamous* would be compared with *Capote*, a United Artists release directed by Bennett Miller from a script by Dan Futterman. On the occasion of the belated UK release of *Infamous*, Craig noted that "My feeling all the way along was I wish they had put the two bloody films out together. I wish they'd had the balls to do that."

Infamous makes a fascinating counterpoint to *Capote*. While the latter is an understated, underplayed film, *Infamous* is brash and arch, with bold colour schemes and a confrontational attitude. It's a darker, more affecting film than *Capote*, despite uncertain touches and a lack of subtlety. Jones' Capote goes beyond high camp to some bizarre new dimension all his own. In some shots, he resembles an immaculately turned-out three-toed sloth. The script doesn't play down Capote's less appealing side, the writer behaving like an insensitive jerk and a spoilt child. It soon becomes clear that Capote the raconteur, acid wit and bitchy gossip is a calculated party-piece that both reflects and conceals the man himself. His relationship with Harper Lee (Bullock) is more abrasive than in *Capote*, emphasising that their long-standing friendship has jagged edges. Talking heads – all characters from the film – fill in Capote's background and character. All in all, Jones' portrayal seems closer to the real thing than Philip Seymour Hoffman's more controlled incarnation.

Where *Capote* begins with the discovery of the Clutters' bodies, *Infamous* opens with a glimpse of Capote's New York social life as he is seated at the swish, ultra-exclusive El Morocco nightclub. Chanteuse Kitty Dean (Paltrow) is performing Cole Porter's 'What Is This Thing Called Love?', thereby establishing the theme of the film. There are already hints of angst beneath the plush surface, Dean turning Porter's upbeat romantic number into a heartfelt confessional session. Porter, a married man who had numerous homosexual affairs, was well acquainted with the twilight world of a desire unacceptable to conventional society.

Third-billed in *Infamous*, Craig makes his entrance after 40 minutes. As with *Capote*, Perry Smith is first seen under police arrest, though in broad daylight rather than at night. The exchange of glances between Smith and Capote is more protracted, the two men instantly drawn to one another. With darkened hair and eyebrows, Craig's Smith bears a passing resemblance to his character in *The Jacket*, a more surreal and superficial examination of a troubled human soul. Craig looks much older than *Capote* actor Clifton Collins Jr, who in fact is only two years his junior.

Collins Jr is 5'8", four inches taller than the real Perry Smith. Robert Blake, who played Smith in the 1967 film of *In Cold Blood*, exactly matched the killer's height of 5'4". (He also went on trial later for murdering his wife, but that's another story.) Rather than disguising Craig's 5'11", director McGrath uses it as an asset. His stature and powerful build make a startling contrast to Toby Jones' diminutive 5'5" frame. Craig's size and stillness evoke a big cat, caged but still able and willing to strike. He also captures an underlying sense of both suffering and brutality. Craig imbues the 'wounded animal' cliché with an extraordinary conviction and vitality.

Craig's Smith is much warier of Capote than the Collins Jr version. At the start, he is downright hostile, saying, "Don't bullshit me. You don't care about my side. You're not trying to help me." During this first conversation, Craig is framed in long shot, semi-obscured by shadow. Smith is as much a mystery to Capote as he is to the viewer. For all Capote's reassurances, Smith isn't easily won over, remaining distrustful and saying, "You've got a hell of a fucking nerve." In one scene, he adopts a threatening posture, towering over the seated writer. In *Capote*, the writer never seems in any physical danger when he visits Smith. *Infamous* shows Capote taking a considerable risk in sharing Smith's cell with the guard out of sight.

Smith's initial hesitation means that Dick Hickock (Lee Pace) plays a more prominent role, giving Capote information about his partner in crime. Hickock notes, with amused contempt, that "Perry Smith fancies himself an artiste." Smith idolises Humphrey Bogart and Marlon Brando, two generations of ultimate macho cool. McGrath has Craig strike some Brandoesque poses, all white vest, muscles and moodiness in a bleak, hostile environment. When Capote sends Smith and Hickock a stash of porn magazines, the former takes exception, requesting art and literature instead.

Smith even ventures to criticise Capote's work, complaining that his writing lacks kindness. He dreamed of being a singer or painter and the film suggests he had some talent in both fields. Smith sings 'Gold Mine in the Sky', his father's favourite song, Craig emphasising the emotion over the technique. Both Capote and Smith aspire to create one great work of art. The irony, of course, is that Smith has become an integral part of Capote's crowning literary achievement. Smith will pay with his life while Capote, by implication, will be steadily eaten away by guilt, remorse and grief.

Smith longs for acceptance and respect. Capote seems to be the one man who will listen to him with sympathy and not make a joke of his romantic aspirations. The deep probing of psyches cuts both ways, Smith forcing Capote to strip away his protective layers of pretension and affectation. In a breakthrough moment, Smith sits down next to Capote on a bunk and apologises for his previous aggression. Flashbacks show parallels in their childhoods, though the emphasis is on Smith's awful relationship with his useless absentee father. Smith retains an element of doubt over Capote's motives, switching from tenderness to savagery in the blink of an eye. His second physical attack on the writer – sparked by the book's title – is a forceful reminder that Capote is dealing with a multiple murderer. Craig captures Smith's cold fury as he clamps a large hand over Capote's mouth and drags him to the back of the cell, out of sight.

From the start, *Infamous* is much more upfront than *Capote* about gay, or 'queer', sexuality. The first physical contact between Smith and Capote is a 'manly' arm-wrestling match, devoid of any sexual or romantic connotations. Smith later grabs Capote and pushes him against a wall, a display of brute strength from a man who is otherwise powerless. When Capote blows on Smith's face to evoke a Mexican breeze, the effect is almost erotic. The dark side of sexuality surfaces when a furious Smith threatens Capote with anal rape. The subsequent revelation that he only wanted to scare and humiliate Capote reveals a calculating mind and complete absence of moral bearings.

Infamous depicts Smith as a man slowly and painfully coming to terms with his long-suppressed homosexuality. It's suggested that Hickock's homophobic slurs goaded Smith into killing Herb Clutter and his teenage son (Hickock shoots the mother and daughter). After 90 minutes, Smith confesses his feelings for Capote: "We really connected, didn't we?" The kiss that follows seems spontaneous and unselfconscious. Craig suggests that Smith is experiencing reciprocated affection for probably the first time in his life.

Ever the opportunist, Capote advises Smith on his final words – an apology for the killings – as the gallows beckon. (This attempt at stage management fails, Smith saying nothing before the black hood goes on and the noose is tightened.) Their historically accurate goodbye kiss is a demure peck on the cheek. The grimmest moment comes when Smith sits in a car, chewing gum, while the prison staff wait for the hanged Hickock to die (over 20 minutes after he fell through the trapdoor). There's nothing noble or romantic about Smith's last moments on earth. He stumbles on the steps to the scaffold and starts to panic as the hood goes on. Unlike *Capote*, *Infamous* remains true to the facts at this point. Having witnessed Hickock's execution, Capote leaves rather than see Smith die.

The exact nature of Capote's relationship with Smith will never be known. Where *Capote* hedges its bets, *Infamous* reflects McGrath's belief that they were lovers. While Capote never admitted to the relationship, McGrath cites the documentary *A Visit with Truman Capote* (1966) as containing clear indications. Moreover, several of Capote's friends and colleagues claimed the writer lost much of his enthusiasm for life after Smith's execution. Capote never finished another book and died prematurely in 1984 from an alcohol-related illness.

Craig agreed that *Infamous* was at heart a love story, albeit a tragic one. While Smith and Capote were never a 'couple' like George Dyer and Francis Bacon, the attraction between them was undoubtedly sexual. Like Dyer, Smith was a man doomed by his status, circumstances and human failings. He could never have fitted in with Capote's elite Manhattan social circle. The appalling crime that sealed Smith's fate was the only reason he met Capote and their relationship unfolded in the shadow of the gallows. As Craig explained to Liz Hoggard:

> *There was never any self-consciousness about it. I always think that's how a love story needs to play out anyway, because it's just this friendship that starts growing, and if it turns into sex, it turns into sex … This is about two human beings really sitting down and trying to figure each other out.*

Infamous was launched at the Venice Film Festival, with Douglas McGrath and Toby Jones in attendance. Questioned about his screen kiss with Craig, Jones kept his comments light-hearted, saying, "I never dreamed I'd kiss James Bond. Now that I've done it, I say I hope I'm just the first of many." Craig was amused – up to a point – by the media attention: "What's he supposed to say? 'Very dry?'" Craig didn't join McGrath and Jones at the festival, citing work commitments. He later admitted that he felt his 007 status would overshadow the film, telling Hoggard, "I had this whole awful debate going on with myself. I thought, I can't go because otherwise it will be all about the new Bond being in town."

Infamous was distributed by Warner Bros, who had little faith in the film's box-office prospects. In the wake of *Capote*, *Infamous* was headed for a DVD premiere, bypassing cinemas altogether. The Warner executives changed their minds after the film's favourable reception in Venice. The theatrical trailer included the tagline, "There is more to the story than you know," which could easily be read as a dig at *Capote*. *Infamous* accordingly opened in the US on 13 October 2006. Inevitably, the film was overshadowed by *Capote*, which had been released a year earlier. Philip Seymour Hoffman had won the Best Actor Academy Award for *Capote* months before *Infamous* hit US screens. In Hollywood terms, Truman Capote was old news. Some critics didn't recognise Craig at first, which gave him great satisfaction. He was being judged as an actor, not a movie star or the new Bond.

Infamous opened in the UK on 19 January 2007, after *Casino Royale*, earning respectful reviews but little else. Craig hoped his new fame as Bond would tempt audiences, saying, "If more people go and see *Infamous* now because I'm James Bond, that's great. But people should go and see it because it's a wonderful movie." How would British audiences react to seeing the new Bond kiss another, less ruggedly handsome man? Answer: they couldn't care less, as they didn't bother seeing it.

After making *Infamous*, Craig's career took a step upwards in June

2005 with *Munich*. Also based on real events, *Munich* was directed by Steven Spielberg, the most commercially successful filmmaker of the past 30 years. A decade earlier, Craig had briefly entered the wider Spielberg universe via his appearance in *The Young Indiana Jones Chronicles*. Second time around, he would be working with the man himself.

Spielberg's career had flagged – by his standards – since *Saving Private Ryan* (1998), which netted him a second Best Director Oscar. His most recent film, *War of the Worlds* (2005), had proved a major hit but did little for his reputation. *Munich* was produced by Spielberg's DreamWorks company, which had backed *Road to Perdition*, with distribution through Universal. The budget was $75 million, modest by Spielberg's standards. Given the subject matter – both downbeat and controversial – this financial caution made sense.

Munich was filmed from 29 June to 29 September 2005 on locations in France, Hungary, Malta and New York. The script was written by Eric Roth, whose credits included *Forrest Gump* (1994) and *Ali* (2001), and playwright Tony Kushner, best known for the two-part epic *Angels in America* (1992-3), in which Craig had appeared 12 years before. The lead role went to Australian actor Eric Bana, with Geoffrey Rush, from *Elizabeth*, Ciaran Hinds, one of Craig's victims in *Road to Perdition*, and French actor Mathieu Kassovitz cast in support.

Munich opens in 1972, when 11 Palestinian terrorists – or freedom fighters – take Israeli athletes hostage at the Munich Olympic village. Negotiations lead nowhere and a botched police counterstrike fails to prevent the murders of all the athletes. The Israeli government identifies Black September as the group responsible and initiates a bloody retaliation. Mossad, the Israeli secret service, dispatches five agents to assassinate the Palestinians held accountable. The Mossad quintet track down their prey in Rome, Paris, Cyprus, Beirut, Athens and London.

Running two and a half hours, Munich is an ambitious attempt to combine a thriller, a character study and an examination of the moral issues raised by the mission. Craig plays the talkative Steve, a South African Jew who acts as the group's getaway driver. His Afrikaner accent recalls both *The Power of One* and *I Dreamed of Africa*, Craig progressing from neo-Nazi racist cop to apolitical ranch manager to Zionist avenger. Steve's blond hair and blue eyes are the Nazi ideal, an irony not addressed in the film.

Interviewed during production, Craig described his character as having a gung-ho, bull-in-a-china-shop attitude. Steve starts out with a clear distinction between good and bad, his conscience untroubled by the state-sanctioned killings. He even dances with a fellow agent to celebrate their first assassination. Steve grouches a lot, frustrated that he's not getting a share of the action. Pointing his gun with a menacing look, he has to be satisfied with shooting out a streetlight (under orders). Craig is barely visible during the pitched gun battle in Beirut. Anyone looking for some pre-Bond gun play will be disappointed. Steve does take part in the killing of a female Dutch assassin who caught one of his team in a lethal 'honey trap', and the sight of Craig and co shooting a semi-naked woman with bicycle-pump guns is bizarre on so many levels.

Craig felt that the cocksure Steve would be gradually caught up in an emotional turmoil he never expected. This side of the character isn't really explored in the final cut. While Steve looks more anxious in later scenes, it's largely because people are out to kill him. Inevitably, the hunters have become the hunted and three of the Mossad agents are killed. A comment on the futility of vengeance, the never-ending cycle that destroys all involved? Maybe so, but we've been here many times before. Sidelined by the script, Craig is even denied an action set-piece. Steve and team leader Avner (Bana) are sent on a major hit which has to be aborted at the last minute. Craig isn't seen again and *Munich* tails off to an unsatisfying conclusion.

Munich opened in the US on 6 January 2006. The film grossed $47 million, way short of its production cost. Released in the UK three weeks later, it took £4.7 million. In theory, *Munich* was Craig's biggest movie to date, and for one of Hollywood's leading directors. It should have been a big deal in his career, yet the end result was strangely muted. Supporting Eric Bana, whose own Hollywood prospects were far from certain, Craig made the most of a limited character, a back-up man who becomes increasingly marginalised as the film progresses. Most reviews gave Craig only cursory mention, focusing on the film's depiction of terrorism, an all-too-topical subject. *Munich* was a Spielberg movie, first and foremost, and the majority verdict lauded the intent rather than the end result.

In the calm before the James Bond storm, Craig's personal life drew more attention than his film roles. The divorced father of one had been settled with Heike Makatsch since 1997. While there was no sign of Craig getting married a second time, he and Makatsch seemed committed to each other. By early 2004, however, their relationship had foundered beyond repair.

Based in London, Makatsch soon found that the stardom she attained in her home country meant little elsewhere. While her career still thrived in Germany, it was going nowhere in Britain and the US, where she remained a relative unknown. Roles in *Longitude* (2000), *Late Night Shopping* (2001) and *Resident Evil* (2002) did little for her industry profile. There was talk of Makatsch hitting the big time with *Love Actually* (2003), an all-star romantic comedy written and directed by Richard Curtis. She played Alan Rickman's seductive secretary, lending a touch of class to a clichéd role. *Love Actually* opened in the UK in November 2003, the same month as *The Mother*. At the time, Makatsch seemed to have picked the winning team, *Love Actually* cleaning up at the box-office. But, while the film was a hit, Makatsch stood little chance of a breakthrough in a cast that included Rickman, Hugh Grant, Bill Nighy, Colin Firth, Emma Thompson, Liam Neeson, Rowan Atkinson and Kiera Knightley. This was no reflection on her talent, looks or personality, just a harsh fact of life.

Craig and Makatsch split in January 2004. A few months later, Craig was linked with supermodel Kate Moss, whose celebrity boyfriends included Johnny Depp and, subsequently, Pete Doherty. They were spotted together in the audience for dancer-choreographer

Michael Clark's show at Sadler's Wells. Craig and Moss initially claimed that there was no relationship between them. They just happened to be mutual friends of Rhys Ifans and Gwyneth Paltrow, Craig's co-stars from *Enduring Love* and *Sylvia*. The press didn't believe a word of it, putting the new celebrity 'couple' on their most-wanted list. Craig soon found himself exiting restaurants through the kitchens he'd got to know so well during his National Youth Theatre and Guildhall days, and, in the end, he decided that he found Moss' behaviour "too wild" for comfort. He also hated the accompanying levels of tabloid coverage, claiming he wouldn't put himself in the same situation again. Craig's wariness of Moss proved justified. Her volatile behaviour and alleged cocaine habit would draw a lot of negative press, though Moss bounced back with minimal damage to her career.

Craig was then seen out and about with Sienna Miller, his supposed lover during the *Layer Cake* shoot. Miller subsequently linked up with Jude Law, Craig's co-star from *Road to Perdition*. They met on the set of *Alfie* (2004), an ill-advised remake of the 1966 Michael Caine movie which failed to launch Law as an international star. Craig and Law had been pals, if not particularly close. While the press were desperate to push the Law-Miller-Craig love triangle, the stars weren't playing ball. As before, Craig and Miller denied being anything more than good friends. *The Mirror* quoted Craig as saying, "Sienna is special, she has chutzpah. I've heard she's considering giving up [acting] because of the pressure, but this is one artist who shouldn't." This sounds like a friend speaking, rather than a lover, which, of course, was exactly the impression Craig wanted to convey.

When Law's affair with his children's nanny became public, Craig took Miller out to dinner, which inevitably set tongues wagging once more. Perhaps Craig was merely offering his distraught friend a sympathetic ear and a shoulder to cry on. Or had Miller embarked on a revenge fling with Craig to get back at the cheating Law? Tabloid editors and the paparazzi preferred the latter option. On one occasion, Craig had to drive away from a night spot with Miller lying flat across the back seat of the car to avoid being caught on camera. This was great ammunition for the press: why were Craig and Miller taking such extreme measures if they had nothing to hide?

Craig's work schedule provided welcome relief from his hectic personal life. He lent his vocal talents to *Renaissance* (2005), an ambitious animated feature film. Years in the making, this co-production between France, Luxembourg and Great Britain was directed by Christian Volckman. Budgeted at 14 million Euros, *Renaissance* was designed in stark, high-contrast black and white, with no shades of grey. The character animation was created with a process known as motion capture, which involved recording live-action material of actors performing the movement required for the film and then transferring the recorded data of the position of the actors' limbs, faces and eyes to computer generated 3D models. The voice cast for the British version also featured Catherine McCormack, Jonathan Pryce and Ian Holm.

Renaissance is set in Paris in the year 2054. There are references to a recent war, though the city appears to be thriving. The skyline is dominated by adverts for Avalon, a mysterious mega-corporation that promotes "Health. Beauty. Longevity." When an Avalon employee goes missing, the future of the entire human race is in jeopardy. Jaded cop Barthélémy Karas is assigned to the case...

As a technical achievement, *Renaissance* is impressive. The doom-laden black and white visuals capture the desired look of a graphic novel. The overall effect is one of claustrophobia, with a succession of dark rooms, narrow corridors and confined spaces. Obvious influences include *Blade Runner* (1982), *Nineteen Eighty-Four* (1956 and 1984), *Metropolis* (1927), *THX 1138* (1971), the *Matrix* trilogy (1999, 2003) and even *Caligula* (1979). The invisible Avalon agents are an ingenious touch and the more imaginative action scenes rival anything in the *Matrix* sequels. The thin story is less successful, involving identity theft and that old science fiction standby, the quest for immortality. The film feels at least 25 minutes too long and the ending falls flat.

Craig voices Karas, a super-cool supercop with a troubled past. Taciturn to the nth degree, Karas is brisk and abrupt. Put on the trail of the missing Avalon scientist, he tells his team, "First we find her. And then we sleep." To be honest, the English version of *Renaissance* suffers by comparison with the French-language original. The tentative vocal performances blend uneasily with the overall style. It doesn't help that the English dialogue, by Michael Katims, is sometimes clunky, making an unsuccessful attempt at futuristic hard-boiled jargon.

While Craig and Pryce come off better than most, even they are constrained by the demands of the script, a questionable translation and the pre-existing animation. Craig's voice doesn't really suit his character, who looks French with a touch of American film noir. In the original version, Karas is voiced by French actor Patrick Floersheim, who, being much older than Craig, couldn't have played Karas in the flesh – but his weary, cynical Gallic inflection is a much better match for the character design. *Renaissance* opened in France on 15 March 2006, the English version arriving in the UK on 28 July to mixed reviews and modest box-office.

After *Munich*, Craig got an offer from Warner Bros of a co-starring role in *The Invasion*, not having worked for the studio since *The Power of One* nearly 15 years earlier. The new film was loosely based on Jack Finney's novel *The Body Snatchers*, previously filmed in 1955, 1978 and 1993. This new take on the story paired Craig with Hollywood superstar Nicole Kidman, who had won an Academy Award for her performance in *The Hours* (2002) but had entered a slump with more recent titles like *The Stepford Wives* (2004), *Birth* (2004), *The Interpreter* (2005) and *Bewitched* (2005). Where had the Kidman magic gone? Given her track record with remakes, some questioned Kidman's wisdom in agreeing to star in a fourth film version of *The Body Snatchers*. Perhaps with this in mind, Warners played down the film's remake status, first announcing it as *The Visiting* until people pointed out that the derivation was too obvious to be overlooked.

Jack Finney's novel centres on a doctor, Miles Bennell, who

discovers a bizarre epidemic in the small California town where he lives and works. Patients are convinced that their relatives and friends have been replaced by impostors. The latter look, sound and behave exactly like the original people yet something is missing. There's no real emotion or warmth, just a pretence of it. At first, Bennell believes he's dealing with an outbreak of mass hysteria. As events escalate, he realises that more sinister, inhuman forces are at work. In *The Invasion*, the main character is Kidman's Carol Bennell, a psychiatrist who has a son who – in the Hollywood way of things – could be the key to saving the entire human race from alien aggressors. Craig was cast as Kidman's colleague and romantic interest, Ben Driscoll.

The Invasion was directed by Oliver Hirschbiegel, a German filmmaker who drew international acclaim with *Downfall* (2004), a compelling, if grim, World War II drama concerning the last days of Adolf Hitler. Hirschbiegel's deal for *The Invasion* allowed him to use cameraman Rainer Klausmann and editor Hans Funck, who both worked on *Downfall*. The supporting cast included Craig's fellow Brit Jeremy Northam, from *Mimic* (1997) and *Gosford Park* (2001), and Veronica Cartwright, who had appeared in *The Birds* (1963), *Alien* (1979) and the second version of *Invasion of the Body Snatchers*.

Warners budgeted *The Invasion* at $50 million, a modest sum for a film with an A-list star; it's a fair bet that Kidman's recent run of flops was starting to hurt her career. Shooting ran from September through December 2005 on locations in Baltimore, Washington and Los Angeles. The idea was to release *The Invasion* in August 2006, during the long summer vacation. This plan had to be scrapped, however, when Hirschbiegel's cut of the film was rejected by producer Joel Silver, who felt it didn't deliver the required excitement and spectacle, especially in its latter stages. It's rumoured that test screenings had gone badly, though Silver denies this. Whatever the case, Warners declared *The Invasion* unreleasable in its original form, with problems that couldn't be fixed through re-editing. With Hirschbiegel out of the picture, Joel Silver hired Andy and Larry Wachowski – best known for creating the *Matrix* franchise – to rewrite the script.

But all this, and the film's eventual fate, lay in the future. For the time being, *The Invasion* proved a memorable shoot for reasons unconnected with the worth or otherwise of the finished film. For it was while on location in Baltimore that Craig learned he was to be the new James Bond.

NINE

BONDAGE...

nterviewed at the time of *Road to Perdition*, Craig remarked, "If I believed it every time someone said, 'This is gonna be your big break,' I'd be a fucking lunatic by now." Still sane after all the hype and let-downs, Craig was finally confronted with a solid gold, bona-fide, once-in-a-lifetime chance to become a superstar. How to cope with being offered the role of James Bond? "My first reaction was, I needed a drink."

After 44 years and 20 films, the Bond series was returning to the screen with *Casino Royale*. Owing to various legal twists and turns, the new film would be co-produced by MGM, Sony Columbia and Eon Productions, which held the film rights to the Bond character. The Bond movie franchise kicked off with *Dr. No* (1962) and, from the start, the family-friendly package of sex, violence, fast cars and high style proved a winner. The brand name proved bigger than the star, Bond number one Sean Connery making way for George Lazenby, Roger Moore, Timothy Dalton and Pierce Brosnan.

Connery's dark good looks, seductive Scottish burr and cold-blooded demeanour proved a tough act to follow and most of his successors were found wanting. Brosnan's more refined Bond was generally regarded as a close second, though all five 007s had their ardent admirers. While the Bond series had been through rough patches – neither *The Man with the Golden Gun* (1974) nor *Licence to Kill* (1989) were big hits in the US – it remained the second most successful movie franchise after the *Star Wars* saga.

In late 2003, word spread that Pierce Brosnan had been dropped from the series. Producers Barbara Broccoli and Michael Wilson, it was said, felt he was too old for the role. There were rumours, too, that Brosnan's salary demands were considered excessive. Whatever the case, Brosnan had lost his 007 licence to thrill. Who would become the next James Bond? According to press reports, front runners included Craig, Ewan McGregor, Jude Law, Orlando Bloom, Colin Farrell, Ioan Gruffudd, Heath Ledger, Clive Owen, Eric Bana, Gerard Butler, Julian McMahon, Hugh Jackman and Dougray Scott, who had acted with Craig in *The Rover*.

Clive Owen was said to be the favoured choice. Many Bond fans felt that his good looks, cool manner and 'classy' demeanour made him an ideal candidate. Others argued that Owen lacked the humour and lightness of touch essential to the role. Sean Connery had supposedly tipped fellow Scot Ewan McGregor for the role. While McGregor wielded a mean lightsabre in the second *Star Wars* trilogy (1999-2005) and assorted hardware in *Black Hawk Down* (2001), action movies weren't really his bag. Nevertheless, it was widely rumoured that McGregor was Eon Productions' number one choice for Bond. Though intrigued by the challenge, he ruled himself out, citing concerns over typecasting.

Movie hard-man Jason Statham, best known for the *Transporter* shoot-and-punch-em-ups, publicly declared his interest in playing Bond. Big mistake. Would Colin Salmon, who played intelligence officer Charles Robinson in three of the Brosnan films, be the first black Bond? *The Sun* seemed to think so, for a day or two. One paper claimed to have a leaked memo from the Eon production office. According to this murky source, some of the bigger names had already been ruled out: McGregor (too short), Jackman (too fey), Farrell (too sleazy). Alternatively, none of these actors was interested in a jaded movie franchise that could stunt their careers. As the shortlist was whittled down, Craig's main rival seemed to be Australian actor Julian McMahon, who had played Doctor Doom in *Fantastic Four* (2005).

By April 2005, the rumour mill was in overdrive: Craig could spend the next ten years as Bond, for a reputed £15 million fee. Craig had been seen in an antiquarian bookshop, looking for a first edition of Ian Fleming's *Casino Royale*. This last story proved to be true. London bookseller Peter Ellis confirmed that Craig had enquired about the book at his shop: "I told him that he should expect to pay about £20,000. He didn't seem particularly surprised at the price, but then he didn't ask me to get him a copy either." By mid-October, Craig's agents at ICM (International Creative Management) were no longer denying the rumours, stating that they couldn't comment until Eon Productions made an official announcement. Craig had been in the business long enough not to be seduced by hype. Meetings and negotiations meant little until a contract had been signed. At one point, he suggested that, while MGM wanted him for the part, Broccoli and Wilson seemed less certain. Would they reconsider over Brosnan and bring him back for a fifth 007 mission?

On Monday 10 October 2005, during filming for *The Invasion*, Craig received the long-awaited phone call from Barbara Broccoli. On the 14th, he signed a three-film contract with Eon Productions. His mother Carol jumped the gun, confirming Craig's casting the day before the official announcement. Questioned by a reporter from the *Liverpool Daily Post*, she seemed unaware that the decision was still under wraps. "Obviously we are thrilled to bits," she said. "It has come at a very good time in his career. He has worked extremely hard all his life and this would be his biggest populist role. I think he could bring something very interesting to the part." She also noted, unnecessarily, that "It will be life-changing."

Taking a break from *The Invasion*, Craig left the Baltimore location and returned to London for the *Casino Royale* press conference. This media junket was held on *HMS President*, moored at a naval training centre on the Thames. Craig arrived in a Royal Marine Rigid Raider speedboat, dressed in an expensive, 007-worthy Brioni suit. He boarded the Raider craft at *HMS Belfast*, then sped under Tower Bridge to the jetty of *HMS President*.

While Craig's grand entrance seemed suitably macho, there were problems. Craig was obliged to wear a life-jacket, which undercut both his suit and the cool image associated with Bond. He hung on to a safety rail, as most civilians would have done under the circumstances. Craig admitted to the press that he disliked fast boat travel. And it didn't help the Bond mystique that Craig's Royal Marine escort looked much tougher than he did. This carefully staged event was supposed to officially reveal the identity of the new 007. Yet the assembled media – and most other interested parties – already knew it was Craig. Inevitably, Craig was asked about his mother spilling the beans a day early. He curtly denied that this slip had spoiled the surprise, saying, "That's not very fair. And not strictly accurate either."

Accompanied by producers Broccoli and Wilson and director Martin Campbell, Craig braved the media circus. He promised to make his mark on the iconic role, bringing a grittier feel to the character. The producers confirmed that they had met over 200 candidates before choosing Craig. Michael Wilson delivered the expected spiel – "Daniel is a superb actor who has all the qualities needed to bring a contemporary edge to the role." Asked about the previous 007 movies, Craig revealed that his favourite Bond was Sean Connery, hardly the most controversial choice. Diana Rigg, who co-starred in *On Her Majesty's Secret Service* (1969), beat out *Live and Let Die*'s Jane Seymour as his top Bond Girl. It probably helped that Rigg had played a more complex and tragic character than the average Bond heroine.

The verdict on Craig's unveiling as Bond was mixed to say the least. More sympathetic journalists suggested that he didn't yet appreciate the off-screen requirements of being Bond. *Mirror* columnist Tony Parsons was unimpressed:

> *Moody, monosyllabic and oozing angst, anyone would think*
> *that Daniel Craig had been selected as the new Hamlet rather*
> *than the new James Bond … Craig is one of our best youngish*

actors. He was brilliant in Our Friends in the North. *But he seems a little too embarrassed by the whole Bond circus. At the press conference to announce his appointment to mythic status, Craig squirmed and did not seem even remotely excited.*

Anyone who can [allegedly] shag Jude Law's girlfriend has the sex appeal of the young Sean Connery. Unfortunately for all us Bond fans, Daniel Craig appears to have the sense of humour of the middle-aged Osama bin Laden.

Independent writer David Lister felt things had gone downhill from the queasy speedboat arrival onwards: "I suspect that no other Bond actor, not even Roger Moore, would have gone so worryingly out of character." Asked about Kate Moss and Sienna Miller, Craig lost his cool, snapping at the offending hack, "I'm not going to get into that." While Lister didn't question Craig's acting ability, he felt the new 007 had much to learn in the PR department:

I've seen Connery at press conferences and he can shoot down a troublemaker with a witty riposte. He doesn't do tetchy … James Bond actors aren't allowed to be irritable, frightened of travelling at speed, or nervous that they might make a hash of things. And they never, never sulk … Daniel Craig is a fine actor and should be given a chance in the role. It's his off-screen persona that needs improving. He needs to start oozing style and panache. Live the dream, Daniel.

Easier said than done. In fairness, Pierce Brosnan's press conference for *GoldenEye* (1995) hadn't been a howling success either. Brosnan looked uneasy at times and forgot the name of Bond's favourite car manufacturer (answer: Aston Martin). When *GoldenEye* was released to general acclaim, this initial awkwardness was soon forgotten.

Craig had expected a certain amount of sniping from the press. But he wasn't prepared for the fan backlash. A small but vocal group of hardcore Bond devotees denounced his casting as a disaster for the franchise. This anti-Craig sentiment was widely reported in the press, with some newspapers adding their own voices of dissent. Craig, it seemed, lacked both the physical attributes and the style to play Bond, on the following counts:

Too short

Standing 5'11", Craig didn't measure up to Connery (6'2"), Lazenby (6'2½"), Moore (6'1", Dalton (6'2") or Brosnan (6'1"). While more charitable sources upgraded Craig to six feet, he still lacked at least an inch. Of course, when *Casino Royale* finally opened, no one even noticed this alleged lack of stature.

Too blond

Ian Fleming's Bond was dark-haired, and the five previous film incarnations had followed suit. News articles such as 'From *GoldenEye* to golden hair' suggested a blond Bond was a radical departure from tradition that bordered on blasphemy. Bond villains could have blond hair – notably Robert Shaw's Red Grant in *From Russia with Love* (1963) and Christopher Walken's Max Zorn in *A View to a Kill* (1985) – but 007 himself? While Craig had darkened his hair for some roles, the end result gave his brooding, rugged countenance an unsettling air that bordered on menacing. This was fine for his villains, such as the whip-happy sadist in *Sharpe's Eagle*, but wouldn't work for good guy Bond. If it matters, Moore had noticeably lighter hair than Connery, Lazenby, Dalton and Brosnan. And unlike Connery, Craig wouldn't require a hair-piece for the role. Not yet anyway.

Alleged inability to drive an Aston Martin DB5

The Daily Star ran an article entitled 'Bond's licence to squeal: 007 wuss Dan can't even change gears'. According to this piece, "superwimp Daniel Craig" couldn't drive the classic Bond car – seen in *Goldfinger* (1964) and *Thunderball* (1965) – because he was only used to automatic transmissions. The 'wuss' and 'superwimp' jibes said more than the discussion of manual gearshifts: Craig wasn't macho enough to play Bond. For the record, Craig claimed he could use a gear-stick as well as the next man.

Ears too large

C'mon people, Craig's ears aren't that huge. Besides, did it harm the careers of Clark Gable and Big Ears? Exactly.

Too similar to a potato

Several columnists, mostly female, compared Craig's looks to Mr Potato Head, the vintage children's toy immortalised in *Toy Story* (1995) and *Toy Story 2* (1999). This minority view suggested nothing more than the sound of a barrel being scraped. According to *The Mirror*, Craig had been nick-named 'Potato Head' since childhood. Spud-related jibes were nothing new.

There was even an anti-Craig website called craignotbond.com, 'home of the *Casino Royale* boycott'. This forum claimed, bizarrely, that Craig resembled American actor Bill Murray, best known for his deadpan comedy roles in *Groundhog Day* (1993) and *Lost in Translation* (2003). Pictures also compared Craig with a lemur, a zombie, Gollum and Ukrainian President Viktor Yushchenko, whose face had been disfigured by dioxin poisoning. (First prize in the bad taste stakes.) Site spokesperson Deanna Brayton summed up her problem with Craig's casting thus: "How can a short blond actor with the rough face of a professional boxer and a penchant for playing killers, cranks, cads and gigolos pull off the role of a tall, dark, handsome and suave secret agent?"

Some of the posts were downright nasty. "Why choose this putrid, ugly man as Bond?" asked one. "He looks like a charmless *Big Issue* vendor," said another. (Second prize in the bad taste stakes.) The site called for all true Bond fans to boycott the new film and claimed to have 15,000 supporters. Is it still up and running? Who cares? Conversely, givecraigachance.com listed nearly 1,000 supporters of the new Bond. Craig later admitted that he'd looked at the Bond internet sites and wished he'd left them alone.

The Sun, which had backed Colin Salmon, waged its own anti-Craig campaign, asking, "Has Daniel Craig got the bottle to play Bond or is he an Octo-pussy cat?" Note the clever play on words. In the tabloid's view, Craig had blown Bond's macho image by wearing a life-jacket at the press launch – never mind that he had no choice – and looking a bit seasick. Tim Craig didn't help matters by jumping in to defend his son's manly credentials: the boy Daniel had worked in rough pubs in Notting Hill and the Portobello Road. Never mind defusing a nuclear warhead or abseiling down a hollowed-out volcano; serving pints of lager to dodgy west London geezers took balls of steel. And what kind of tough guy needed his dad to fight his battles? Ernst Stavro Blofeld must have been quaking in his boots.

The Mirror ran an interview with Canadian actress Lois Maxwell, who played the lovelorn Miss Moneypenny in every Bond film from *Dr. No* to *A View to a Kill*. Shown a photograph of Craig, Maxwell expressed doubts about his suitability for Bond. "He's not as handsome as Roger or Sean, is he?" she observed. "He has what you'd call an interesting face…" Ouch.

Craig received support from Catherine Zeta Jones, who'd been a friend since they worked together on *Young Indiana Jones*. She argued that Craig had the right intensity for James Bond. Sienna Miller, another friend and possibly more, also weighed in.

> *I think he is a brilliant actor, a very strong, powerful actor. And I think it's exciting that they will be taking Bond back to being more of a misogynist … more interesting than he has become. And I think Daniel has a kind of gritty realism that will be really interesting in that role.*

Clive Owen, the man some felt should have been Bond, graciously backed Craig: "The thing that is really exciting is … they have cast a really serious actor and I think that when the film comes out everyone will see what a great choice he was." More crucially, Sean Connery gave Craig the thumbs-up, calling him "a terrific choice … He's a good actor. It's a completely new departure." Craig appreciated the gesture, noting that "Connery set and defined the character. I wanted his approval and he sent me messages of support, which meant a lot to me." Even Roger Moore stepped in to silence the naysayers. "I am fed up with everybody attacking poor Daniel Craig," he complained. "I am sure he is going to be absolutely super."

The media was having a field day debating whether or not Craig was right for Bond. But Craig had taken a long time to decide if Bond was right for him. A successful, sought-after actor in theatre, television and films, he had never seen himself becoming associated with a particular character. The role of Bond brought many benefits, mostly financial, yet it could also become a curse. Most actors were wary of typecasting, especially in the one role. Did Craig really want to carry the tag of 'James Bond star', then 'former James Bond star', for the rest of his career? Would his reputation as a serious actor be undermined if he assumed the 007 mantle? Craig had appeared in over 15 feature films, displaying talent, charisma and versatility. He'd won acclaim for his stage performances in *Angels in America* and *A Number*, among others. If he took on the role of James Bond – with whatever degree of success – his options as an actor could be severely restricted by the brand image.

How would Craig's non-Bond film career progress during his stint as 007? Not forgetting his post-Bond career; even if he proved a smash hit in the role, the time would come to hand in the weaponry and tailored suits and park the Aston Martin in the garage. In both cases, the precedents were not encouraging. Whether in 'Bondage' or after, all five of his predecessors had had problems sustaining their stardom without the Bond image. Craig was well aware of the risks:

> Sean Connery obviously defined the part, and even he struggled for a while to get rid of the mantle. That's the pitfall and it could happen to me. I've been working so hard, for however

*long it is I've been doing this, to try and stick to doing stuff I
totally believe in and that would be wiped out.*

When first approached by Broccoli and Wilson, Craig had been
flattered rather than enthusiastic. He sought advice from Roger
Michell, who directed him in *The Mother* and *Enduring Love*. A good
friend of Craig, Michell felt Bond would be a mis-step in his career.
Interviewed by Sandi Chaitram for filmexposed.com, Michell
explained:

> *I think he'd make a great Bond. But I've advised him against
> it. I just feel that Daniel is beginning to come into his own
> now, especially with the work he's done in* The Mother *and*
> Layer Cake. *I think to take on Bond now will pigeon-hole him,
> and as an actor that can be difficult to recover from.*

Leaving aside Michell's baffling enthusiasm for *Layer Cake*, his
wariness over the James Bond role struck a chord with Craig.
Promoting *Layer Cake* in the US, he was frank about his doubts over
becoming Bond: "I'd like to be able to be in both big and small
movies and I wonder that if I do Bond whether or not directors
would employ me, which would be a big shame."

Nevertheless, he agreed to a meeting with Broccoli and Wilson,
where the producers outlined their plans for the Bond character and
franchise. According to Craig, they wanted a more vulnerable 007
than the Brosnan incarnation. Audiences had embraced a new
generation of flawed action heroes, notably Kiefer Sutherland's Jack
Bauer in the TV hit *24* and Matt Damon's Jason Bourne (can the 'JB'
initials be coincidence?) in *The Bourne Identity*. Craig's Bond would
be a complex, psychologically troubled man. This rebranding was a
blatant box-office ploy, yet Craig was intrigued by the acting
challenge.

While Craig liked what he heard from Broccoli and Wilson, they
didn't have a script on offer. He felt the producers wanted him to

accept the role without seeing even a first draft screenplay. Unable to make this leap of faith, Craig told them he wasn't interested at this stage. This caution was understandable, as the Bond movies had a history of script problems.

Committed to making *Munich*, Craig tried to put Bond out of his mind but found it impossible. He had been a fan of the Bond movies since watching *Live and Let Die* with his father back in 1973. He cited *Dr. No* and *From Russia with Love* as two of his favourite films, also claiming that even the worst Bond movies had "something to love about them." As a professional actor, he had never expected to be involved with the franchise, not even as third-thug-on-the-left. Discussing Bond with Steven Spielberg, Craig felt the 007 franchise lacked the dramatic gravitas of a film like *Munich*. Spielberg told him to wait for the final screenplay before making a firm decision. If Craig liked the script and the deal on offer he should take the role.

The screenwriters for *Casino Royale* included Neal Purvis and Robert Wade, who had both worked on the two most recent Bond films, *The World is Not Enough* (1999) and *Die Another Day* (2002). Their *Casino Royale* script was polished by Paul Haggis, who made his name as the writer-director of the Oscar-winning *Crash* (2004). Haggis explained that the 21st Bond film would offer something new. "We're trying to reinvent Bond," he maintained. "It's very difficult to think of new ways of blowing things up. It's the journey that's the thing – finding a new journey for the character." Haggis delivered the revised screenplay in September 2005.

Craig hadn't been too impressed by the original novel, Ian Fleming's first. He read it initially while travelling on the Piccadilly line, prior to his first meeting with Barbara Broccoli, and finished it just as he arrived at Piccadilly station, tossing the book in a bin. His reaction to Fleming's masterpiece: it was okay. But when Craig received Haggis' draft of the screenplay, his attitude changed dramatically. He later revealed that he wanted to hate the script, as this would have made his decision much easier. But the Haggis version gripped him from page one. As Craig admitted to Stuart

Jeffries, "I thought, this is a great story, probably because it adhered to the book quite closely, and I just thought, 'You've got to be really silly not to have a think about this.'"

In September 2005, Craig shot a screen test at Pinewood Studios, longtime home of the Bond movies, along with four other actors. For years, potential Bonds had been auditioned with a *From Russia with Love* scene in which 007 first meets Soviet defector Tatiana Romanova, who may not be all she seems. This encounter required an actor to deliver all the desired Bond elements: romance, drama and action. When the footage was screened by the producers, Craig stood out as the clear winner.

Craig soon decided that the pros of becoming Bond number six outweighed the cons. Yes, he might become typecast, reducing the non-Bond roles on offer, but the benefits could be extraordinary. While deliberating the matter, Craig attended a BAFTA (British Academy of Film and Television Awards) event. He found himself seated at the same table as Pierce Brosnan, recently ousted as the reigning 007. Despite his public discontent over the matter, Brosnan proved friendly, giving Craig the advice he needed to hear: "Go for it. It's a ride." Craig came to the Bond series with a far more substantial body of film work than Brosnan had prior to *GoldenEye*. People already knew there was more to Daniel Craig than Bond. Signing the contract with Eon Productions brought an immense feeling of relief. "I thought, God, this is all right: I'm doing what I want to do. And that was a huge weight off my shoulders."

Committed to the Bond franchise, Craig underwent exhaustive preparation for his first 007 mission. He stopped smoking and hired personal fitness trainer Simon Waterson, who had worked with him on *The Invasion*. Waterson was famous – or perhaps notorious – for his Commando Workout programme. He also had sterling Bond credentials, having got Pierce Brosnan into shape for *The World is Not Enough* (1999) and *Die Another Day* (2002). Interviewed in *GQ* magazine, Waterson explained that Craig needed 'functioning muscle' for Bond: "There's no point in having great muscles if they can't be used in a beneficial way like speeding across the ground, climbing, jumping and fighting." Under Waterson's supervision, Craig put on 20 pounds of muscle. He would call on Waterson again for *His Dark Materials* (2007).

Casino Royale was first published in 1953 and was for many years the only 007 book not owned by Eon Productions, as Fleming sold the rights before making his deal with Harry Saltzman. It had been adapted twice before – as a 1954 CBS TV drama and, in 1966, as a bloated Bond parody courtesy of Columbia Pictures, a film described by Craig as "a psychedelic mess," which is being charitable. In 1999, MGM paid Sony – Columbia's parent company – $10 million for the film rights to *Casino Royale*. As things turned out, by the time the film was ready to shoot, Sony Columbia were the new owners of MGM/UA. Craig had starred in the Columbia-financed *Layer Cake*, which failed to yield either stardom for him or significant profits for the company. Second time out, Craig needed to deliver a hit, and on a much larger scale.

The director of *Casino Royale* was New Zealander Martin Campbell, who had been responsible for reviving the 007 franchise after a six-year hiatus with *GoldenEye* (1995), the first Brosnan Bond film. Campbell's key team for *Casino Royale* included cameraman Phil Meheux, who had shot *GoldenEye*, editor Stuart Baird (the Mr Fixit on *Lara Croft Tomb Raider*) and production designer Peter Lamont, who had worked on most of the Bond films from *Goldfinger* (1964) onwards, starting out as a humble draughtsman.

For a long time, the identity of Craig's leading lady was a matter of wild speculation. *Casino Royale* featured a strong female character, Vesper Lynd, played by *Dr. No* star Ursula Andress in the earlier film. Campbell's first choice for Lynd was South African actress Charlize Theron, but she passed on *Casino Royale*, perhaps wary that the producers would use her status as a counter to Craig, a relative unknown in the United States. Eon Productions also supposedly approached Angelina Jolie, star of *Lara Croft Tomb Raider* and its sequel. But, having played a female James Bond, Jolie wasn't interested in a demotion to Bond Girl.

Sienna Miller was also mentioned as a possible candidate. In October 2005, several tabloids had reported that Craig had enjoyed another fling with his *Layer Cake* co-star. Miller denied being interested in a Bond-sanctioned reunion, saying, "I don't think it's the right time for me to be a Bond Girl. I think it may undo the hard work that I have been doing this year." Miller was referring to her leading roles in *Casanova* (2005), opposite Heath Ledger, and *Factory Girl* (2006), which cast her as Edie Sedgwick, Andy Warhol muse and doomed drug addict. (In the event, neither film proved a breakthrough.) The role of Vesper Lynd finally went to French actress Eva Green, who had appeared in Ridley Scott's epic *Kingdom of Heaven* (2005).

Le Chiffre was played by Danish actor Mads Mikkelsen, who'd fought alongside Bond contender Clive Owen in *King Arthur* (2004). Judi Dench returned as 'M', a role she'd played from *GoldenEye* onwards, making her the only Brosnan-era regular to appear in *Casino Royale*. The producers also secured a cameo from Chinese actress Tsai Chin, who'd appeared in the pre-credits sequence of *You Only Live Twice* (1967) nearly 40 years earlier. The role of Felix Leiter, Bond's CIA contact, went to acclaimed stage actor Jeffrey Wright, who had worked with Craig on *The Invasion*; he was the second African-American to play Leiter, following Bernie Casey, who appeared in the 'unofficial' – ie, non-Eon – Bond film *Never Say Never Again* (1983).

Casino Royale was in production from 30 January to 21 July 2006. The Bond series had long been based at Pinewood Studios, which had its own '007' stage. Location work was done in Prague, London, Venice and the Bahamas. When filming commenced in Prague, Eon Productions held another press conference, with Craig flanked by Judi Dench and Eva Green. Compared with his media debut as the new 007 star, Craig seemed much more assured, with positive use of body language. The lessons of the uneasy Bond launch had been taken on board.

Craig pushed to do as many of his own stunts as possible. While insurance problems ruled out the more dangerous stunts, Craig took his share of hard knocks. "If you don't get bruised playing Bond," he claimed, "you're not doing it properly." He lost a crown filming his first punch-up, though tabloid reports turned this into two teeth knocked clean out of his head. The worst was yet to come, Craig being hit in the groin with a knotted rope while shooting the torture scene. Interviewed on ITV, he recalled that "I just jumped like eight feet in the air shouting 'Stop!' and left the room rather hastily." After taking some painkillers, Craig went back on set and resumed filming. Interviewed by *Digital Spy*, stunt co-ordinator Gary Powell, who had been with the franchise since *GoldenEye*, lavished praise on Craig: "Daniel really took some hits on *Casino Royale*. I'd see him bruised and cut up, fight after fight. And he'd just say, 'Oh shit, that smarted a bit, let's go again.' He did everything we asked of him and more."

Craig's gun instructor was ex-soldier Joss Skottowe. Like Powell, he felt Craig's dedication to the role went beyond the call of duty. "I brought in some SAS chums to give Daniel some extra training," he reported. "And even they were impressed. Daniel is the only Bond who in real life could pass SAS selection. He's fit, he looks like a killer and he's smart." Given Craig's aversion to guns and violence, these compliments could be seen as double-edged, especially the 'killer' tag. In the context of a Bond movie, Craig wanted to look like he could use a weapon with lethal force if the occasion demanded. Off screen, he had no wish to develop an aggressively macho image.

Craig knew that some Bond fans wanted him to fail. "You take it in, you can't help it," he admitted. "I've been trying to give 110 per cent since the beginning but, after all the fuss, maybe I started giving 115 per cent." Whatever their claims to the contrary, the Bond producers had been rattled by the anti-Craig faction. In early March 2006, they released clips from the Bahamas shoot in which Craig was seen in action, jumping from a moving truck. And, despite his novice status, Craig felt he was well qualified in assessing what made a good Bond film: "I'm a Bond fan. If I go and see a Bond movie there are certain things I think should be in it. And they're there. We've got them in spades. Nobody knows more than I do how important this is, and it's my job to get it right."

The script originally featured suicide bombers, a sadly topical ingredient. Craig persuaded the producers to drop this angle, as he feared it could provoke anti-Muslim sentiment. Craig felt the bad guys should be motivated by cold hard cash alone. As he explained, "Every terrorist in this movie is non-political ... the connotations of a suicide bomber are something that lie within religion and politics." On the film's release, however, some critics would note another uncomfortable element – that of neo-colonialism – in *Casino Royale*'s action scenes. Early on, Bond takes out a squad of black soldiers with a combination of fists, bullets and explosives. He later takes care of two black hitmen, in more prolonged and graphic kills. Craig had been here before, beating and shooting the 'kaffirs' in *The Power of One*. This time they were in a position to fight back, not that it made much difference to the outcome. No one suggested that the Bond producers were promoting a white supremacist agenda, but the producers could have paid more attention to the ethnic spread of their rogues' gallery.

Six days before *Casino Royale*'s US release, Craig and director Martin Campbell gave a press conference in a Manhattan hotel. The assembled journalists noted that Craig was in a good mood, far removed from his awkward, defensive manner at the first Bond media junket. *Toronto Sun* reporter Liz Braun described Craig as "fairly glittering with good cheer. He may be cool, calm and collected as James Bond, but in person, Craig is humorous and down-to-earth and seemingly unaffected by it all." Now much wiser in the ways of Bond, Craig pushed *Casino Royale* as a team effort:

> We set out to make a good movie. That's all we did. Everyone was on the same page. And the criticisms came in and we just got on with what we were doing. There's obviously a lot more heat on this one, probably because of some of the criticism that's happened, but I'm still saying the same thing – go see

the movie. Go see the movie. See what you think.

Campbell felt Craig had handled the adverse criticism well:

I think he had a hill to climb, psychologically. With critics, you say, 'Well, to hell with them, I don't give a damn,' but you sort of do. There's not a person who isn't affected by that … That was a huge problem for him, just in the back of his mind – are you going to sink a 50-year franchise? Now he's got over that hump, he's more relaxed. But he'll never be a star. The public will see him as a star, of course, but not him. He's very shy. It's all about the work with him, and the praise that's being heaped on him now, I think it just embarrasses him.

Craig's advance press coverage for *Casino Royale* hadn't always seen him so sunny. Interviewed for *Entertainment Weekly* magazine, he was frank about the anti-Craig sentiment. "They hate me. They don't think I'm right for the role. It's as simple as that. They're passionate about it, which I understand, but I do wish they'd reserve judgment." In GQ magazine, he was less diplomatic:

Some of the stuff that's been said is as close to a playground taunt as you are going to get. "You've got big ears!" Fucking hell! There is a part of me that would love to turn it around and shove it up their arse. The only way I can do that is to get this right. Believe me, no one cares about this more than I do.

Interviewed on the US entertainment show *Extra*, Craig pushed the boundaries of acceptable language on network TV. "When it [the film] comes out, if they still feel the same way then, you know, screw them!" As the show went out live, the producers couldn't delete the 'screw'. Deanna Brayton of craignotbond.com expressed righteous dismay at Craig's 'shocking' behaviour:

I believe that Daniel Craig has disgraced himself with his brusque remarks. It only goes further to support the position held by many fans that Daniel Craig has neither the class required for the role of Bond, nor the character to be the caretaker of such a beloved and iconic movie hero. Our only hope is that Bond fans who have been on the fence about Mr Craig will now realise that we who were unhappy with him from day one were right all along.

Too late, Deanna. Nobody cared any more. Craig's Bond was about to roll and no force on earth could stop him.

TEN

...AND BEYOND

Casino Royale received its UK premiere at the Odeon Leicester Square on Tuesday 14 November 2006. As usual, Queen Elizabeth II and the Duke of Edinburgh were on hand for the launch of the new Bond movie. (Incidentally, the Queen was crowned in 1953, the year Fleming's book was published.) The premiere also marked Craig's first public appearance with his new girlfriend, 29-year-old Satsuki Mitchell.

Craig had met Mitchell when she served as a production executive on *The Jacket*. While his role in that film was little more than a cameo, he evidently made an impression. They started dating in October 2004, two years before *Casino Royale* opened. Craig felt that, with Mitchell's agreement, the James Bond premiere was the right time to declare himself "happily not single." Resplendent in a black Versace dress, with halterneck, Mitchell looked uneasy at times, with nervous backward glances. While she dutifully answered press questions, she preferred to remain in the background, letting Craig do most of the talking. As he explained to Liz Hoggard:

> She's been with me all through this, and all the way through
> filming. So why exclude her? She's up to it; she's an adult ...
> Bond has been too big an experience, it might not come around
> again. We had to do that amazing thing in Leicester Square,
> and walk round all that craziness, just because it may never
> happen again.

Leaving Mitchell behind, Craig later attended *Casino Royale* premieres in Zurich, Paris, Tokyo and Beijing, among many others. At the Sydney premiere, he encountered an old classmate in the crowd, who announced her Craig connection with an excitement that bordered on hysteria. Arriving in Beijing, Craig was offered a pirate DVD of the film for a bargain 75 pence. "Someone tried to sell me a copy," he reported. "I was wearing a hat and glasses so they didn't recognise me. It saddens me." (The piracy, presumably, not the lack of recognition.) *Casino Royale* was the first Bond movie to be shown in China. The notoriously strict government censor had few problems with the film, though a reference to the Cold War was deleted.

Budgeted at a hefty $150 million, *Casino Royale* had to be a blockbuster. The Bond franchise had always drawn a mixed response from the critics. From the start, *Casino Royale* received some of the best reviews of any Bond film. According to *Guardian* critic Peter Bradshaw:

> *Daniel Craig is a fantastic Bond, and all those whingers and nay-sayers out there in the blogosphere should hang their heads in shame. Craig was inspired casting ... he brings a serious actor's ability to a fundamentally unserious part; he brings out the playfulness and the absurdity, yet never sends it up. He's easily the best Bond since Sean Connery, and perhaps even – well, let's not get carried away ... For the first time in ages, I am actually looking forward to the next James Bond movie.*

A longtime *Guardian* reader, Craig was "thrilled" by Bradshaw's response, quoting sections of the review word for word. Fellow *Guardian* writer Steve Rose felt that Craig's back-to-basics Bond had revived a tired franchise in the nick of time: "Tired of suave, smirking, product-placement playboy James Bond? Then try new hard-hitting, merciless, torture-loving Bond Dark, as modelled by Daniel Craig in *Casino Royale*!"

Most British critics were similarly impressed: "Daniel Craig is brilliant, oozing the kind of edgy menace that recalls Sean Connery at his best" (David Edwards in *The Mirror*). "Craig is up there with the best. His sex appeal is off the scale. The stunts are more physical and the violence raw" (Wendy Ide, *The Times*). "Craig's Bond has been rebooted as a man not quite secure within his own tuxedo and the result is a nervier epic. It could have been off-puttingly dark but Craig holds the screen" (Sinclair McKay, *The Daily Telegraph*). *Observer* critic Philip French felt the film displayed a tension between capturing the book's seriousness while retaining the classic Bond movie ingredients, noting "an uncertainty of tone that, as with *Dr. No*, the franchise's modest beginning in 1962, is not unendearing." And Craig's Bond was damned with faint praise: "Certainly he's the most athletic and agile 007 since Connery … He's also one of only two Bonds (the other being Timothy Dalton) to hint at an inner life. At present, Craig seems happier with the serious aspects of the role … Anyway, he'll do."

Writing in *The Independent*, Anthony Quinn took a firmly dissenting view of Craig's debut:

> *I remain unconvinced by his Bond, not least because 'good acting' is wasted on such a fantasy role; what's really required is a presence, an ability to look the part and to carry off its essential foolishness. That might not be the man Fleming created, but it sure as hell is the man that cinema has, and it's too late to change him now … What I miss in Craig's incarnation is a lightness of touch, and a sense of fun … A touch of the pugilist is fine so long as he retains his pertness, the truly distinctive quality of a man so frequently called upon to save the world. Bond is brought back from the dead in* Casino Royale, *but his long-term prospects aren't encouraging.*

So, does *Casino Royale* deliver the goods? Whatever the film's failings, the answer is a definite 'yes'. It's notable that *Casino Royale* is closer in spirit to the standard-issue Bond movie than the dark re-imagining of the franchise promised by the producers. (Did anyone really expect anything different?) The black and white prologue has moody, noirish lighting and some shaky hand-held camerawork when the going gets rough. From the start, Craig handles the action well, putting the boot in with conviction. He looks impressively athletic during a construction site chase, bursting through a partition wall. While Craig had a stunt double for some scenes, this doesn't detract from his achievement.

Craig's Bond is as flirtatious, confident and shrewd as any of his predecessors. At the same time, Craig believed Bond should make mistakes and show his emotions. His encounter with Le Chiffre at the Casino Royale sees 007 at his most vulnerable. Bond's brisk manner and muscular physique is effectively contrasted with the effete, slender Le Chiffre, an asthmatic master villain who weeps bloody tears. Looking sharp in a dinner jacket, Bond is distracted by Vesper Lynd at a crucial poker game, letting his feelings over-ride his professionalism. Outwitted by Le Chiffre, he allows himself to be poisoned, Craig becoming the first 007 to throw up in the line of duty.

Bond's relationship with Vesper Lynd is efficiently handled without delivering the promised depth or sense of tragedy. Like virtually every so-called Bond Girl before her, Lynd is promoted as 007's equal. She turns the tables on her sexist colleague, noting Bond's "perfectly formed arse." Green meets the requirements of the role, which often proves a thankless task. The Bond-Lynd romance lacks resonance partly because it can't get in the way of either the plot mechanics or the established 007 persona. *On Her Majesty's Secret Service* encountered the same problem, though George Lazenby's doomed love affair with Diana Rigg had an unexpected pathos. At their best, Craig and Green have an edgy chemistry and their fully clothed shower scene is a far cry from the usual Bond canoodling. Holding Lynd in his arms, Craig's Bond displays a tenderness and compassion only hinted at in earlier films.

Craig's scenes with Judi Dench have more bite, despite the lack of sexual frisson. When Bond breaks into M's apartment, her indignation is tempered with a grudging admiration. Craig felt that his Bond – an orphan by implication – related to M as a mother figure. The newly anointed 007 seems nervous and apologetic towards his boss, before his natural insolence reasserts itself.

Several critics would cite 24's Jack Bauer as an inspiration for Craig's Bond: tough, blond and able to both inflict and withstand near-superhuman levels of pain and violence. While Bond had been tortured in several films, *Casino Royale* raised the bar to an unprecedented level. It's hard to imagine Sean Connery or Pierce Brosnan tied naked to a chair and thrashed about the testicles. Roger Moore would have surely passed out at the mere thought. The torture scene in Fleming's book was praised by fellow novelist Raymond Chandler as heralding a brutal new realism in crime fiction. The equivalent scene in the film is more stylised and less graphic, Le Chiffre substituting a knotted rope for the original cane carpet-beater. Careful lighting casts the crucial area in shadow, though Craig's anguished howls leave little doubt as to what is going on and where. The sado-masochistic, homoerotic result resembles a bizarre out-take from *Love is the Devil*. Obscured in semi-darkness, Craig's trussed naked form and anguished features are a Francis Bacon study made flesh ('The Screaming Bond'). Perhaps wisely, the sequence is cut short before the implications become too strong.

Craig is seen to better advantage in the earlier airport sequence. Handcuffed, bloodied and bruised, Bond allows himself a small satisfied smile as a bomber-for-hire blows himself up. Once again, the spectre of Steve McQueen is invoked, the airport setting and bloody showdown recalling the finale of *Bullitt* (1968). This time, Craig is up to the comparison, leaving *Layer Cake* far behind.

Craig wanted his Bond to be a more complex figure than previous incarnations. "I think true good guys have to step into the dark side to do their job," he suggested. "I wanted people to question Bond's morals and his judgment." The end result is a compromise, the script at times overdosing on psychobabble. Having fallen for Lynd hook, line and sinker, Bond writes M a letter of resignation while relaxing in Venice. This doesn't convince for a moment and even Craig looks doubtful as he plays these scenes. The film gets back on track with a betrayal, and few actors do pissed-off-and-angry better than Craig. As he removes a metal spike from his back with a dismissive grunt, we realise this Bond is the real deal. Lynd meets her death in Venice and Bond comments, "The bitch is dead," the closing sentence of Fleming's book. (Strictly speaking, "The bitch is dead now.") The line doesn't work so well in the context of the film, as Lynd acted from love, not greed or malice. *Casino Royale* brushes aside these uncertainties for a neat pay-off. When Craig utters the immortal words, "The name's Bond, James Bond", few will doubt it.

Released in the UK on 16 November, *Casino Royale* grossed an astonishing £54.6 million during its British run. The film opened in the US a day later, to generally strong reviews. According to Kenneth Turan in the *Los Angeles Times*, "Craig … has both the physicality and presence to make this film's more brutal, less suave Bond, a man who would do anything to get the job done, completely persuasive." In *Variety*, Todd McCarthy claimed that "Craig comes closer to the author's original conception of this exceptionally long-lived male fantasy figure than anyone since early Sean Connery." And Roger Ebert, in the *Chicago Sun-Times*, called Craig "a superb Bond: leaner, more taciturn, less sex-obsessed, able to be hurt in body and soul, not giving a damn if his Martini is shaken or stirred."

In the US, *Casino Royale* was beaten to the weekend number one spot by *Happy Feet* (2006), an animated tale of lovable penguins. The latter grossed $41.53 million, while *Casino Royale* took $40.83 million, losing out by just $700,000. Despite this early disappointment, *Casino Royale* went on to make a respectable $170 million in North America. The previous Bond film, *Die Another Day*, had taken $432 million worldwide. *Casino Royale* grossed nearly $600 million. Craig claimed that he'd never bothered with box-office receipts prior to *Casino Royale* (though his agent probably did). He paid close attention to the opening weekend grosses for his first Bond movie, however, telling Liz Hoggard that "Watching the numbers coming in, and it steadily going up, I thought, 'It's okay, we've got away with it.' It was like the fucking *Blue Peter* appeals."

Speaking of appeal, Craig's pumped-up 007 physique won him a lot of press coverage and countless new fans. Indeed, *Casino Royale* will doubtless be remembered for the swimming trunks scene. Craig had previously donned the trunks for *Some Voices*, *Sword of Honour*, *Sylvia* and *Enduring Love*. He was already in good shape some years before the 007 workout, though, for dedicated Craig followers, his emergence from the sea in *Casino Royale* made an amusing contrast to the scene in *Elizabeth* where he wades to shore in a full priest's habit. On reflection, the latter appearance was never going to make him a sex symbol.

A still from the beach scene soon became the iconic image from *Casino Royale*, showing Craig's credentials as the new James Bond. Taken by Jay Maidment, the picture captured Craig's dazzling blue eyes, well-built shoulders, six-pack stomach and finely honed pectoral muscles. The photo was compared to the famous shot from the first Bond film, *Dr. No*, where Ursula Andress emerges from the sea in a fetching bikini. (In the book, she's wearing even less.) Some suggested that Craig's Bond was now the series' official 'eye-candy', in place of the legions of bikini-clad Bond Girls. Craig's stripped-down 007 was certainly a hit with his gay fans. "I was out recently and all these gay guys were over me like a rash, but they never ask about the Bond plot." Clever gender subversion, shrewd marketing or sheer fluke?

Craig argued that his new muscular look was both justified and essential in the context of the movie: "If Bond should at some point take his shirt off, we should feel that he's physically imposing, that he's done the things he's supposed to have done, like being a commander in the navy." Whatever the reasoning, his training sessions with Simon Waterson had certainly paid off. Craig's Bond also sits bare-chested at his laptop, tapping away with undeniable machismo.

Writer-performer Charlie Higson, author of several novels about the young Bond, felt that Maidment's photo "captures the birth of a new James Bond." Interviewed in *The Independent*, Higson seemed almost breathless with excitement:

> *It's a fantastic image, and I actually think it could end up changing the history of British cinema. Since about 1972 [post-*Get Carter*?], we've been inundated with wimps like Jude Law [ouch!] and Orlando Bloom [wince!]. Even in Bond films, you had Roger Moore who, let's be honest, never looked like much of a threat to man nor woman. But Daniel Craig has real physical presence. I think this image may lead to a re-birth of the tough-guy action hero, the sort of character that was last seen in the days of people like Stanley Baker and Richard Burton.*

The light-blue front-tie swimming trunks were made by Italian underwear manufacturer La Perla. The normally tie-in-astute Eon Productions hadn't made a sponsorship deal with La Perla, suggesting the 'swimwear effect' was both unplanned and unexpected. A spokesman for La Perla explained that they'd also created the orange bikini worn by Halle Berry in *Die Another Day*, a deliberate homage to Andress and *Dr. No* that didn't have the intended impact. Craig's trunks were called 'Lodato', or 'praised', from the Grigioperla, or 'grey pearl', men's range. La Perla claimed the star had chosen them himself from the selection on offer. On the film's release, upmarket boutiques across Britain and continental Europe announced that the trunks were selling out fast. A buyer for Selfridges commented, "Everyone's seen the clips of Bond emerging from the water, and everyone wants to look that good. The 'Bond factor' is really true; all girls want to go out with James Bond, and all men want to be him."

As a rule, the Bond films were rarely contenders for major awards, or awards of any kind. *Casino Royale* looked set to buck the trend, earning nine nominations at the 2007 BAFTAs. Craig was up for Best Actor and his 007 debut seemed a strong contender for Outstanding British Film of the Year (never mind that it was American-produced and financed). Craig faced stiff competition in the form of Leonardo DiCaprio (*The Departed*), Richard Griffiths (*The History Boys*), Forest Whitaker (*The Last King of Scotland*) and Peter O'Toole (*Venus*). This was distinguished company for Craig to be keeping: one of Hollywood's biggest names, one of Britain's best – and biggest – character actors, a respected African-American actor and director, and a hellraising legend whose wildly uneven career was touched by greatness.

The results were announced on 11 February, during a ceremony held at London's Royal Opera House. Craig lost out to Forest Whitaker, whose fearsome portrayal of crazed Ugandan dictator Idi Amin had been widely tipped to take the prize. Under the circumstances, Craig could be proud of his nomination, given the calibre of both the winner and his fellow losers. *Casino Royale* took just one award, for Best Sound. One rash journalist suggested Craig might have won if he'd turned up for the ceremony in his *Casino Royale* swimming trunks. Craig's response was terse: "You're a fucking fool." Sean Connery might have handled it with more finesse, but it's hard to disagree with Craig's sentiment.

Months before *Casino Royale*'s release, Craig joined the cast of *The Golden Compass*, based on the first book in Philip Pullman's acclaimed fantasy trilogy, *His Dark Materials*. In production from September 2006 through to the following January, the film version was produced by New Line, who scored a big hit with Peter Jackson's *Lord of the Rings* trilogy (2001-3). New Line had enough confidence in the Pullman property to sanction a $150 million budget.

Craig was cast as Lord Asriel, an enigmatic, coldly rational figure. The seemingly benevolent uncle of young heroine Lyra, Asriel was modelled on the Devil in John Milton's epic poem *Paradise Lost* – and was also Craig's first bearded film character since Darren in *The*

Mother. (In some shots, the beard gave Craig a passing resemblance to retired tennis champion Boris Becker.) The role had been played on the London stage by Timothy Dalton, a fellow member of the exclusive 007 club. Craig would also be playing a father for the first time since *Sylvia*, where Ted Hughes' parenting skills were more impressive than his behaviour as a husband. The self-centred Lord Asriel was an even worse role model. As the father of a 14-year-old daughter, Craig was more amused than appalled by Asriel's paternal failings: "I'm a bad dad," he quipped, hinting at one of the plot twists for those who hadn't read the book.

The Golden Compass reunited Craig with Nicole Kidman, cast as elegant villainess Mrs Coulter. Pullman approved of Kidman's casting, but made it known he had favoured Jason Isaacs for Lord Asriel. (Coincidentally, Isaacs had played Craig's lover in the 1993 National Theatre production of *Angels in America*.) Writing in *The Sunday Times*, Pullman endorsed New Line's choice for the role: "Asriel requires someone who has the physical presence of a man of action and the quick intelligence of a scholar, and the charisma to dominate the screen while apparently doing nothing. When the name of Daniel Craig was mentioned, I leapt at the idea, and he is ideal." A fan of the book, Craig had nothing but praise for Pullman, describing the writer as "such a passionate, great guy." The cast also included newcomer Dakota Blue Richards as Lyra, Eva Green from *Casino Royale*, Tom Courtenay, Sam Elliott, Ian McKellen, Christopher Lee, Kathy Bates, Kristen Scott Thomas and Derek Jacobi, from *Love is the Devil*.

Having rejected a script by Tom Stoppard, New Line assigned the project to writer-director Chris Weitz, who'd found fame and fortune producing the gross-out *American Pie* comedies. During pre-production, however, Weitz quit *The Golden Compass*, citing insurmountable technical challenges. In August 2005, he was replaced as director by Anand Tucker, who had worked with Craig on the TV docudrama *Saint-Ex* in 1994. Pullman approved the choice of Tucker, who had a clear idea of the film's theme: "Lyra's search for self-discovery and for a family." By May 2006, Tucker, too, had left the film, owing to 'creative differences' with New Line. Remarkably, Weitz agreed to return and the production got back on track. Pullman seemed happy with Weitz. "I watched his film *About a Boy* [2002, based on Nick Hornby's novel], from which I could tell that he knew how to direct children, and what's more he put the camera in the right place."

The Golden Compass was shot on location in Switzerland and the UK, with interiors mounted at Shepperton Studios. Craig's new star status was reflected in the production credits: 'Security for Mr Craig' (step forward Dave Lindsay). Craig met Pullman on set and was impressed by the writer's passion for life beyond his literary universe. Pullman's book had been attacked as anti-religious by some Fundamentalist groups, prompting speculation that the film version would be toned down to avoid upsetting Christian sensibilities (and reducing the box-office take). During filming, Craig pushed hard to preserve the subversive edge of Pullman's work. He also felt the book had been misunderstood, telling Liz Hoggard "There's nothing antireligious about this film. It's antiestablishment in a big way and antitotalitarian and anti-controlling. But essentially it's a film about growing up, and how difficult that can be." Was Craig being deliberately naïve here?

With its release set for December 2007, *The Golden Compass* was first unveiled, in incomplete form, at the Cannes Film Festival in May. While the scenes on offer amounted to little more than an extended showreel, the response was generally positive. Craig was on hand to support the film, still sporting an impressive beard. During post-production, key scenes were cut from the film's final act. New Line explained that the deleted footage would appear in the sequel, a show of faith in the first film's box-office potential.

In the meantime, Craig had returned to the almighty ongoing mess that was *The Invasion*, which had apparently wrapped in December 2005. Having engaged the Wachowski Brothers, creators of the *Matrix* franchise, to refashion the script, Warner Bros now hired

The *Casino Royale* press photocall
at The One and Only Ocean Club,
Nassau, Bahamas, 8 March 2006

Craig as a US Army Sergeant with Marcell Nagy as Gyura Köves in *Sorstalanság* (*Fateless*, 2005)

Murderer Perry Smith (Craig) is apprehended in Las Vegas in Douglas McGrath's *Infamous* (2006)

Craig with director Steven Spielberg and co-stars Hanns Zischler and Eric Bana (right) during filming on *Munich* (2005)

Ben Driscoll (Craig) and Carol Bennell (Nicole Kidman) discover an alien takeover in *The Invasion* (2007)

Bond comforts Treasury agent Vesper Lynd (Eva Green) in *Casino Royale* (2006)

James Bond (Craig) is cornered at the Nambutu Embassy in Madagascar in *Casino Royale*

As explorer and experimental theologist Lord Asriel in *The Golden Compass* (2007)

On location for his role as Hollywood actor Joe Scot in *Flashbacks of a Fool* (2008)

Craig as Tuvia Bielski with Jamie Bell as his brother Asael in Edward Zwick's *Defiance* (2008)

Bond pursues an MI6 traitor in Sienna's underground cisterns in *Quantum of Solace* (2008)

Bond with Agent Fields (Gemma Arterton) at Dominic Greene's fundraising party in *Quantum of Solace*

On location in Chile with Olga Kurylenko (as Camille) during filming on *Quantum of Solace*

The iconic image from *Casino Royale*:
Craig in La Perla swimming trunks at West Shore,
New Providence Island, Bahamas

James McTeigue to direct some re-shoots. McTeigue had worked as an assistant director on the *Matrix* trilogy before making his directing debut with Warner's *V for Vendetta*. Both Kidman and Craig were called back to film new scenes in January 2007. This extra footage cost Warners nearly $10 million. According to rumour, one third of the final cut was McTeigue's work, though the long-gone Oliver Hirschbiegel retained sole director credit.

Aside from problems with a runaway car – the handbrake wasn't engaged properly – the reshoots proceeded smoothly enough. The press made much of Craig leaping into the moving vehicle to save the day, yet *The Invasion* needed more than passing media coverage. The internet buzz was mostly negative, with gripes over allegedly poor special effects. The completed film finally opened in the US on 17 August 2007, followed by a British release on 12 October. Significantly, Warners didn't launch *The Invasion* with a big premiere, despite the presence of Kidman and Craig – another sign that the studio had little faith in its revamped science fiction thriller. After all the delays and reshoots, many expected the film to be a dud. It certainly had an illustrious pedigree to live up to. Jack Finney's 1950s fantasy of human beings being reproduced as soulless facsimiles, or 'pod people', had sired a bona-fide classic in its first film version (1955) and two intriguing remakes – a 1978 reading called, like the first film, *Invasion of the Body Snatchers*, and a 1993 reimagining simply called *Body Snatchers*.

The 21st century version opens in jumbled flashback, with jittery camerawork and editing, mumbled dialogue, a weak script and flat performances. Displaying its production woes like gaping wounds, *The Invasion* splices chunks of high concept sf thriller onto the remains of an existential psychodrama. The editing is often choppy, with notably poor continuity for a major studio release. Key moments from the other *Body Snatchers* films are replayed to little effect. *The Invasion* also gives short shrift to its Big Themes: family break-up, nationalist antagonism, psychiatry as mind control and the fragility of civilization. There are car chases and foot chases *ad nauseam* yet the tension doesn't ratchet up until the last ten minutes. Small moments are effective and *The Invasion* has one potent message: don't drink the complementary coffee.

Playing second fiddle to Kidman, Craig emerges from *The Invasion* with modest credit but no great distinction. An engaging presence, he has little to do as Dr Ben Driscoll, a friend of heroine Carol Bennell (Kidman). Retaining his British accent, Craig is initially abrasive yet soon warms up into a regular nice guy and the obvious partner for Kidman's uptight single mother. Craig's performance recalls some of his early films, before he found his feet as a movie actor. There's nothing wrong with his portrayal, technically speaking, but it gives no hint of his true ability. Looking relaxed in a white coat, t-shirt and jeans, Craig does earnest and concerned to a tee and that's all the script requires of him. In one scene, he dons a police uniform, though the effect is more leather bar than cop shop.

By contrast, Kidman resembles a spooky CGI version of herself, an unintentional reflection of the alien takeover plot. Even allowing for the slice-and-dice production, her screen chemistry with Craig is negligible. Having rebuffed Driscoll's advances after a dinner party, Bennell calls him for help when a census taker proves to be an alien. The next morning, Driscoll is still in Bennell's house, cooking her breakfast. Critic Gary Kramer felt Craig "has the role of the female lead, since Kidman is the hero (a single mother and postmodern feminist, too)."

The character names are the giveaway. Kidman's Carol Bennell is named after Miles Bennell, hero of the 1955 film, while Craig's Ben Driscoll is the reverse-gender version of Becky Driscoll, Miles' doomed love interest. Several reviewers noted the curious way in which Craig's rugged machismo was undercut by the film. *Entertainment Weekly* critic Owen Gleiberman observed that "Craig gets little chance to show his unruly charisma." *Premiere*'s Glen Kenny went further: "This movie makes a gelding out of Daniel Craig." The producers compensated for Craig's minimal, 'feminised' role by having him burn Kidman's breakfast pancakes. Clearly, he's too much of a man to be a good cook.

Most US critics dismissed *The Invasion* as a redundant, poorly conceived remake that wasted the story's potential. The film even dispensed with the giant seed pods of earlier versions, substituting vomiting aliens. References to the Iraq war – a burning issue for Craig, among many others – amounted to little more than background TV news broadcasts and the dubious suggestion that the quickest route to world peace is alien invasion. Mankind, it seems, is meant to be selfish, aggressive and murderous. If director Hirschbiegel intended *The Invasion* as a pointed allegory, it got lost on the cutting-room floor.

"Here is a great story born to be creepy," observed Roger Ebert in the *Chicago Sun-Times*, "and the movie churns through it like a road company production. If the first three movies served as parables for their times, this one keeps shooting off parable rockets that fizzle out. How many references in the same movie can you have to the war in Iraq and not say anything about it? … OK," he concluded facetiously. "Now we've had *Invasion of the Body Snatchers* twice, *Body Snatchers* once and *The Invasion* once. Somebody should register the title *Of The*."

In *The Village Voice*, Scott Foundas was even more brutal, decrying the film's innovation of "using actual pod people as actors" (referring, alas, to Kidman and Craig) and therefore proposing "a Razzie Award for worst casting … for this fourth, spectacularly lousy screen version of Jack Finney's 1954 novella *The Body Snatchers*, which some bright light envisioned as the ideal starring vehicle for the Cold Mountain herself, Nicole Kidman, and for Daniel Craig, last seen as poker-faced James Bond. Earth to Hollywood: the whole point is that these characters are supposed to have a difficult time camouflaging their emotions."

More sympathetic reviewers rated *The Invasion* as a moderately intriguing update, a flawed effort rather than an outright disaster. Writing in the *Boston Globe*, Ty Burr argued that "Buried somewhere within the bipolar extravaganza that is *The Invasion* is an awfully good movie that got away." So, if the film was ultimately a failure, it provided reasonable entertainment along the way. But the poor box-office returns suggested audiences weren't sufficiently intrigued to check it out for themselves. The film took barely $6 million during its crucial opening weekend, proving another flop for Nicole Kidman. *The Invasion* opened in the UK without a press screening, shielding the film from further critical barbs. Far from boosting the movie's box-office chances, this desperate tactic merely underlined its turkey status, deserved or otherwise. TV pundit Jonathan Ross was one of the few UK critics to cover *The Invasion*'s theatrical release. Far from damning the film, Ross saw it as an intriguing take on Finney's story that lacked the courage of its convictions.

Craig was marking time with *The Invasion*, though the pay cheque probably kept him cheerful. Had the film been released before *Casino Royale*, as originally planned, it could have been a backward step in his career. As with *Lara Croft Tomb Raider*, Craig was taking a back seat to a high-powered leading lady. While Kidman's box-office appeal had declined, she remained on the Hollywood A-list. Craig was still just another British hopeful, playing the token boyfriend-with-a-twist role. As things turned out, the inadequacies of *The Invasion* – and especially his character – hardly mattered.

Promoting *The Golden Compass*, Eva Green had nothing but praise for her *Casino Royale* co-star, telling *The Observer*'s Craig McLean: "He's working like a dog. He really wants to prove that he can do other stuff. It's great for him. I mean, everyone wants him. He doesn't have the 'Bond curse' at all. He's great. He deserves it." As promised, Craig used his new level of fame to get more offbeat projects off the ground. Interviewed in late 2006, shortly before returning to *The Invasion* shoot, he outlined his plans for the new year. "There are a couple of things I'm going to do next year, and they're small and they're independent and they're about movie-making. There are hugely positive things out there which I'm going to grab with both hands."

First up in 2007, Craig took the starring role in *Flashbacks of a Fool*, which began filming on 28 May with location work in South Africa and London. The film was written and directed by Baillie Walsh, best known for his music videos for the likes of Massive Attack and INXS, including the latter's 'Taste It' (1992). The former partner of director John Maybury, Walsh had played a bit part in *Love is the Devil*, meeting Craig during production. Craig took to Walsh straight away, as he explained to *Independent* writer Liz Hoggard: "We just hit it off immediately. Baillie is my closest male friend."

Walsh made his film debut as writer, director and co-cameraman with *Mirror, Mirror* (1996), a documentary exploring aspects of gay culture, notably drag queens and male prostitution. *Flashbacks of a Fool* would be his first feature film. Walsh had written the script several years earlier, with Craig in mind for the lead. Their attempts to get the project off the ground led nowhere, until the 007 factor kicked in. As Craig conceded to Hoggard, "It just so happened that I did James Bond, and I think that helped a little bit."

Flashbacks of a Fool could not have been made without Craig's support. In addition to starring in the film, he served as executive producer, securing a budget of £5.5 million. The premise was intriguing, if liable to self-indulgence. Craig played a hedonistic actor whose career hits the skids when he turns 40. Given the state of Craig's own career, life was unlikely to imitate art in this instance. Craig felt the film was about a man haunted by past mistakes, telling Hoggard "I know in my life there's stuff that will come back because I haven't dealt with it, and it's the same with everybody." Hoggard didn't press Craig for further details, in print at least, though more obvious past traumas included the breakdown of his parents' marriage when he was a child and the failure of his own marriage.

Craig's co-stars included Olivia Williams, Emilia Fox, Mark Strong from *Our Friends in the North*, and Helen McCrory, who appeared in *Hotel Splendide* and *Enduring Love*. Good friends with Strong, Craig was godfather to the latter's two year old son. Craig's younger self was played by Harry Eden, an experienced television actor whose film credits included Nibs in *Peter Pan* (2003) and the Artful Dodger in

Roman Polanski's *Oliver Twist* (2005). The 18-year-old Eden was flattered to be cast as the teenage Craig, telling *Observer* writer Jason Solomons "They didn't make me try on blue swimming trunks at the audition, but I was happy to be thought of as a little James Bond."

Much of the film took place in an English seaside town during the mid 1970s. Recreating the heat wave of 1976, Walsh and Craig decided to shoot the beach scenes in South Africa, achieving an ultra-bright, 'hyper-real' effect. As Craig explained to Hoggard "we chose a place that we could make look like England – Suffolk, Dorset – but not."

Olivia Williams had a new baby son and often brought him on set. Cast as Craig's mother, Williams wore heavy old-age make-up in some scenes. This created some bizarre moments, as she explained to *The Guardian*'s Maddy Costa. "It was surreal. There I was with wrinkles and grey hair, breastfeeding. I thought: all in all, this isn't going to be the one where I get to shag Daniel Craig."

Filming with Walsh, Craig sometimes found it difficult to juggle the roles of friend, star and producer. As he admitted to Hoggard: "It's a tough process. And it brings out the worst and the best in people... you cross those little boundaries that normally you wouldn't with friends." Whatever their on-set spats, Walsh showed great loyalty to Craig in the press. Openly gay, Walsh dismissed accusations of homophobia leveled at Craig after he clashed with gay journalist Johann Hari at the BAFTA awards ceremony. As Walsh told Hoggard: "He's so not homophobic. I don't think he ever for a moment considers someone's sexuality when he's talking to them. It's never, ever been an issue between me and Dan." Craig could also point to his sympathetic portrayals of gay characters in *Angels in America*, *Love is the Devil* and *Infamous*.

Craig was also linked with an ambitious science fiction allegory called *Blindness*, a Brazilian-Japanese-Canadian co-production based on the book *Ensaio Sobre a Cegueira* [*Essay on the Blindness*] by Portuguese writer José Saramago. Saramago's acclaimed novel deals with an epidemic of sudden 'white' blindness, where victims can see only a dazzling light, and details the resultant social breakdown. The book was optioned by Canadian actor-writer Don McKellar, who chose Brazilian Fernando Meirelles as director and Julianne Moore as Craig's co-star, also casting himself in a key supporting role.

In late May 2007, however, the *Hollywood Reporter* announced that Craig had withdrawn from *Blindness*. According to the article, he'd been in talks to play the lead without giving a definite commitment to the film. In the wake of *Casino Royale*, Craig had been inundated with film offers. Even as promising a project as *Blindness* had to be weighed carefully. The source material, script, director and leading lady were all first rate. Unfortunately, the projected filming dates couldn't be reconciled with Craig's Bond schedule. The main character in *Blindness* was struggling to survive in an apocalyptic world; half-starved, he needed to have an emaciated appearance. There was no way Craig could lose weight for *Blindness*, then put the bulk and muscle back on in time to shoot the so-called *Bond 22*. As Craig expected, the Bond deal was constricting his wider career, if only for logistical reasons.

Craig did sign up for *Defiance*, a harrowing World War II drama casting him as one of three Jewish brothers in Nazi-occupied Poland who join forces with Russian resistance fighters. Based on a true story, the film was written, produced and directed by Edward Zwick. Craig's co-stars included former child actor Jamie Bell, best known for *Billy Elliot* (2000). Budgeted at $50 million, *Defiance* began shooting in September 2007 at authentic locations in Lithuania. Craig seemed genuinely excited by the project, telling Liz Hoggard "It's an action-adventure movie, but it's not. It's a story about a group of Jews who survived in the forest at Belarus and it touches a great nerve with me because things such as racism and anti-Semitism are still not, sadly, things of the past in Europe." In *Fateless*, Craig's Jewish-American sergeant witnessed the aftermath of the Holocaust in World War II Europe. In *Defiance*, his Jewish character fought back against the Nazis and their appalling 'Final Solution'. The US previews for the film proved highly favourable, with especial praise for Craig's performance.

Craig was also attached to *I, Lucifer* (2009), a diabolical fantasy that had been in development for several years. Directed by Dan Harris, this £14 million British production was set to reunite Craig with Ewan McGregor, his fellow student at the Guildhall School of Music and Drama. Based on a novel by Glen Duncan, *I, Lucifer* had an intriguing premise: God offers Satan one last shot at redemption, sending him to Earth to perform good deeds.

There were rumours that Craig would star in a sequel to *Layer Cake*, entitled *Viva La Madness*. Promoting his fantasy epic *Stardust*, director Matthew Vaughn told *Observer* writer Jason Solomons that plans for the follow-up were well underway. "I'd like to make a British version of *Scarface* but Daniel will have to be less showy than Bond for this one. His character likes to go unnoticed, be discreet and shouldn't be buff and handsome." Vaughn wanted to exploit Craig's Bond-appeal but turn him into an anti-Bond. In terms of hard economics, *Layer Cake*'s mediocre box-office hardly cried out for a sequel. Even with Craig attached, would audiences be interested in a second installment of the XXXX saga five years down the line?

Craig would never go for the easy roles or the easy money. If nothing else, he knew it would bring out the worst in him. As Craig explained to Martyn Palmer: "I mustn't get complacent, because if I start relaxing about all of this, then I'm going to turn into a dick." He'd shown this determination in his pre-Bond days, turning down *Lara Croft Tomb Raider: The Cradle of Life* (2003). Who knows where Craig's career would have gone if he'd returned as Alex West?

In the meantime, Craig wanted to do more theatre, citing Bill Nighy, who appeared in *Enduring Love*, and *Casino Royale* co-star Judi Dench as role models. Could Britain's hottest movie actor take time out for the theatre? Would critics and audiences put the 007 image to one side and give Craig a fair chance? It's certainly possible. Nicole Kidman appeared in Sam Mendes' production of *The Blue Room*, a critical and commercial hit. And Ewan McGregor starred in a revival of *Guys and Dolls*, winning deserved acclaim.

As expected, Craig used his new celebrity status to promote good causes. He was asked to take part in *Little Britain's Big Night*, a live show staged to raise money for the Comic Relief charity. The hit BBC comedy *Little Britain* had made stars Matt Lucas and David Walliams two of the biggest names in entertainment. A big 007 fan, Walliams had also co-written and presented the ITV documentary *David Walliams: My Life with James Bond 007* (2006). Walliams and Lucas were keen for Craig to appear as a Bond-type villain in a show to be staged at the Hammersmith Apollo on 22 November 2006. The BBC would record the performance, showing highlights as part of its *Comic Relief* marathon on 16 March 2007. The projected celebrity guest cast also included Kate Moss, Craig's ex-girlfriend. In the event, Craig's work commitments meant he wasn't available for the show. The tabloid press, hoping for a Craig-Moss reunion, were disappointed.

Still eager to contribute, Craig agreed to guest star in a pre-filmed sketch for *Comic Relief* night. He appeared opposite Catherine Tate, one of Britain's leading comedy performers and a respected dramatic actress. The sketch took the form of a mock documentary. Tate played the frumpy Elaine Figgis, whose search for romance in internet chat rooms leads her to 'BondBoy68' (1968 is the year of Craig's birth). Now saddled with actor Daniel Craig as her live-in boyfriend, Figgis has no idea who he is and feels a little disappointed: "I was hoping for someone slightly better looking." Unable to deal with Craig's obsessive devotion, Elaine finally ends their affair. She even admits that she'd prefer to date ageing TV cop John Nettles, a joke lost on those who haven't seen either *Bergerac* or *Midsomer Murders*. Craig leaves alone on his tandem, a broken man. For a throwaway comedy skit, it's almost poignant.

Playing along with a straight face, Craig gives a good-humoured performance. There's none of the self-consciousness or uneasiness that some 'serious' actors have brought to their rare comedy excursions (charitable or otherwise). Craig even agreed to be depicted as a Celine Dion fan, which is surely way beyond the call of duty.

His painfully earnest declarations of love evoke *Obsession*, *Love is the Devil* and *Enduring Love*, though none of those films featured jokes about foul smelling lavatories or Carphone Warehouse.

Interviewed back in 2005, Craig seemed adamant that he would remain an actor rather than a star, insisting that "I don't want to be a celebrity because that sucks. It's just madness." Too bad. Craig had become a fully-fledged celebrity and the only way he could get out of it – for now – would be to quit the movie business and become a recluse. Given his contract with Eon Productions, and several other film deals, this didn't look like a viable option.

EPILOGUE

Everybody seems to think I'm suddenly a multi-millionaire. It doesn't happen overnight, you know. And, no, they didn't give me an Aston Martin. There's no such thing as a free lunch.
DANIEL CRAIG, ON BECOMING JAMES BOND

Craig's new level of celebrity doesn't always run in his favour. He took some media flack, for example, for attending Elton John's 60th birthday party. The press wanted to know why he was there. Did Craig have a longstanding friendship with Elton? Was he a die-hard fan who regularly danced to 'Crocodile Rock'? Or had the Bond-era Craig become the kind of celebrity who turned up at all the big showbiz events? Elton had attended the *Casino Royale* premiere in Leicester Square, so, arguably, Craig was merely returning the courtesy. According to *The Mirror*, John's partner David Furnish confessed to having a major crush on Craig. Judging from the response to Craig's Bond, he was in good company.

The Sun reported that Craig had bought a 2.5-ton Cadillac Escalade for use in Los Angeles. According to the article, he had problems parking the deluxe four-wheel drive vehicle, often leaving it at strange angles. Local residents were canvased for their amused reactions. The new Bond might be able to handle his Aston Martin but his kerb-side manoeuvres needed some work. Interviewed in *Elle* magazine, Craig denied any plans to take up permanent residence in the movie capital:

> LA is always a good place to visit, but also a good place to get out of. It doesn't feel like a proper city. You can't party in Los Angeles. Everything closes at ten o'clock! The studios made that happen, to stop actors staying in bars until three in the morning.

The immediate Bond effect placed severe constraints on Craig's social life. As he explained to Liz Hoggard, "The truth is I can't really go out at the moment … I just get shouted at. It's not anything bad, and it will die down eventually. And if it stops me walking into too many bars, that's no bad thing." He could still hang out in New York and Soho, however: "Anyone can walk round Soho." Elsewhere, fans – usually male – would inevitably rush up to him.

Craig had problems with less respectful fans, including one who took a picture of his backside. Craig's response was unfiltered outrage rather than movie star cool: "What the fuck are you doing that for? You've got a fucking nerve. Can you delete that?" Under the circumstances, a fierce order of "Delete that now!" would have sounded better. While the press noted Craig's grasp of digital camera technology, his insults were felt to lack style. More to the point, did the offending fan delete the photo as requested? Probably not. But what's a superstar to do? Grabbing the camera would have been risky, inviting charges of theft or perhaps assault. Even if the matter went no further, imagine the tabloid headlines: "Cheeky 007 Fan Left Shaken and Stirred by Bruiser Bond!" While Craig wanted to avoid movie star pique, he was offended by some people's behaviour, telling Martyn Palmer "Trying to take pictures of me when I'm having a piss is not welcome and never will be. And yes, that's happened."

Craig has only just joined the celebrity A-list and the media will be watching for signs of weakness. Can the Buff Blond Bond hack it in the big league? Some would argue that he merits no special sympathy. Craig knew that playing Bond would change his life. If the trappings of fame seemed too heavy a price, he could have walked away from the franchise. Now, as Craig adjusted to the harsher glare of the media spotlight, he had to brace himself for a few rough patches. Even the most hardened stars couldn't play the gracious celebrity 24 hours a day.

Craig envied colleagues who could promote worthy causes without being scrutinised in the popular press. He greatly admired old friend and fellow actor Nick Reding, who put a successful career on hold to run the Kenyan theatre company SAFE (Sponsored Arts For Education), promoting HIV and AIDS awareness and education. "It's what I fantasise about doing," Craig confessed, "if situations were different. I'd like to think I would react in that way. But I'm not sure I would. I'm scared of that. But Nick has that personality." In mid-2007, Craig became the voice of Barnardo's 'Believe in Children' campaign. The long-established charity wanted to counter misconceptions about troubled kids. Research had revealed a widespread adult fear of wild, 'uncontrollable' children, who were seen as beyond help by the age of 13. Craig recorded a series of radio spots aimed at changing these negative attitudes.

To date, Craig's post-*Casino Royale* career had met with a mixed critical and commercial response. He emerged from the *Invasion* car wreck largely unscathed, which is more than can be said for Nicole Kidman. In any case, the film properly belonged to his pre-007 days. There were no ready excuses for *The Golden Compass*, though Craig couldn't be blamed for the film's failings. For one thing, he was barely in it.

The Golden Compass glitters aplenty, yet seldom heads in the right direction. While Pullman's literary concepts don't translate easily to film, this stumbling adaptation creates problems of its own. Chris Weitz's clunky, episodic script is weighed down by the exposition-heavy dialogue. The anti-Christian slant is still there, for those who care to look. Depicting the soul as an animal spirit was asking for trouble with the religious right, frustrated over its failure to nail the *Harry Potter* series. Heroine Lyra lacks ready appeal, not helped by

DANIEL CRAIG – ULTIMATE PROFESSIONAL

Dakota Blue Richards' come-and-go accent and awkward line readings. Nicole Kidman plays Mrs Coulter as a 1930s vamp yet still resembles a digital facsimile of her old self. Strong points include the ice bears, Sam Elliott's engaging Lee Scoursby and some effective battle scenes. Spread over two hours, this isn't enough. Lavish to the nth degree, *The Golden Compass* is uninvolving, charmless and, dare one say it, lacking in soul. The ending screams "To Be Continued…" Don't count on it.

Prominent on the film's poster, Craig has little more than a cameo. The closing credits give the game away, billing the alleged co-star in 19th place. Asriel is the first character to appear, strolling along with his leopard familiar. Could this bold scholar be something of a predator? Looking good in a suit and tie, the bearded Craig plays Asriel as terse and confident, with the occasional quiet smile. After the first 15 minutes, Asriel largely disappears. At the 40 minute mark, he is shown being ambushed in the frozen wastes, a brief burst of 007-style action. After 85 minutes, Asriel reappears in his secret laboratory, a wordless scene that merely patches a gaping hole in the story.

Craig does well with his limited character and screen-time, capturing Asriel's conviction, determination and courage. His barely concealed fear of the Magisterium conveys the darkness and menace of this organization, sorely lacking in Kidman's slinky villainess and the guy with a bad comb-over. Craig also lifts some clumsy dialogue, notably "Lyra, dust is none of your business." He has no scenes with Kidman, though after *The Invasion* no-one begged for a reunion. Craig makes a final, spectral appearance in the closing minutes, a silent vision in Lyra's compass. It's a tribute to Craig's performance that he flits in and out of the story, seemingly at random, and still steals the movie.

The Golden Compass premiered in London on 27 November 2007, with a general release on 5 December. Attending the premiere with Nicole Kidman, Craig fielded the expected questions about Pullman's anti-Christian bias:

I'm not surprised at the criticism. I get that. But I think the majority of people who are criticising it haven't read it. These books are not anti-religious. Mainly they're anti-misuse of power – whether it's religious or political. It's interesting that people should get so angry because the morals in this book are solid and really good. Any child should read this.

The British press response was mixed, to say the least. *Guardian* critic Peter Bradshaw seemed impressed and disconcerted in equal measure. "It's a convoluted, enjoyable, very mad, deeply conservative and, at one moment, horribly violent extravaganza." Appreciating Nicole Kidman's "glamorous and arresting turn" as Mrs Coulter, he made little mention of Craig. Both Bradshaw and *The Independent's* Anthony Quinn felt *The Golden Compass* was too blatant in its borrowings from other fantasy epics. As Quinn noted: "The collegiate atmosphere has a hint of Hogwarts, which gives way to a nip of Narnia, a touch of Tolkien and a pinch of *Pirates of the Caribbean.*"

Going further back, *The Golden Compass* could be compared with David Lynch's *Dune* (1984), another big budget fantasy based on a supposedly unfilmable novel. Like *Dune, The Golden Compass* has an opening voiceover conveying a ridiculous amount of information in a short space of time. Where *Dune* has a prophecy and Spice, *The Golden Compass* has a prophecy and Dust. In both cases, these crucial substances amount to little more than a baffling plot device. New Line and Chris Weitz could have learned a valuable lesson from the Lynch film: don't create fantasy worlds where the ground rules and key plot points require laborious and repeated explanation. *Dune* proved a box-office disaster and its long-term cult success brought little comfort to Lynch.

Opening in the US on 7 December, *The Golden Compass* earned some positive reviews. *Chicago Sun-Times* critic Roger Ebert was impressed: "*The Golden Compass* is a darker, deeper fantasy epic than the Rings trilogy, *The Chronicles of Narnia* or the Potter films. It springs from the same British world of quasi-philosophical magic, but creates more complex villains and poses more intriguing questions. As a visual experience, it is superb. As an escapist fantasy, it is challenging." Ebert also praised the lead performances, which held their own amid the CGI wizardry. "Nicole Kidman projects a severe beauty in keeping with the sinister Mrs Coulter, and Daniel Craig and Sam Elliott give her refined and rough surfaces to play against."

Overall, the US critics were middling, with an undercurrent of disappointment. *Variety*'s Todd McCarthy rated the film as an "impressively rendered but oddly uninviting adventure". Writing in *Rolling Stone*, Peter Travers dismissed *The Golden Compass* as a dud: "The Catholic League thinks it's anti-Catholic. Admirers of Philip Pullman's 1995 *His Dark Materials* trilogy think Chris Weitz's film guts the backbone of the book. Me, I just think it blows." Noting the 'cheesy' effects and messy script, Travers saved much of his venom for the stars: "Kidman and co-star Daniel (007) Craig strike as many sexual sparks as they did in *The Invasion*, which was none." *San Francisco Chronicle* critic Mick LaSalle felt Craig's "commanding and swaggering" performance was wasted on an underused character.

As things turned out, negative reviews were the least of New Line's worries. In most countries, the film's alleged anti-Christian bias generated media coverage but few protests. Within the US, the powerful and influential religious right declared war on *The Golden Compass*. The Catholic Church felt it was being equated with the evil Magisterium, which practiced a bizarre form of child abuse. Months before the film's release, the US-based Catholic League urged a boycott of *The Golden Compass*. For all the departures from Pullman's book, New Line were still guilty of peddling atheism to kids. The stars had done their best to defend both book and film. Nicole Kidman emphasized her Catholic upbringing, stating she would never appear in a film she regarded as anti-Christian. Craig also denied the perceived anti-Catholicism, though his remark to Martyn Palmer that "faith always needs to be questioned" didn't help the cause.

The League's tactics seemed to have worked. *The Golden Compass* grossed just $70 million in the US, way short of expectations. A number of critics had predicted this, Todd McCarthy commenting "It's doubtful *Compass* will find a B.O. [box office] path anywhere near Narnia, much less Middle-earth." There's a case for arguing that, regardless of the religious controversy, New Line had overestimated *The Golden Compass*'s domestic appeal. Pullman's book had always been more popular in the UK than the US.

Interviewed by Martyn Palmer for *The Times*, Craig had joked about starring in a second huge movie franchise. "I know", he groaned with mock despair. "Who'd have guessed?" Guess again. Outside the US, *The Golden Compass* took around $300 million, which didn't cover its production, marketing and distribution costs. Even allowing for television and home video sales, the film was unlikely to show a significant profit. New Line and Chris Weitz had planned to release the first sequel in late 2009. *The Golden Compass*'s commercial failure in the crucial US market left the intended series dead and buried. Blockbuster fantasy epics are a high-risk game and the $370 million take was nowhere near enough to warrant a sequel, especially in the face of organized Christian protests.

While *Flashbacks of a Fool* inspired no boycotts, it had problems being noticed at all. The film premiered in London on 13 April 2008, with a general release five days later. Craig promoted his pet project with a series of interviews. Liz Hoggard felt Craig was eager to shake off his Bond image, for the time being. "The man who dragged Ian Fleming's suave, chilly secret agent into the 21st century seems keen to remind us that he's not to be mistaken in any way for his best-known character."

For all Craig's good intentions, he didn't have much to say about his new character, talking mainly in clichés. "I play someone who's had a huge amount of success and hasn't really learnt anything… you'd imagine he'd have supreme happiness, but he's a fuck-up. He has no direction in life." Craig made light of his role as producer-star, with the commercial muscle and high-powered connections beyond the reach of most actors. "When I was younger the idea of networking was a big luvvy joke, and on a basic level it's about self-interest… on a more generous level, it really is the sharing of information… It's lending weight, and it's me going and shaking hands with people." Director Baillie Walsh emphasized that Craig was still a serious dramatic actor, unconstricted by his 007 status. "It was a brave choice for Dan. He's Bond and he wants to protect that, but he throws himself into the role. I think it's good for him to take those risks. I think he needs to."

Despite Craig's presence, *Flashbacks of a Fool* needed a lot of critical goodwill to find an audience. This support wasn't forthcoming, most reviewers dismissing the film as at best a curiosity and at worst a tedious failure. *Observer* critic Philip French saw only "a curiously pointless exercise". Writing in *The Guardian*, Xan Brooks rated *Flashbacks of a Fool* as a curate's egg, "a woozy rites-of-passage drama that seems one-part languorous to two-parts drunk… an intriguing bit of driftwood, an exotic wreck." By the end of the film, Brooks argued, Craig had taken a curious side-trip that didn't amount to much: "he shakes his head, picks up his bag and prepares to return to Bond". Reviewing the film in *The Independent*, Anthony Quinn noted "moments of tenderness and warmth" but not much else. In *The Times*, Wendy Ide felt the main character was misconceived. "Self-absorbed, self-pitying and self-destructive… Joe's lack of evolution is unsatisfying." Several critics noted Craig's friendship with Walsh and his personal commitment to getting the film made. While the producer-star deserved points for loyalty and tenacity, the end result was an interesting failure. Fans were doubly disappointed that Craig appeared in the film for barely 25 minutes. Shown on 272 screens, *Flashbacks of a Fool* took just £246,072 on its opening weekend.

No one, least of all Craig, expected a blockbuster but the critical sniping and meagre returns must have stung. At the time of writing, the film remains unreleased in the United States, with most pundits predicting a belated DVD premiere. Even Craig's star status couldn't stir much distributor interest in a poorly reviewed character drama.

As Sean Connery discovered between Bond pictures, the 007 lustre didn't necessarily extend to other film roles. While *Flashbacks of a Fool* had been badly received, Craig showed no regrets about his involvement, telling Martyn Palmer "to be able to make films like this is important to me. I have to be all these other things now and acting starts dropping down the list, which is bizarre. You go, 'Hang on a minute, I just want to be an actor, I want to just turn up and do the gig.'"

Whatever causes Craig chose to promote, the James Bond factor would work in his favour for the time being. The only downside to *Casino Royale*'s success was that the next 007 film had to be even better. It was rumoured that the script would be based on Ian Fleming's short story 'Risico', from the *For Your Eyes Only* collection first published in 1960. In this 41 page thriller, Bond targets a heroin smuggling ring in Italy, only to find himself double-crossed. The title refers to the way one character pronounces 'risk'. Sharper Bond fans soon realised the rumour was false, as elements of 'Risico' had already been used in the film *For Your Eyes Only*. Moreover, the Venice locations central to the story featured heavily in the last act of *Casino Royale*.

On 24 January 2008, Eon announced the film's title as *Quantum of Solace*, taken from a Fleming story first published in 1959 and subsequently included in the book *For Your Eyes Only*. Only the title would be retained, as the plot centred on the aftermath of a dull dinner party, with a long anecdote that did not involve Bond. Fleming defined a quantum of solace as 'the amount of comfort' necessary for the relationship between two people to survive.

This appears to have been a last-minute decision, as the title 'Quantum of Solace' had been considered for a Bond film in the past and rejected as unsuitable. Some felt audiences wouldn't understand it. *Licence Revoked* had become *Licence to Kill* when market research revealed that many people didn't know what 'revoked' meant. Craig admitted to doubts about the title, but felt it fitted the tone of the new film:

It's grown on me. I was unsure at first. Bond is looking for his quantum of solace and that's what he wants, he wants his closure. Ian Fleming says that if you don't have a quantum of solace in your relationship then the relationship is over. It's that spark of niceness in a relationship that if you don't have you might as well give up. Bond doesn't have that because his girlfriend has been killed, therefore he's looking for revenge to make himself happy with the world again.

According to media reports, Craig would receive £5 million for *Quantum of Solace*, with a guaranteed £3 million raise for his third Bond appearance.

Eon Productions hoped to release the second Craig Bond film the year after *Casino Royale*, as the combination of 007 and 2007 seemed too good to miss. These plans soon proved over-optimistic. The production would not be ready to roll in time, and Craig's other commitments meant he wouldn't be available. The new release date was announced as November 2008, two years after *Casino Royale*. 2008 was the centenary of Ian Fleming's birth, which seemed a suitable anniversary. The Imperial War Museum in London marked Fleming's centennial with the first major exhibition devoted to his life and work. 007 film props on display included Sean Connery's overcoat from *Doctor No*, the bladed shoes used in *From Russia With Love*, Goldfinger's golf shoes, a spear gun from *Thunderball*, a wing mirror dart gun from *Live and Let Die*, a bullet-riddled cello from *The Living Daylights* and Craig's bloodstained shirt from *Casino Royale*.

Speaking at the 2007 Cannes Film Festival, Craig admitted that he'd let himself go after his tough fitness regime for *Casino Royale*. "I had some down time. I got to enjoy myself a bit. I'm getting back into shape now. I'm kind of building myself up again." Craig had around six months to achieve Bond-level fitness, as shooting was set to begin in London in December. Interviewed by Martyn Palmer, he detailed his new 007 workout programme. "Last time I did a lot of weights to bulk up because I had to do it quickly. This time I'm going to do more boxing and more running. I won't look physically much different, but I won't be as 'no neck' as I was last time."

Eon's first choice for director was Roger Michell, who worked with Craig on *The Mother* and *Enduring Love*. This was somewhat ironic, given Michell's advice to Craig to turn Bond down. Eon approached Michell in mid-2006, months before *Casino Royale*'s release. Tempted by the pay cheque on offer, he had concerns over the projected eighteen-month schedule. Perhaps director and franchise were never meant to unite, as Michell soon dropped out. Interviewed for *The Times* by Dominic Maxwell, Michell gave his reasons for leaving the film:

> *In the end I didn't feel comfortable with the Bond process, and I was very nervous that there was a start date but really no script at all. The Bond people are used to going into these massive productions in quite a chaotic way. I just decided eventually that I'd be doing it for the wrong reasons. I'd be doing it for my friendship with Daniel Craig. I'd be doing it for the money. And not really because I yearned to do it.*

Who would replace Michell? *Casino Royale* director Martin Campbell seemed to have ruled himself out. He and Craig had clashed a few times during filming, though this was hardly unusual. *The Mirror* quoted Campbell as saying he "wasn't totally convinced" by Craig at first, which probably didn't help. Craig supposedly fought with Campbell to give Bond a stronger emotional centre. Whatever the case, they emerged from the experience with a healthy mutual respect. More importantly, Campbell was wary of being typed as a Bond director. A Bond film per decade was one thing. A Bond film every two years – with nothing else in between – would suggest there were few other offers. *Casino Royale* co-writer Paul Haggis also declined to direct, as he wanted to focus on other projects.

On Craig's recommendation, Eon signed a deal with Marc Forster, German-born director of *Monster's Ball* (2001), *Finding Neverland*

(2004), *Stay* (2005) and *Stranger Than Fiction* (2006). A fan of Forster's work, Craig felt he would be in tune with a flawed, humanised Bond. The director would also work on the script, alongside Paul Haggis and 007 regulars Neal Purvis and Robert Wade. Some questioned Forster's qualifications as a Bond director. He had little experience with high-concept action movies, focusing more on offbeat character-based pieces. Forster felt he was well suited to the new style of Bond movie, which emphasised a tougher, darker quality in the character, saying "I have always been a Bond fan, so it is very exciting to take on this challenge. The new direction that the Bond character has taken offers a director a host of fresh possibilities."

Quantum of Solace would be a direct sequel to *Casino Royale*, picking up plot threads left unresolved at the end of the previous film. This was touted by some as a new departure for the series, though *Diamonds are Forever* opens with Bond taking revenge for the murder of his wife at the end of *On Her Majesty's Secret Service*. Judi Dench returned as M, her sixth outing in the role. In addition, *Quantum of Solace* was set to reintroduce the character of René Mathis, played by sometime Italian movie idol Giancarlo Giannini. In *Casino Royale*, Le Chiffre named Mathis as the double agent who betrayed Bond. While subsequent events suggested otherwise, Bond felt that Mathis' innocence remained unproven. Given Bond's mood as the closing credits rolled, Mathis needs to provide some convincing answers in the new film. There were internet rumours that Eva Green would reappear as Vesper Lynd, presumably in flashback. Green dismissed these stories, telling Craig McLean "There will be pictures [of Vesper] and things like that. I don't know who the Bond girl's gonna be. I'm a bit jealous!"

Craig announced that he wanted *Live and Let Die* co-star Jane Seymour to return for the new Bond film. Her performance as Solitaire, the psychic Tarot card reader, had made a big impression on him back in 1973. Craig hoped Seymour would reprise the role three-and-a-half decades on, though his logic seemed contradictory, to say the least. "*Casino Royale* was about early Bond and I love the idea of him revisiting his past and meeting up with ex-loves. That has to include Jane Seymour. I'm a huge fan, I thought she was fantastic."

While Jane Seymour's Solitaire didn't appear in *Quantum of Solace*, Jeffrey Wright returned as Felix Leiter, while Jesper Christensen reprised his role as Mr White. Wright was only the second actor to play Leiter more than once, following David Hedison in *Live and Let Die* and *Licence to Kill*. Bond completists noted that he was the first to take the role in consecutive films.

Marc Forster wanted the chief villain to be played by Swiss actor Bruno Ganz, who starred in *Saint-Ex* and, more recently, *Downfall*. Ganz's extraordinary portrayal of Adolf Hitler in the latter showed he had a flair for megalomaniac villains. In fact, Eon had already contracted French actor-director Mathieu Amalric, who appeared in *Munich* and *Marie Antoinette* (2006). He won acclaim for his performance in *The Diving Bell and the Butterfly* (2007), a harrowing drama based on real events. Amalric was surprised that his character had no unusual physical characteristics, such as Doctor No's metal hands, Largo's eyepatch, Blofeld's scar (in *You Only Live Twice*), Tee Hee's claw hand, Scaramanga's third nipple, Jaws' teeth or Le Chiffre's bloody tears. "I said to Marc: No nothing? A beard? Can I shave my hair? He said: No, just [use] your face." Forster felt the new Bond villain would be more sinister if he looked perfectly normal, his twisted genius hidden behind a calm façade. As Amalric put it at a Pinewood press call: "The director saw something in me that had to do with the devil. That was a compliment." Amalric's bad guy would also lack fighting skills, much to Bond's surprise. "Sometimes anger can be much more dangerous. I'm going to fight like in school." Few of the classic Bond *uber* villains could handle 007 *mano a mano*, though Red Grant gave him a hard time in *From Russia with Love*.

The supporting cast included Gemma Arterton, who had recently appeared as one of the bad schoolgirls in *St Trinians* (2007). Cast as Agent Fields, a novice MI6 operative, Arterton showed her own inexperience in the ways of the press. Discussing details of the plot, she seemed to reveal her character's fate, drawing a parallel with Diana Rigg's Tracy Di Vicenzo in *On Her Majesty's Secret Service*.

Budgeted at around $230 million, *Quantum of Solace* was in production from 2 January to 21 June 2008, with studio work at Pinewood and location filming in Italy, Spain, Mexico, Panama, Chile, Austria and the UK. Forster wanted his cast to make script suggestions, hiring writer Joshua Zetumer to incorporate the new dialogue on a daily basis. Craig suffered several injuries, claiming that *Casino Royale* was "a walk in the park" compared to his second Bond venture. On a lighter note, Craig turned 40 during the Panama shoot and threw a big party for 300 guests, including the cast and crew. Craig's presence in Panama drew hordes of paparazzi and he switched hotels several times to keep them off his back. Craig described Bond in *Quantum of Solace* as "an unfinished article with a sense of revenge, who is still headstrong and doesn't always make the right decisions."

The first trailer for *Quantum of Solace* was suitably sombre, highlighting vengeance, damaged goods, the world's most precious resource and a mysterious global organization that poses a terrible threat. Vesper Lynd's Algerian Knot pendant also featured, suggesting that Bond will be visiting his lost love's treacherous former boyfriend. The action highlights were present and correct, Felix Leiter commenting "James, move your ass."

Given his left-wing sympathies, Craig had become surprisingly protective of establishment figure Bond, a man of few liberal instincts. British director Paul Greengrass, who handled two of the Jason Bourne films, had supposedly dismissed Bond as a cruel imperialist, an unwelcome remnant of the long-dead British Empire. Interviewed in *Empire* magazine, Craig leapt to his character's defence. "I am not going to get into a pissing competition with the Bourne fans. You have the monarchy, you have government and then you have the civil service. The reason the civil service remains a non-political organization is that if the shit hits the fan you hope the civil

service will turn around and go 'We've got it covered.' That's Bond."
Perhaps Craig was starting to take his secret agent alter ego too
seriously. Whatever his roots in real life, 007 is still a fantasy figure.
Quantum of Solace received its charity royal world premiere in
Leicester Square, London on 29 October 2008, in the presence in
Princes William and Harry. Craig trod the red carpet once more,
accompanied by co-stars Judi Dench and Gemma Arterton.

So is Craig now the still, calm centre of the relentless Bond
juggernaut? It has been suggested that he still harbours doubts about
the role. Maybe so, but, having made his decision, Craig seems fully
committed to the franchise. For the next few years at least, Craig's
career will be thriving. He now enjoys a level of choice and control
that was unthinkable just a few years ago. Craig's personal life seems
similarly settled, Satsuki Mitchell having been introduced to the
world on the same night Craig was launched as James Bond. Mitchell
accompanied Craig throughout most of his worldwide and whirl-
wind *Casino Royale* promotional tour. She kept him grounded – and
sane – when the media and fan attention threatened to overwhelm
him. Interviewed by Martyn Palmer, Craig paid tribute to his supportive girlfriend. "I couldn't get through it without her. You've got to
have a sense of perspective and she gives me that. Being on your own
would be sad, sick and weird. I need that balance, it's crucially
important. And we've been to some amazing places. You have to have
someone to share this stuff with."

Barely 40, Craig seems nostalgic for his youth, feeling that people
today are less inclined to stand up and make their voice heard. As he
explained to Liz Hoggard: "We all seemed to be politically savvy,
protesting about things. We [now] have a general malaise…
Individuals with a passion are rare." Still passionate about political
issues, Craig appreciates the limitations on his opportunities to speak
out in public. "I'm an actor, not a politician… I can't straddle both
places and expect to be taken seriously." Perhaps Craig's star status
has made him overly cautious. Many actors have been open about
their political beliefs and campaigned accordingly: John Wayne,

Charlton Heston, Paul Newman, Marlon Brando, Sidney Poitier, Jane Fonda, Vanessa Redgrave, Susan Sarandon. Even Sean Connery openly supported the Scottish National Party.

Not that Craig will become complacent in any sphere of his life. For most people, Craig is an actor, albeit a hugely successful one. He's also a father who worries that teenagers now grow up too fast, faced with too many ways to spend their leisure time and, via the internet, too much exposure to a potentially risky adult world. On a lighter note, Craig has tried to get his daughter Ella interested in The Rolling Stones, only to find she's stuck on The Beatles. It seems that 1960s pop culture still exerts a powerful hold over the younger generation. Which prompts the question: who is Ella's favourite James Bond?

WHO'S THE DADDY? CRAIG VERSUS CAINE

I n 2008, Daniel Craig turned 40. For some men, this milestone heralds an era of leather jackets, motorbikes and unsuitable younger girlfriends. Not for Mr Craig. His career and personal life are on a roll and he looks set to become one of the major British film actors of his generation. Craig's second James Bond movie will draw large audiences, whatever the reviews are like. His other film projects are sure to attract attention, if not guaranteed big box-office.

In the introduction to this book, I noted that Craig had common ground with the working class British actors who broke through in the 1960s, becoming major film stars with a worldwide following: Albert Finney, Terence Stamp, Michael Caine and Sean Connery. Sir Sean's career was examined in the 'Bondage' chapter, up to *The Untouchables*. There's not much to add, other than noting Connery's continued employment in high profile American movies. He scored a big hit as Harrison Ford's dad in *Indiana Jones and the Last Crusade* (1989), and added much needed gravitas to *The Rock* (1996), which made knowing reference to Connery's Bond persona. Connery's last film to date is the disappointing *The League of Extraordinary Gentlemen* (2003). No-one was that surprised when Connery announced his retirement from acting. Though tempted by the fourth Indiana Jones film, he has – so far – stuck to his decision.

Albert Finney made his film breakthrough as working class rebel

Arthur Seaton in *Saturday Night and Sunday Morning* (1960), one of the British 'kitchen sink' movies. He consolidated his stardom with the more fanciful period romp *Tom Jones* (1963). Craig ventured into similar territory with *The Fortunes and Misfortunes of Moll Flanders*, though with greater sexual frankness and less blatant symbolism. After *Two for the Road* (1967), Finney seemed to lose interest in his film career, concentrating on the theatre and occasional television appearances. His more notable post-1960s movies include *Gumshoe* (1971), *Wolfen* (1981), *The Dresser* (1983) and *Miller's Crossing* (1990). More recently, Finney lent a touch of class to *Erin Brockovich* (2000), *Big Fish* (2003) and *The Bourne Ultimatum* (2007).

Terence Stamp made an Oscar-nominated film debut in *Billy Budd* (1962), as a heroic martyred sailor, and had nowhere much to go but down. Stamp relied largely on his smouldering good looks rather than the dramatic muscle of a Finney, or a Craig. Even at the height of his fame in the 1960s, Stamp's film roles were a mixed bag, the best including *The Collector* (1965), *Far from the Madding Crowd* (1967), *Poor Cow* (1967) and *Theorem* (1968). At the end of the decade, for reasons well-documented elsewhere, Stamp largely quit the business to seek peace and enlightenment in India. Returning to full-time acting a decade later, Stamp scored a memorable comeback as General Zod in *Superman* (1978) and *Superman II* (1980). He was also on good form as an enigmatic fugitive ex-con in *The Hit* (1984). From this point on, Stamp lent his aristocratic good looks and hint of exquisite decadence to a string of mostly mediocre movies, notably *Young Guns* (1988). Highpoints included *The Adventures of Priscilla, Queen of the Desert* (1994) and *The Limey* (1999), which gave Stamp his first good starring role in years. His TV work included hosting *The Hunger*, introducing Craig's misadventures in 'Menage a Trois'. Stamp has expressed regret that he wasn't offered the role of James Bond. The closest he got was playing Monica Vitti's sidekick in *Modesty Blaise* (1966).

Of these four actors, the most interesting comparison with Craig is Michael Caine. How does Craig's career to date compare with that of Sir Michael? Blond hair and blue eyes aside, they seem very different people in both their professional and personal lives. Unlike Craig, Caine favoured ostentatious displays of wealth during the early days of his success, notably a Rolls-Royce, for which he employed a chauffeur as he couldn't drive at the time. Politically, Caine is to the right of Craig by some distance. He was a long time Conservative supporter, only switching sides with the rise of New Labour in 1997.

While Craig regards himself as an actor first and foremost, Caine always wanted to be a star. Interviewed for *Films and Filming* in the late 1960s, he explained "While the star system lasts, I shall do everything in my power to be a star, at the highest price that I can screw out of anybody." This hard-headed attitude could be attributed to a deep-rooted insecurity, especially over money. Caine endured a tough childhood, followed by years of poverty as he struggled to establish himself in the acting profession. While Craig was often short of money during his early days as an actor, he never brushed his teeth with salt or worked as a bouncer in a brothel.

Craig has a reputation for turning roles down – often with big money attached – if he can't see himself as the character. Caine, on the other hand, seems willing to take almost anything, even movies intended for James Caan. Rare exceptions include *Women in Love* (1969), as Caine was uncomfortable with the full-frontal nudity, and *Frenzy* (1972), because he despised the proffered role of a psychopathic rapist and murderer. In his autobiography, Caine's professed attitude to his film career is disarmingly straightforward: "I have a definite standard by which I choose films: I choose the best one available at the time I need one...You get paid the same for a bad film as you do for a good one." Caine has stated, somewhat optimistically, that "No one remembers unsuccessful pictures because no one goes to see them. At the end of the day you are remembered for your hits."

Praised for his 'unactorish' quality, Caine's screen persona made virtues of his working class background and pronounced Cockney intonation. The golden era of Caine's film career ran just over ten years, from *Zulu* (1964) to *The Man Who Would Be King* (1975). His best movies of this period constitute a strong body of work that endures and resonates to this day. While good or at least watchable films followed, Caine seemed to lose his edge as an actor, settling for comfortable, unsurprising professionalism. Late in his career, Caine won two Academy Awards (Best Supporting Actor), for *Hannah and Her Sisters* (1986) and *The Cider House Rules* (1999). While neither performance can be counted among his best, Caine's work in these movies stood out against the bulk of his later output.

Michael Caine was born in South London on Tuesday, 14 March 1933, just under 35 years before Craig. As a lot of people know, Caine's birth name is Maurice Joseph Micklewhite, which he still uses in his personal life. His parents worked as a fish market porter and a charlady. A keen amateur actor as a teenager, Caine returned from National Service in the Korean War determined to turn professional. Bypassing stage school – a near impossible dream for someone of his background – he served his apprenticeship with the Horsham repertory company for three years and began winning small roles in television dramas. Like Craig, Caine married young, to actress Patricia Haines, and had a daughter, Dominique. The marriage lasted only three years.

Caine began his career at a time when the British film industry was still turning out a large number of movies on a regular basis. He made his film debut in *A Hill in Korea* (1956), with only eight lines of dialogue, most of which were cut from the release print. Caine went on to play bit parts, often uncredited, in such films as *Yield to the Night* (1956), *How to Murder a Rich Uncle* (1957), *Carve Her Name with Pride* (1958), *The Bulldog Breed* (1960) and *The Day the Earth Caught Fire* (1961). There was little sense of progression to his roles, which remained small, and few saw Caine as potential star material. In *The Day the Earth Caught Fire*, made five years after his debut, Caine appeared in one scene as a policeman directing traffic in a thick mist. He had one line of dialogue and, by his own admission, screwed it up so badly that director Val Guest advised him to quit the business. Now in his late twenties, Caine felt – with some justification – that any chance for a shot at the big time had passed him by.

While Craig faced a depressed local film industry when he left the Guildhall in 1991, he developed his career in the theatre and television, attracting attention while still in his mid-20s. Craig's film debut, *The Power of One*, came at the same age as Caine when he appeared in *A Hill in Korea*. Caine had appeared in 17 films before being cast in *Zulu*, his first big movie. By contrast, Craig's 17th film was *The Jacket*, by which time he had already made *Elizabeth*, *Love Is the Devil*, *Some Voices*, *Road to Perdition*, *Enduring Love* and *Layer Cake*.

Zulu gave Caine fifth billing and a special 'introducing' credit. He was cast against type as Gonville Bromhead, an inexperienced upper class officer. Caine works hard to generate sympathy for Bromhead, who initially seems vain, patronising, racist and arrogant. He handles the shadings of the character well, conveying the cynical, hesitant and insecure man underneath the mannerisms and pomposity. Craig donned the scarlet uniform and posh accent for *Sharpe's Eagle*, cast as the dastardly Lieutenant Berry, an utter swine with no redeeming features.

By the end of *Zulu*, Bromhead has shown himself to be both professional and courageous, barking orders through gritted, if gleaming, white teeth. Caine convinces the audience that Bromhead has acquired a hard-won lesson in wisdom and humility. His upper class accent is mostly sound, though East End vowels sometimes emerge in moments of high emotion (Craig has a similar problem when attempting an American accent). Caine also made good use of Bromhead's pith helmet, pulling it forward to put his eyes in shadow much of the time. Eyes can reveal more of a person than they would wish and Bromhead is not a man to give too much away.

Caine's fair hair and eyebrows are undeniably distinctive, contrasting with co-star Stanley Baker's dark complexion. Whether or not they worked in his favour is another matter. Some casting directors felt Caine looked too effeminate for a leading man. *Zulu's* executive producer Joseph Levine told Caine that he looked 'queer' on screen. Craig faced a similar problem from the other end of the macho spectrum. He looked too rough and tough to play the dashing hero.

When Christopher Plummer and Richard Harris turned down the lead in *The Ipcress File* (1965), Caine got a shot at his first starring role. The film was produced by Harry Saltzman, who, alongside Albert Broccoli, had brought James Bond to the big screen in *Dr No*, *From Russia with Love* and *Goldfinger*. *The Ipcress File* was based on a novel by Len Deighton, which treated espionage in a cynical, downbeat fashion, far removed from the escapist romanticism of the Bond series. While James Bond jets around the world's most glamorous locations, Sergeant Harry Palmer is stuck in London pulling shifts on tedious surveillance jobs.

As Palmer, Caine peers out from behind glasses and his distinctly droopy eyelids, caused by a disease called blefora. The deadpan Palmer is cocky, insolent, insubordinate and flirtatious. He makes his own coffee, shops in supermarkets and bets on horses picked from the sports pages of *The Sun* (pre-Rupert Murdoch).

Palmer enjoys cooking and classical music, which caused the producers some concern. What if audiences thought he was gay? In the mid-1960s, when homosexuality was still a criminal offence, this would have been commercial suicide. To assuage any doubts over Palmer's heterosexual credentials, he has an otherwise redundant affair with a female agent. He also proves handy in a fist fight, first removing his glasses.

Many regard Harry Palmer as the definitive Caine performance. Though set up as the dupe and fall guy, Palmer proves smart and intuitive, if recklessly impulsive. He emerges as a tough, sympathetic Everyman, light years away from the super-heroic, super-human Bond. Palmer is the working class hero – or anti-hero – to Bond's upper class public schoolboy adventurer. The joke, of course, is that Palmer is as much a fantasy figure as 007. For once, the trailer hyperbole proved accurate: "His name is Michael Caine and no-one will forget his name."

Caine's career took off into the stratosphere with *Alfie* (1966), which cast him as a hedonistic Cockney lothario. Bigger names such as Terence Stamp, Laurence Harvey, Anthony Newley and *Zulu* actor James Booth had passed on the role. Many actors refused to be associated with a film containing an abortion scene, fearing it would harm their images. How wrong they were. *Alfie* was the number two film at the UK box-office, beaten only by the Bond movie *Thunderball* (1965). It also scored a hit in the US and took Caine to Hollywood.

So how did Caine do it? From the opening scene, Alfie treats the camera – and the audience – as his confidante, creating a sense of intimacy and camaraderie. For the most part, Caine gets by on sheer charisma. A specialist in smooth talk and easy charm, Alfie is vain, shallow, cold and amoral. While Harry Palmer's screw-you attitude masks a man of decency and courage, Alfie is a selfish prick with a perpetual smirk on his face. His conquests are referred to as 'birds' or just 'it'. He seems to care for his illegitimate infant son, but can't wait to push the mother out of his life. He slaps a pregnant ex-lover – a one afternoon stand – when she cries out in pain after having an abortion induced.

Alfie's 'comeuppance' is hardly devastating, dumped by an older lover for a younger model. The self-recrimination also rings hollow, Alfie lamenting that he doesn't have 'peace of mind'. Caine's achievement is not so much to make Alfie sympathetic, as to stop him becoming utterly loathsome. He also does well with the direct addresses to the camera, a trick Craig repeated in the final scene of *Layer Cake*. Caine later remarked of *Alfie*: "To be a movie star, you have to carry a movie. And to carry a movie where you play the title role is the supreme example. The third thing, for a British actor, is to do it in America. The fourth is to get nominated for an award. That picture did all four things for me."

Caine made his US debut with *Gambit* (1966), a caper movie that now looks dated. The leading lady was Shirley MacLaine, who chose

Caine as her co-star. While *Gambit* suffers from a thin plot and clunky script, it's still one up on *Lara Croft: Tomb Raider*, Craig's US 'breakthrough'. At the time he made *Gambit*, Caine was around the same age as Craig when he appeared in the *Lara Croft* movie. For all its faults, *Gambit* launched Caine in America. Caine stumbled with *The Wrong Box* (1966), a clumsy all-star comedy, and took a headlong plunge with *Hurry Sundown* (1967), his first film to be shot in the United States. This Deep South melodrama cast him as a dastardly landowner. Caine's Southern accent was derided by many critics, which seems to irk him to this day.

Caine returned as Harry Palmer in *Funeral in Berlin* (1966). After a brief ride on London's public transport, Palmer is transposed to the divided German city, becoming the international secret agent he conspicuously wasn't in *The Ipcress File*. There are shades of *Alfie* in a few scenes, a 007-style office flirtation, and some curious gay undertones. The US trailer re-emphasised that Palmer was a new and different kind of hero, "Horn-rimmed. Cockney wit. Iron fist… Girls always make passes at spies in glasses."

The third Palmer film, *Billion Dollar Brain* (1967) flirts with being Bond-lite, complete with Maurice Binder titles. Yet Palmer is set up – once again – as the errand boy and fall guy, in a way that would be anathema to Bond. While the dry wit and sharp tongue are still present and correct, Palmer spends much of the film in a state of bewilderment. Palmer's increasingly passive nature seemed to turn off audiences, as *Billion Dollar Brain* proved a box-office disappointment. Harry Palmer never enjoyed the commercial or cultural impact of James Bond, played by Caine's good buddy Sean Connery. It's worth noting that Craig's Bond has some traits in common with Palmer: the class consciousness, the cockiness, the vulnerability and the capacity to make potentially fatal errors of judgement.

Craig can rest easy in the knowledge that he will never make a film as bad as *The Magus* (1968). Based on an acclaimed novel by John Fowles, this oddity is set in Greece, where Caine's English schoolteacher falls under the spell of Anthony Quinn's mysterious doctor. Caine admits that he didn't understand the book, the script or the final cut. His bemused performance suggests he had no idea what was going on and had given up hope of finding out. In his defence, Caine didn't want to make the film but had no choice under the terms of a deal with Twentieth Century Fox. Caine also came a cropper with *Deadfall* (1968), a psychological thriller, and *Play Dirty* (1968), a *Dirty Dozen* rip-off, both critical and commercial flops. *Deadfall* almost matches *The Magus* for ham-fisted 'sophistication'. As Caine noted, something went badly awry between the writing of the script and the completion of the movie.

Now in his mid-thirties, Caine risked tarnishing the stardom he'd worked so long to acquire. *Variety* observed that Caine seemed "to have lost much of the spark which launched his career so promisingly." Was Caine simply overexposed, appearing in too many movies, or had his trademark underplayed style started to wear thin with audiences? A third possibility was Caine's apparent ill-luck – or ill-judgement – at picking projects.

The light-hearted crime caper *The Italian Job* (1969) is mainly notable for the line "You're only supposed to blow the bloody doors off!" Caine's Charlie Croker is preoccupied with clothes, cars and 'birds', who come a poor third. There are nods to *Alfie* (off-screen orgies) and *Zulu* (posh accent assumed for subterfuge). His performance verges on both camp and self-parody, though he and the rest of the cast are upstaged by French stuntmen in Mini Coopers. It's arguable that *The Italian Job* is the film *Layer Cake* tried to be: a hip, flip crime caper that hides its dubious subtexts under a glossy sheen of ingenious stunts and humorous banter. *The Italian Job* proved popular in the UK and Europe, but flopped in the US. The iconic title was reused for a largely unrelated 2003 remake, which did well enough to merit a sequel.

Caine's US career marked time with the World War II drama *Too Late the Hero* (1970), where the action took a back seat to meaningful statements about the insanity of war. Caine delivered another of his mouthy, insubordinate Cockney rebels, to diminishing returns.

While the mannerisms were getting familiar, he did evoke a conflicted character, torn between his sense of self-preservation and growing sense of duty.

As the 1960s came to an end, Caine returned to form with *The Last Valley* (1970), set in seventeenth-century Switzerland, during the Thirty Years War. Sporting a beard and a convincing German accent, Caine gives a precise, controlled performance with just the right amount of humour. His unnamed mercenary captain is cultured and intelligent, offering a rational, philosophical brand of barbarism. (Craig would also be well suited to the part, though who would make a film like this now?) *The Last Valley* is a flawed, exasperating film with extraordinary elements. More to the point, it showcases one of Caine's best performances and he cites the film as a personal favourite. *The Last Valley* was an expensive flop, at a time when the British film industry was starting to implode, as the American studios withdrew their financial backing.

Caine turned producer with *Get Carter* (1971), playing a London gang enforcer who returns home to Newcastle when his brother dies in suspicious circumstances. Caine felt that most British crime films depicted gangsters as stupid, silly or funny. Growing up in London's rough Elephant and Castle district, he knew the truth was very different. Jack Carter's ice cold stare combines with character quirks (eye drops, hygiene conscious, slow reader, phone sex) and a vicious sense of humour. Caine conjures an extraordinary aura of menace, even when ordering a drink, "Pint of bitter… in a thin glass" (in case he needs to use it as a weapon). A smart man, Carter is a strong believer in applied thuggery. Every conversation is an interrogation and each pleasantry carries an implied threat. One confrontation includes the famous line: "You're a big man but you're in bad shape. With me it's a full-time job. Now behave yourself."

Whatever its faults, *Get Carter* is a genuine British gangster movie classic. Craig gave it his best shot in *Layer Cake* but the script, direction and most other things were against him. That said, Jack Carter is perhaps the one archetypal Caine character that Craig could refashion in his own image: Geordie Peacock's harder, nastier older brother.

Kidnapped (1971) is notable for two things: Caine knew the film would be a dud and he didn't get paid for it. Miscast as Jacobite rebel Alan Breck, Caine struggles with a dodgy moustache and a wavering Scots accent. He does well during the sparse action scenes, proving a fine swashbuckler with a ruthless streak. Caine also conveys Breck's pride, and a naivety that borders on delusion, yet the feeling persists that his heart wasn't in it. Craig could certainly do something with the role of Breck, though he'd need a better script and direction than Caine received.

Pulp (1972), co-produced by Caine, is slight but hugely enjoyable. Caine plays Mickey King, a British expatriate settled on the island of Malta. A writer of lurid pulp thrillers, King finds his life turned around – and in danger – when he accepts a mysterious commission. Caine's assured voiceover, an amusing parody of the pulp fiction style, puts *Layer Cake* to shame. Despite his name, King is an amiable loser, with overlong hair, mauve-tinted glasses and a crumpled white suit. A hapless dupe, he makes a dismissive Bond reference, yet clearly longs for a chance to sort out the bad guys and restore his macho pride.

Caine re-established his acting credentials with *Sleuth* (1972). Aiming high, he shared the screen for nearly two and a half hours with Laurence Olivier, widely regarded as the greatest actor of the twentieth century. Caine plays Milo Tindle, an Anglo-Italian hair salon entrepreneur who has nouveau riche aspirations but lacks the capital to realise them. Smart and witty, Tindle contends with the snobbery, racism and resentment of crime novelist Andrew Wyke (Olivier). Caine conveys the bemusement, unease and defensiveness of a man out of his depth. While Caine does his best with a crucial charade scene, it was designed for the stage, not the big screen. His distinctive eyes also give the game away, despite the use of contact lenses. Caine handles the final act with assurance, portraying a newly confident and insolent Tindle, whose smooth surface conceals –

barely – a seething rage. Critic Alexander Walker described *Sleuth* as "a fulfilment of the Cockney boy's curiously dated yet still powerful aspiration to gain the 'respectablility' of the class above him." Given Caine's avowed hatred for the class system – also a major theme in *Sleuth* – this seems unlikely. Surely he was more concerned with proving himself as a dramatic actor, holding his own against Olivier. Craig would be denied this opportunity – Olivier died in 1989 – though he looked comfortable opposite John Gielgud in *Elizabeth*. Caine agreed to co-star in the 2007 remake of *Sleuth*, directed by Kenneth Branagh, in the role played by Olivier. The part of Milo Tindle went to Craig's former friend Jude Law.

Caine turned forty in 1973, an atypically quiet year in his career. His last released film before hitting the big 4-0 was *Sleuth*, after which Caine took time out from making movies to focus on his personal life. With the honourable exception of *The Man Who Would Be King* (1975), opposite Sean Connery, Caine's later films lack the spark of his work in the sixties and early seventies. Having fought his way to the top, he had little left to prove, the former bit player now an established movie star who had earned the respect of Olivier. Settled in his professional and personal lives, financially secure, Caine seemed content to work as a technically adroit, highly professional leading man.

Unlike most of his contemporaries, Caine is still working regularly, usually on high profile movies such as *The Quiet American* (2002), *Austin Powers in Goldmember* (2002), *Batman Begins* (2005), *Bewitched* (2005), *The Weather Man* (2005), *Children of Men* (2006), *The Prestige* (2006) and *The Dark Knight* (2008). *Bewitched* aside, this is an impressive recent CV for an actor pushing 75.

What are the most important lessons Caine could teach Craig? Don't become a movie star for hire, don't let your bank balance blunt your sense of adventure, don't appear in inferior remakes of your best films, and think twice before releasing your own compilation CD, whatever Elton John may say.

TELEVISION AND FILM CREDITS

In the text, Daniel Craig's credits are discussed, wherever possible, in production order. The following filmography, however, lists them in order of first transmission (television) or release (film).

THE POWER OF ONE

[French title: *La Puissance de l'ange*]
127 minutes
Warner Bros / Alcor Films / Canal+ / Regency Enterprises / Village Roadshow Pictures (France / USA / Australia)
Director: John G Avildsen; *Executive producers:* Graham Burke, Greg Coote, Steven Reuther; *Producer:* Arnon Milchan; *Associate producer:* Doug Seelig; *Screenplay:* Robert Mark Kamen (based on the novel by Bryce Courtenay); *Director of photography:* Dean Semler; *Production design:* Roger Hall; *Editing:* John G Avildsen, Trevor Jolly; *Music:* Hans Zimmer.
Cast: Stephen Dorff (PK aged 18), Morgan Freeman (Geel Piet), Armin Mueller-Stahl (Doc), John Gielgud (Headmaster St John), Simon Fenton (PK aged 12), Winston Ntshona (Mlungisi), Dominic Walker (Morrie Gilbert), Fay Masterson (Maria Marais), Alois Moyo (Gideon Duma), Ian Roberts (Hoppie Gruenewald), Marius Weyers (Professor Daniel Marais), **Daniel Craig (Sergeant Jaapie Botha)**, Paul Tingay (grandfather), Tracy Brooks Swope (mother), Nomadlozi Kubheka (nanny), Brendan Deary (PK as an infant), Guy Witcher (PK aged seven), Robbie Bulloch (Jaapie Botha as a teenager), Tonderai Masenda (Tonderai), Jeremiah Mnisi (Dabula Manzi), Hywell Williams (Captain), Clive Russell (Sergeant Bormann), Agatha Hurle (midwife), Nigel Ivy (newborn PK), Winston Manwarra (Tonderai as an infant), Cecil Zilla Mamanzi (ranch foreman), John Turner (Afrikaaner minister), Gordon Arnell (minister at mother's funeral), Michael Brunner (Kommandant Van Zyl), Gert van Niekerk (Lieutenant Smit), Ed Beeten (prison Commander), Robert Thomas Reed (school fight opponent), Roy Francis (referee), Clare Cobbold & Natalie Morse (Maria's friends), John Osborne (school gate guard), Simon Shumba (man without past), Stan Leih & Rod Campbell (van cops), Adam Fogerty (Andreas Malan), Tony Denham (boxing partner), Eric Nobbs & Edward Jordan (city cops), Colonel Bretyn (Brian O'Shaughnessy), Faith Edwards (Miriam Sisulu), Raymond Barreto (Indian referee), Liz Ngwenya (Nganga ancient woman), Andrew Whaley (ticket taker), Dominic Makuwachuma (Joshua), Lungani Sibanda, Akim Mwale, Pesedena Dinah, Rosemary Chikobwe Sibanda, Martha Gibson Mtika, Joel Phiri, Peggy Moyo,

David Khabo & David Guwaza (students), Robin Annison (Anita), Christien Anholt (dinner date), Nigel Pegram (guest), Jon Cartwright (Jacob), Reverend Peter Van Vuuren (minister at Maria's funeral), Marcia Coleman (woman guest), Banele Dala Moyo (boy who reads).
US release: 27 March 1992
UK release: 4 September 1992

ANGLO-SAXON ATTITUDES
three x 90 minutes
Euston Films / Thames Television
(Great Britain)
Director: Diarmuid Lawrence; *Producer:* Andrew Brown; *Script:* Andrew Davies (from the novel by Angus Wilson); *Art Director:* Charmian Adams; *Editor:* Donald Fairservice.
Cast: Richard Johnson, Elizabeth Spriggs, Dorothy Tutin, Douglas Hodge, Tara Fitzgerald, Nicholas Jones, Deborah Findlay, Briony Glassco, Simon Chandler, Simon Mattacks, Carmen du Sautoy, Paudge Behan, Amanda Mealing, Jane How, David Savile, Oliver Ford Davies, Edna Doré, Paul Firth, David Ryall, Lila Kaye, Julie Legrand, **Daniel Craig**, Helen Cherry, Rosalie Crutchley, Jay Benedict, John Boswell, Pat Keen, John Cater.
UK tx: 12, 19, 26 May 1992

COVINGTON CROSS
pilot episode
45 minutes
Thames Television /
Reeves Entertainment / Capital Cities
(Great Britain)
Director: William Dear; *Executive producer:* Gil Grant; *Producers:* Aida Young, Joel Surnow; *Script:* Gil Grant; *Director of photography:* Alan Hume; *Music:* Carl Davis.
Cast: Nigel Terry (Sir Thomas Grey), Cherie Lunghi (Lady Elizabeth), Jonathan Firth (Richard Grey), Glenn Quinn (Cedric Grey), Ione Skye (Eleanor Grey), James Faulkner (Sir John Mullens), Paul Brooke (Friar), Ben Porter (William Grey), Jad Mager (Jasper), Rosalind Bennett (Genevieve De La Croix), Greg Wise (Henry of Gault), Miles Anderson (King Edward), Richard Cordery (village leader), Terence Beesley (peasant father), Oliver Haden (guard), **Daniel Craig (walkway guard)**, Shay Gorman (servant), Devon Dear (peasant girl).
US tx: 25 August 1992
UK tx: 31 August 1992

BOON:
MACGUFFIN'S TRANSPUTER
Season 8, Episode 1
50 minutes
Central Independent Television
(Great Britain)
Director: Nicholas Laughland; *Executive producer:* Ted Childs; *Producer:* Michele Buck; *Script:* Peter Palliser; *Director of photography:* Don Perrin; *Lighting director:* Keith Reed; *Production design:* Jeff Tessler; *Editing:* Nigel Miller.
Cast: Michael Elphick (Ken Boon), David Daker (Harry Crawford), Neil Morrissey (Rocky Cassidy), Saskia Wickham (Alex Wilton), Peter McEnery (Robert MacGuffin), Mark Benton

(Charlie Hardiman), Lucy Briers (Maggie), John Pennington (Mr Wilton), **Daniel Craig (Jim Parkham)**, Julia St John (Liz Kennedy), Tilly Blackwood (Shirelle), Bruce Alexander (Henry Maple), Denzil Pugh (drunk).
UK tx: 8 September 1992

DROP THE DEAD DONKEY: GEORGE AND HIS DAUGHTER

Season 3, Episode 10
24 minutes
Channel 4 / Hat Trick Productions (Great Britain)
Director: Liddy Oldroyd; *Executive producer:* Denise O'Donoghue; *Producers:* Andy Hamilton, Guy Jenkin; *Script:* Andy Hamilton, Guy Jenkin; *Additional material:* Nick Revell, Malcolm Williamson; *Senior cameraman:* Tony Keene; *Lighting director:* Keith Reed; *Designer:* Graeme Story; *Title music:* Matthew Scott; *Choreography:* David Toguri.
Cast: Robert Duncan (Gus), Ingrid Lacey (Helen), Neil Pearson (Dave), Jeff Rawle (George), David Swift (Henry), Stephen Tompkinson (Damien), Victoria Wicks (Sally), Susannah Doyle (Joy), Stephen Greif (Valdez), Louisa Milwood Haigh (Deborah), **Daniel Craig (Fixx)**, Patsy Palmer (Bev), Connie Hyde (Sheila), Wolf Christian (bouncer), Matthew Hodgson (Vin), Danny Midwinter (Lonny).
UK tx: 11 March 1993

SHARPE: SHARPE'S EAGLE

Season 1, Episode 2
100 minutes

Celtic Films Entertainment / Central Independent Television / Picture Palace Productions (Great Britain)
Director: Tom Clegg; *Executive producers:* Ted Childs, Muir Sutherland, *Producer:* Malcolm Craddock; *Screenplay:* Eoghan Harris (based on the novel by Bernard Cornwell); *Director of photography:* Ivan Strasburg; *Production design:* Andrew Mollo; *Editing:* Robin Sales; *Music:* Dominic Muldowney, John Tams.
Cast: Sean Bean (Captain Richard Sharpe), Brian Cox (Major Hogan), Daragh O'Malley (Sergeant Patrick Harper), Assumpta Serna (Teresa Moreno), Michael Cochrane (Colonel Sir Henry Simmerson), David Troughton (General Sir Arthur Wellesley), Martin Jacobs (Colonel Lawford), Katia Caballero (Countess Josefina), Michael Mears (Cooper), John Tams (Hagman), Paul Trussell (Tongue), Lyndon Davis (Perkins), Gavan O'Herlihy (Captain Leroy), David Ashton (Lennox), Neil Dudgeon (Gibbons), **Daniel Craig (Lieutenant Berry)**, Nolan Hemmings (Ensign Denny).
UK tx: 12 May 1993
US tx: 28 November 1993

THE YOUNG INDIANA JONES CHRONICLES: PALESTINE, OCTOBER 1917

aka *Young Indiana Jones: Daredevils of the Desert* (expanded home video version)
Season 2, Episode 21
45 minutes (original version),
80 minutes (home video version)
Amblin / Lucasfilm / Paramount (USA)

Director: Simon Wincer; *Executive producer:* George Lucas; *Producer:* Rick McCallum; *Co-producer:* Doris Kirch; *Screenplay:* Frank Darabont (based on the character created by George Lucas and Steven Spielberg); *Director of photography:* David Tattersall; *Production design:* Gavin Bocquet; *Editing:* Ben Burtt; *Music:* Laurence Rosenthal.

Cast: Sean Patrick Flanery (Indiana Jones), Catherine Zeta-Jones (Maya), Julian Firth (Richard Meinertzhagen), Cameron Daddo (Jack Anders), Douglas Henshall (T E Lawrence), Haluk Bilginer (Colonel Ismet Bey), **Daniel Craig (Schiller)**, Kerem Atabeyoglu (Rashid), Colin Baker (Major General Harry George Chauvel), Tony Bonner (Lieutenant Colonel M W J Bouchier), Terrence Hardiman (Fitzgerald), Stuart Bennett (Kevin), Todd Boyce (Dex), Bernard Brown (General Hodgson), Vincenzo Nicoli (Kazim), Robert Swann (Brigadier General William Grant), Alan Talbot (Sergeant Porter), John Vine (Allenby), Ali Yalaz (greasy man), James Bowers (British artillery spotter), Halil Dogan (Turkish sentry Captain), Okan Bayülgen (Turkish spotter), James McMartin (British artilleryman), Ozgur Erkekli & Kanat Tibet (Turkish artillerymen), Ben Miller (French officer), Tolga Yalcinkaya (Turkish adjutant), Simon Murray (German officer).

US tx: 14 August 1993
UK tx: 29 January 1994 (Sky One), 11 February 1995 (BBC1)

BETWEEN THE LINES: NEW ORDER
Season 2, Episode 1
50 minutes
British Broadcasting Corporation / Island World Productions / World Productions (Great Britain)
Director: Alan Dossor; *Executive producer:* Tony Garnett; *Director of photography:* Graham Frake; *Editing:* Colin Goudie, St. John O'Rorke; *Music:* Hal Lindes, Colin Torms.

Cast: Neil Pearson (Detective Superintendent Tony Clark), Tom Georgeson (Detective Inspector Harry Naylor), Siobhan Redmond (Detective Sergeant Maureen Connell), Tony Doyle (Chief Superintendent John Deakin), Robin Lermitte (Superintendant Graves), Elaine Donnelly (Joyce Naylor), Bob Mason (Richard Newman), **Daniel Craig (Joe Rance)**, Michael Cronin (Derek Lee-Metford), Angus MacInnes (Patrick Ingram), John Carlisle (Douglas Carter MP), Philip McGough (Norman), Dev Sagoo (Khan), James Clyde (Police Constable Tulloch), Alison Sterling (Sergeant Judy Prescott), Steve Swinscoe (Inspector Cole), Richard Ireson (Chief Inspector Lodge), Brian Southwood (personnel Chief Inspector), Bill Bingham (studio interviewer), Stuart Bunce & Richard Buss (reporters), Angela Catherall (neighbour), Hilary Dawson (solicitor), Nicholas Gecks (defence counsel), Norman Hartley (clerk of court), Grace Mattaka (secretary), Kate O'Connell (TV interviewer), Lucy Tregear (Home Office official).
UK tx: 5 October 1993

HEARTBEAT: A CHILLY RECEPTION

Season 3, Episode 5

50 minutes

Yorkshire Television (Great Britain)

Director: Catherine Morshead; *Producer:* Steve Lanning; *Script:* Eric Wendell.

Cast: Nick Berry (PC Nick Rowan), Niamh Cusack (Dr Kate Rowan), Derek Fowlds (Sergeant Oscar Blaketon), Bill Maynard (Claude Jeremiah Greengrass), William Simons (PC Alf Ventress), Tricia Penrose (Gina Ward), Stuart Golland (George Ward), Mark Jordan (PC Bellamy), Victoria Scarborough (Susan Siddons), Edward Clayton (Jack Siddons), Jane Wood (Beth Siddons), Anne Stallybrass (Eileen), **Daniel Craig (Peter Begg)**, George A Cooper (Walter Pettigrew).

UK tx: 31 October 1993

SCREEN TWO: GENGHIS COHN

79 minutes

British Broadcasting Corporation / A&E Television Networks (Great Britain / USA)

Director: Elijah Moshinsky; *Executive producer:* Mark Shivas; *Producer:* Ruth Caleb; *Screenplay:* Stanley Price (based on the novel by Romain Gary); *Director of photography:* John Daly; *Production design:* Tony Burrough; *Editing:* Ken Pearce; *Music:* Carl Davis.

Cast: Robert Lindsay (Otto Schatz), Anthony Sher (Genghis Cohn), Diana Rigg (Baroness Frieda von Stangel), John Wells (Dr Eckhardt), Frances de la Tour (Dr Helga Feuchtwanger), Paul Brooke (Herr Hans-Dieter Pohl), Patrick Godfrey (Herr Mueller), Rowland Davies

(Otto Kellner), Cara Konig (Frau Martha Kellner), Matthew Marsh (Herr Kruger), Peter Penry-Jones (Dr Brauner), Cheryl Fergison (Frau Langer), **Daniel Craig (Lieutenant Guth)**, Alwyne Taylor (Frau Inge Heller), Charles Dale (Herr Heller), Heather Canning (librarian), Ben Bazell (Hans Schumberg), Jay Benedict (Dr Burkhardt), Shaun Dingwall (Sergeant Hubsch), Chris Jenkinson (Lieutenant Weiss), Peter Jordan (Stein).

UK tx: 2 March 1994

APPROACHING LITERATURE: APHRA BEHN'S THE ROVER

181 minutes

BBC Open University Production Centre [in association with Women's Playhouse Trust] (Great Britain)

Director/producer: Tony Coe; *Director/ designer of stage version:* Jules Wright; *Author of original work:* Aphra Behn

Cast (in alphabetical order): **Daniel Craig,** Danny John-Jules, Morgan Jones, Hakeem Kae-Kazim, Vicky Licorish, Cecilia Noble, Maya Krishna Rao, Dougray Scott, Andy Serkis.

UK tx: unknown; released to VHS in 1995 and DVD in 1997

A KID IN KING ARTHUR'S COURT

89 minutes

Walt Disney Pictures / Trimark Pictures / Tapestry Films (USA)

Director: Michael Gottlieb; *Executive producer:* Mark Amin; *Producers:* Peter Abrams, J P Guerin, Robert L Levy; *Co-producers:* Andrew Hirsh, Jonathon Komack Martin; *Associate producer:* Megan Ring; *Screenplay:* Michael Part,

Robert E Levy (inspired by Mark Twain's *A Connecticut Yankee in King Arthur's Court*); *Director of photography:* Elemer Ragalyi; *Production design:* Laszlo Gardonyi; *Editing:* Anita Brandt-Burgoyne, Michael Ripps; *Music:* J A C Redford.

Cast: Thomas Ian Nicholas (Calvin Fuller), Joss Ackland (King Arthur), Art Malik (Lord Belasco), Paloma Baeza (Princess Katey), Kate Winslet (Princess Sarah), **Daniel Craig (Master Kane)**, David Tysall (Ratan), Ron Moody (Merlin), Barry Stanton (blacksmith), Michael Mehlmann (shop owner), Melanie Oettinger (peasant woman), Rebecca Denton (washer wman), Michael Kelly (apprentice), Louise Rosner (lady in waiting), Paul Rosner (peasant boy), Béla Unger (head guard), Shane Rimmer (coach), Tim Wickham (Ricky Baker), Daniel Bennett (Howell), Debora Weston (Mom), Vincent Marzello (Dad), Catherine Blake (Maya), J P Guerin (umpire).

US release: 11 August 1995

OUR FRIENDS IN THE NORTH

623 minutes (nine x 75 minutes)
British Broadcasting Corporation
(Great Britain)

Directors: Simon Cellan Jones, Pedr James, Stuart Urban; *Executive producer:* Michael Waring; *Producer:* Charles Pattinson; *Associate producer:* Melanie Howard; *Script:* Peter Flannery; *Directors of photography:* John Daly, John Kenway, Simon Kossoff; *Production design:* Rob Hinds; *Editing:* Greg Miller, David Spiers, Paul Tothill; *Music:* Colin Towns.

Cast: Christopher Eccleston (Nicky Hutchinson), **Daniel Craig (George 'Geordie' Peacock)**, Gina McKee (Mary Soulsby), Mark Strong (Terry 'Tosker' Cox), David Bradley (Eddie Wells), Peter Vaughan (Felix Hutchinson), Freda Dowie (Florrie Hutchinson), Alun Armstrong (Austin Donohue), Neil Armstrong (Ben), Phil Atkinson (councillor), Roger Avon (Mr Braniff), Joanna Bacon (female transvestite), Angeline Ball (Daphne), Melvyn Barnes (Sean Collins), Matthew Baron (Anthony Cox, 1967), Tony Barton (Herbert Sidebottom), David Begg (Billy Shaughnessy), Margery Bone (Barbara Cox), Steph Bramwell (Beattie), Colette Brown (Alice MacDonald), Angela Bruce (Nursing Sister), Denise Bryson (Pat West), Siobhan Burke (Lucille), Doyne Byrd (chairman), Johnny Caesar (Eric Burdon lookalike), Daniel Casey (Anthony Cox, 1987 & 1995), Gez Casey (Frank), Peter Cellier (judge), Elspeth Charlton (Mrs Soulsby), Craig Conway (Christopher Collins), Trevor Cooper (Detective Chief Superintendent Dennis Cockburn), Frank Couchman (Patrick Soulsby), Simon Coury (journalist), Rod Culbertson (Bede Connor), John Dair (Charlie Dawson), Eileen Daly (dancer), Ron Davies (Police Superintendent Harrop), Libby Davison (Sarah), Sophia Diaz (Mercedes), Anna Maria Donofrio (Frances), Gwen Doran (Cynthia), Mark Drewry (Michael Frisch), Miles Edwards (Jason), Julian Fellowes (Claud Seabrook MP), Danny Ferguson (Cooper), Nick Figgis (Anthony Cox, 1979), Trevor Fox (Harry), McKenzie

Fraser (returning officer), Evie Garratt (ticket lady), Rory Gibson (Tosker's assistant), Alan Gilchrist (Christopher Collins), Andrew Grainger (Detective Constable Black), Paul Greenwood (Roy Bennett), Michael Gunn (John Clark), David Haddow (Detective Inspector Martin Oldfield), Peter Halliday (Speaker of the House of Commons), Julia Hampson (Olive), Charlie Hardwick (Paula Bennett), Steven Hawksby (Stan), Tony Haygarth (Deputy Chief Constable Roy Johnson), Harry Herring (Arthur Watson), Jean Heywood (woman in market), Stephen Hillman (Police Constable), Tony Hodge (Brian Cox), William Hoyland (Commander Arthur Fieldson), Keith Hutcheon (journalist), Geoffrey Hutchings (John Edwards), Peter Jeffrey (Commissioner Sir Colin Blamire), Tracy Keating (nurse), Harriet Keevil (Helen Windsor), Toby Kensett (Andrew), Gavin Kitchen (Police Inspector), Bobby Knutt (Les), Larry Lamb (Alan Roe), John Larsen (fire safety officer), Sam Lathem (bouncer), Frank Lazarus (psychiatrist), Pete Lee-Wilson (Colin Butler), Emma Lightfoot (Bernadette Cox), Leon Lissek (Walensky), Joanna MacInnes (Francine Volker), Richard Makepiece (TV interviewer), Doreen Mantle (Mrs Wilson), Stephen Marcus (Cyril Hellyer), Jack McBride (Mr Soulsby), Glen McCrory (bouncer), Malcolm McDowell (Benny Barratt), Douglas McFerran (Detective Sergeant Croxley), Peter McGowan (Detective Sergeant Conway), Val McLane (Rita Cox), Kate McLoughlin (Moira), Richard Morton (singer in club), Paul McNeilly (Ernie), Valerie Minifie (solicitor), Roger Monk (drunk), John Morton (Archie), Gavin Muir (Father Kyle), Nicholas Nancarrow (Roy Cox), Tony Neilson (waiter), Christopher Northey (MP in sex shop), Anne Orwin (Mrs Weightman), Nicholas Palliser (stockbroker), Judith Parker (Mrs Noble), Adam Pearson (Anthony Cox, 1974), Mark Pegg (Detective Constable Tony Weir), Barbara Peirson (Brenda Friel), Shaun Prendergast (Frankie), Siôn Probert (journalist), Robert Putt (Taylor), Pierce Quigley (Detective), Paul Rainbow (Inspector), Terence Rigby (Berger), Dirk Robertson (vagrant), Willie Ross (Gordon Peacock), Louise Salter (Julia Allen), Granville Saxton (Commissioner Michael Jellicoe), David Schall (prison officer), David Schofield (Detective Sergeant John Salway), Nicholas Selby (Sir Edward Jones), Peggy Shields (old lady), Jan Southern (Mrs Rashleigh), Miriam Stockley (singer), Donald Sumpter (Commander Harold Chappie), George Sweeney (Detective Sergeant Leonard Morris), Tony Tarrats (Nigel), Catherine Terris (Mrs Merriman), Malcolm Terris (Mr Knox), Stephen D Thirkfeld (journalist), Tim Thompson (political correspondent), Heather Tobias (female vagrant), Sarah Turnbull (Christopher's girlfriend), Alan Turner (Dr Russell), Simon Tyrell (Dave), Arturo Venegas (restaurant manager), Chris Walker (Detective Chief Inspector Paul Boyd), Danny Webb (Detective Sergeant Ron Conrad), Saskia Wickham (Claudia Seabrook MP),

Tracey Wilkinson (Elaine Craig/Cox), Mary Woodvine (Alison).

UK tx: 15 January to 11 March 1996

TALES FROM THE CRYPT: SMOKE WRINGS

Season 7, Episode 9

23 minutes

Home Box Office / Tales From The Crypt Holdings (USA)

Director: Mandie Fletcher; *Executive producers:* Robert Zemeckis, Joel Silver, Walter Hill, David Giler, Richard Donner; *Producer:* Gilbert Adler; *Co-producer:* A L Katz; *Associate producers:* Karyn Fields, Richard Mirisch, Lisa Sandoval, Ed Tapia; *Script:* Lisa Sandoval; *Director of photography:* Robin Vidgeon; *Production design:* Peter Mullins; *Editing:* Jeremy Strachan; *Music:* Tay Uhler.

Cast: Gayle Hunnicutt (Ellen), Denis Lawson (Frank), Ute Lemper (Jacquelyn), **Daniel Craig (Barry)**, Paul Freeman (Alistair), Tres Hanley, Chris Stanton, Julian Kerridge (policeman), John Kassir (Crypt Keeper, voice only).

US tx: 21 June 1996

KISS AND TELL

100 minutes

London Weekend Television / A&E Television Networks

(Great Britain / USA)

Director: David Richards; *Executive producers:* Delia Fine, Sally Head; *Producer:* Sarah Wilson; *Script:* Heidi Thomas; *Director of photography:* Alan Almond; *Production design:* Cecilia Brereton; *Editing:* Nick McPhee; *Music:* Hal Lindes.

Cast: Rosie Rowell (Jude Sawyer), Peter Howitt (Graham Ives), **Daniel Craig (Detective Constable Matt Kearney)**, Ralph Ineson (Sgt Beddowes); Nicola Stephenson (WPC Alex Reynolds); David Bradley (Superintendent Hines), Gillian Bevan (Barbara Ives), Danny Worters (James Ives), Hilda Braid (Gloria Summer), Peter Pacey (Roland Burke), Clare Cathcart (Steph), Helena Little (Dr Garnett), Rosie Cavaliero (Maggie Wallace), Caroline John (Avril Owens), Mark Tandy (barrister), Stephen Ilett (solicitor), Liam McKenna (constable), Patsy Peters (singer), Felicity Chilver (child), Annelise Lovell (child's mother).

UK tx: 9 November 1996

US tx: 15 June 1997

THE FORTUNES AND MISFORTUNES OF MOLL FLANDERS

120 minutes (shown in two parts in UK)

Granada Television / WGBH Boston

(Great Britain / USA)

Director: David Attwood; *Executive producers:* Rebecca Eaton, Gub Neal; *Producer:* David Lascelles; *Screenplay:* Andrew Davies (based on the novel by Daniel Defoe); *Director of photography:* Ivan Strasburg; *Production design:* Stephen Fineren; *Editing:* Edward Mansell; *Music:* Jim Parker, Mark Springer.

Cast (in alphabetical order): Geoffrey Beevers (Judge), James Bowers (gaoler); Colin Buchanan (Rowland), Chrissie Cotterill (Mrs Fairley), **Daniel Craig (James 'Jemmy' Seagrave)**, Ian Driver

(Robin), Lucy Evans (Little Moll), David Fough (Major Bagstock), Ronald Fraser (Sir Richard Gregory), Sam Halfpenny (thin sea captain), Caroline Harker (Maria), Mary Healey (Mrs Baggot), Milton Johns (Mr Meikeljohn), Alex Kingston (Moll Flanders), Nicola Kingston (Moll's mother), James Larkin (Captain Stephens), Dawn McDaniel (Emily), Ken McDonald (Mr Baggot), Trevyn McDowell (Mrs Seagrove), Roger Morlidge (fat sea captain), Maureen O'Brien (Mrs Richardson), Diana Rigg (Mrs Golightly), Struan Rodger (Mr Richardson), John Savident (clergyman in coach), Guy Scantlebury (Captain O'Malley), Bill Thomas (Lancaster innkeeper), Nicola Walker (Lucy Diver), Tom Ward (Lemuel).
US tx: 13 October 1996 (in full)
UK tx: 1 and 2 December 1996

BOOKMARK: SAINT-EX
82 minutes
British Broadcasting Corporation /
Majestic Films International /
The Oxford Film Company
(Great Britain)
Director: Anand Tucker; *Executive producers:* Andy Paterson, Nicolas Kent, Roland Keating; *Producer:* Jake Lloyd; *Co-producer:* Mark Bentley; *Associate producer:* Anna Campeau; *Script:* Frank Cottrell Boyce; *Director of photography:* David Johnson; *Production design:* Alice Normington; *Editing:* Peter Webber.
Cast: Bruno Ganz (Antoine de Saint-Exupery), Miranda Richardson (Consuelo de Saint-Exupery), Janet McTeer (Genevieve de Villefranche), Ken

Stott (Prevot), Eleanor Bron (Marie de Saint-Exupery), Katrin Cartlidge (Gabrielle de Saint-Exupery), Bríd Brennan (Simone de Saint-Exupery), Karl Johnson (Didier Daurat), **Daniel Craig (Guillaumet)**, Dominic Rowan (Aeropostale clerk), Anna Calder-Marshall (Moisy), Aidan Cottrell Boyce (young Antoine), Joe Cottrell Boyce (François), Alex Kingston (chic party guest), Rosalie Crutchley (aunt), Lucy Abigale Smith (young Simone), Hannah Taylor-Gordon (young Gabrielle).
UK tx: 25 December 1996

THE ICE HOUSE
172 minutes (two parts)
British Broadcasting Corporation /
WGBH Boston (Great Britain / USA)
Director: Tim Fywell; *Executive producer:* Chris Parr; *Producer:* Suzan Harrison; *Associate producer:* Michael Darbon; *Script:* Lizzie Mickery (based on the novel by Minette Walters); *Director of photography:* John Daly; *Production design:* Michael Trevor; *Editing:* Roy Sharman; *Music:* David Ferguson.
Cast: **Daniel Craig (Detective Sergeant Andy McLoughlin)**, Corin Redgrave (Chief Inspector George Walsh), Kitty Aldridge (Anne Cattrell), Frances Barber (Diana Goode), Penny Downie (Phoebe Maybury), Dave Hill (Fred Phillips), Ann Bell (Molly Phillips), Luke Garrett (Police Constable Gavin Williams), Geoffrey Greenhill (Sergeant Bob Rogers), Gerard Horan (Detective Sergeant Nick Robinson), Danny Midwinter (Detective Constable Ian Blackshaw), Niven Boyd (Dr Webster),

Paul Jerricho (David Maybury), Helen McCarthy (Mrs Ledbetter), Karen Murden (Mrs Fowler), Krysia Pepper (WPC Susan Brownlow), Jack Galloway (Paddy Clarke), Belinda Sinclair (Eileen Clarke), Anthony May (Peter Barnes), Liam McKenna (Eddie Staines), Sara Stephens (Tracy Fowlds), Laura Girling (Kelly McLoughlin), James D'Arcy (Jonathan Maybury), Alexandra Milman (Jane Maybury), Lynne Farleigh (Mrs Thompson), Jan Shand (Ward Sister), Ian Price (Bill Stanley), Willie Ross (Wally Ferris).
UK tx: 5 and 6 April 1997
US tx: 26 February 1998

THE HUNGER: MENAGE A TROIS

Season 1, Episode 2
30 minutes
Scott Free Productions /
Telescene Film Group Productions /
The Movie Network
(Great Britain / USA)
Director: Jake Scott; *Executive producers:* Jeff Fazio, Bruce Moccia, Paul E Painter, Ridley Scott, Tony Scott, Robin Spry; *Producers:* Chris Burt, Wendy Grean; *Script:* Jordan Katz, Vincent Ngo (based on a story by F Paul Wilson); *Director of photography:* John Mathieson.
Cast: Karen Black (Miss Gati), **Daniel Craig (Jerry Pritchard)**, Lena Headey (Steph Reynolds), Jason Flemyng (young man), Terence Stamp (host).
US tx: 20 July 1997

OBSESSION

[alternative German titles: *Sucht / Obsession – Besessene Seelen*]

[French title: *Berlin Niagara*]
105 minutes
Hollywood Partners (Munich) /
Multimedia Gesellschaft für Audiovisuelle Information / High Speed Films (Paris) / TiMe Medienvertriebs (United Germany / France / Austria)
Director: Peter Sehr; *Executive producers:* Martine Kelly, Rainer Mockert; *Producers:* Wolfgang Esterer, George Hoffmann, Dagmar Rosenbauer; *Co-producer:* Wolfram Tichy; *Screenplay:* Marie Noelle, Peter Sehr; *Director of photography:* David Watkin; *Production design:* Jerome Latour; *Editing:* Britta Paech; *Music:* Micki Meuser.
Cast: Heike Makatsch (Miriam Auerback), Charles Berling (Pierre Moulin), **Daniel Craig (John MacHale)**, Seymour Cassel (Jacob Frischmuth), Allen Garfield (Simon Frischmuth), Marie-Christine Barrault (Ella Beckmann), Daniel Gélin (Xavier Favre), Inga Busch (Ise).
German release: 28 August 1997
French release: 26 April 2000

LOVE IS THE DEVIL: STUDY FOR A PORTRAIT OF FRANCIS BACON

90 minutes
BBC Films / Première Heure / Uplink / Arts Council of England / British Film Institute Production / Partners in Crime / State (Great Britain / France / Japan)
Director/screenplay: John Maybury; *Executive producers:* Takashi Asai, Ben Gibson, Patrice Haddad, Frances-Anne Solomon; *Producer:* Chiara Menage; *Director of photography:* John Mathieson; *Production design:* Alan MacDonald;

Editing: Daniel Goddard; *Music:* Ryuichi Sakamoto.

Cast: Derek Jacobi (Francis Bacon), **Daniel Craig (George Dyer)**, Tilda Swinton (Muriel Belcher), Anne Lambton (Isabel Rawsthorne), Adrian Scarborough (Daniel Farson), Karl Johnson (John Deakin), Annabel Brooks (Henrietta Moraes), Richard Newbold (Blond Billy), Ariel de Ravenel (French official), Tallulah (Ian Board), Andy Linden (Ken Bidwell), David Kennedy (Joe Furneval), Gary Hume (Volker Dix), Damian Dibben & Anthony Cotton (Brighton rent boys), Anthony Ryding (London rent boy), Christian Martin (bell-hop), Ray Olley (boxing referee), Wesley Morgan & Nigel Travis (boxers), Eddie Kerr (tailor) George Clarke & David Windle (wrestlers), William Hoyland (Police Sergeant), Mark Umbers (Police Constable Denham), Hamish Bowles (David Hockney), Jibby Beane, Gentuca Bini, James Birch, Tim Burke, Liz Clarke, Jemima Cotter, Fiona Dealey, John Dunbar, Victoria Fernandez, Natalie Gibson, Caroline Hardy, Charlie Hayward, Miles Johnson, Kate St Johnston, Ulla Larson, Alistair Mathieson, Chiara Menage, James Mitchell, Gregor Muir, Lorcan O'Neill, Jon Spiteri, Francesco Vezzoli, Thalia Valeta, Marjorie Walker & Gillian Young (Parisian art world), Maria Bjornson, Judy Blame, John Byrne, Les Child, Jake Dodds, Daniel Farson, Sandy Hawkes, David Harrison, Malcolm Key, Phillipe Krutchley, Steven Linard, Alan MacDonald, Norman Rosenthal, Thomasina Smith, Yolanda Sonnabend, Annie Symons, Davd Symons, Sue Tilley, Virginia Wetherell, Winford & Michael Wojas (Colony Room Club), Roger Bowdler, Duggie Fields, Pam Hogg, Ben Martin, Amanda Menage, William Middleton, Christina Moore, Elspeth Thompson & Tu Tu (restaurant), Suzie Bick, Lucy Ferry, Simon Goldberg, David Harvey, Rifat Ozbek, Anita Pallenberg, Jimmy Trindy & Andy Walsh (casino), Gaby Agis, Melanie Arnold, Matt Cogger, Angus Fairhurst, Georgie Hopton, Marco Jackson, Sarah Lucas, Jean Mortimore, Lance Patterson, Johnnie Shand Kydd & Josephine Soughan (French pub), Dave Baby, Sam Chapman, Andrew Coltrane, Daniele Minns, Tracey Emin, Caron Geary, Sam Hawkins, Darren King, Donald McInnes, Martin Meister, Gillian Wearing, Johnathan Williams, Steven Zivanovic, April & Sheena (Brighton pub).

UK release: 18 September 1998
US release: 7 October 1998

ELIZABETH

124 minutes

Working Title Films (Great Britain)

Director: Shekhar Kapur; *Producers:* Tim Bevan, Eric Fellner, Alison Owen; *Co-producers:* Liza Chasin, Debra Hayward; *Screenplay:* Michael Hirst; *Director of photography:* Remi Adefarasini; *Production design:* John Myhre; *Editing:* Jill Bilcock; *Music:* David Hirschfelder.

Cast: Cate Blanchett (Elizabeth I), Geoffrey Rush (Sir Francis Walsingham), Christopher Eccleston (Duke of Norfolk), Joseph Fiennes (Robert Dudley, Earl of Leicester), Richard

Attenborough (Sir William Cecil), Fanny Ardant (Mary of Guise), Kathy Burke (Queen Mary Tudor), Eric Cantona (Monsieur de Foix), James Frain (Alvaro de la Quadra), Vincent Cassel (Duc d'Anjou), **Daniel Craig (John Ballard)**, Angus Deayton (Waad, Chancellor of the Exchequer), Edward Hardwicke (Earl of Arundel), Terence Rigby (Bishop Gardiner), Amanda Ryan (Lettice Howard), Kelly Macdonald (Isabel Knollys), Emily Mortimer (Kat Ashley), John Gielgud (the Pope), Liz Giles (female martyr), Rod Culbertson (Master Ridley), Paul Fox (male martyr), Peter Stockbridge (Palace chamberlain), Valerie Gale (Mary's dwarf), George Yiasoumi (King Philip II of Spain), Jamie Foreman (Earl of Sussex), Wayne Sleep (dance tutor), Sally Grey, Kate Loustau, Elika Gibbs, Sarah Owen & Lily Allen (ladies in waiting), Joe White (Master of the Tower), Matt Andrews & Liam Foley (Norfolk's men), Ben Frain (young French man), Lewis Jones (priest), Michael Beint (Bishop Carlisle), Kenny Doughty (Sir Thomas Elyot), Hayley Burroughs (Elizabeth's dwarf), Joseph O'Conor (Earl of Derby), Brendan O'Hea (Lord William Howard), Edward Highmore (Lord Harewood), Daniel Moynihan (first bishop), Jeremy Hawk (second bishop), James Rowe (bishop in cellar), Donald Pelmear (third bishop), Tim Bevan (handsome man), Charles Cartmell & Edward Purver (Dudley's men), Vladimir Vega (Vatican cardinal), Alfie Allen (Arundel's son), Daisy Bevan (Arundel's daughter), Jennifer Lewicki (Arundel's nursemaid), Viviane Horne (Arundel's wife), Nick Smallman (Walsingham's man).
UK release: 23 October 1998
US release: 6 November 1998

LOVE & RAGE

100 minutes
Isle of Man Film Commission / Nova Films / Bord Scannán na hÉireann / Cathal Black Productions / Schlemmer Film
(Great Britain / Ireland / United Germany)
Director: Cathal Black; *Producers:* Cathal Black, Rudolf Wichmann; *Screenplay:* Brian Lynch (based on the book *The Playboy and The Yellow Lady* by James Carney); *Director of photography:* Slawomir Idziak; *Production design:* Ned McLoughlin; *Editing:* Ulrike Leipold; *Music:* Ralf Weinrich.
Cast: Greta Scacchi (Agnes MacDonnell), **Daniel Craig (James Lynchehaun)**, Stephen Dillane (Dr Croly), Valerie Edmond (Libby), Donal Donnelly (Sweeney), David Walshe (Martin), Lalor Roddy (Eamon), Olivia Caffrey (Julia), Charlotte Bradley (peasant woman), Noel O'Donovan (glass workman), Kieran Aherne (vicar), Oliver Maguire (hotel manager), Paul McGlinchey (Constable), John Whelan (potter), Ray McBride (three card huckster), Mike Copley (fire eater), Eamon Carlisle (barrel man), Christy Burke (barrel man's assistant), Don Foley (custom's official).
first shown: 15 April 1999
(Dublin Film Festival)

TX: THE MUSEUM OF MEMORY

40 minutes

British Broadcasting Corporation
(Great Britain)

Director: John Maybury; *Producer:* Keith Griffiths; *Series editor:* John Wyver; *Music:* Daniel Goddard.

Cast: **Daniel Craig**, Heike Makatsch, Derek Jacobi (voice).

UK tx: 24 June 1999

THE TRENCH

[French title: *Tranchée*]

98 minutes

Arts Council of England / Blue PM / Bonaparte Films / British Screen Productions / Canal+ / Galatee Films / Portman Entertainment Group / Skyline Films (Great Britain / France)

Director/screenplay: William Boyd; *Executive producer:* Xavier Marchand; *Producer:* Steve Clark-Hall; *Director of photography:* Tony Pierce-Roberts; *Production design:* Jim Clay; *Editing:* Jim Clark, Laurence Mery-Clark; *Music:* Evelyn Glennie, Greg Malcangi.

Cast: Paul Nicholls (Private Billy Macfarlane), **Daniel Craig (Sergeant Telford Winter)**, Julian Rhind-Tutt (2nd Lieutenant Ellis Harte), Danny Dyer (Lance Corporal Victor Dell), James D'Arcy (Private Colin Daventry), Tam Williams (Private Eddie Macfarlane), Anthony Strachan (Private Horace Beckwith), Michael Moreland (Private George Hogg), Adrian Lukis (Lieutenant Colonel Villiers), Ciaran McMenamin (Private Charlie Ambrose), Cillian Murphy (Rag Rookwood), John Higgins (Cornwallis), Ben Wishaw (James

Dennis), Tim Murphy (Bone), Danny Nutt (Dieter), Charles Cartmell (Harold Faithfull), Tom Mullion (Nelson), Jenny Pickering (Maria Corrigan), Tom Silburn, Dahren Davey, Jamie Newell, Liam King, Stan Charity, Luke Ducket, Chris Bridgeman & Guy Barrett (additional platoon members).

UK release: 17 September 1999

US release: 22 November 2000

SHOCKERS: THE VISITOR

Season 1, Episode 2

50 minutes

Tiger Aspect / Channel 4 (Great Britain)

Director: Audrey Cooke; *Executive producers:* Greg Brennan, Julia Ouston; *Script:* Guy Burt; *Director of photography:* Alasdair Walker; *Production design:* Gillian Miles; *Editing:* Victoria Boydell; *Music:* Nick Bicat.

Cast: **Daniel Craig ('Richard')**, Miranda Pleasence (Louise), Shaun Parkes (Matt), Claire Rushbrook (Terri), Theo Fraser Steele (Tom's cousin), Stuart Milligan (Mr Jefferson), Dean Byfield (Charlie), Clare Bifford (first publisher), David Holdaway (second publisher), John Drummond (unemployed man), Toby Mace (first waiter), Nick Fletcher (second waiter), Rupert Ward-Lewis (young man in pub).

UK tx: 26 October 1999

I DREAMED OF AFRICA

114 minutes

Jaffilms / Global Entertainment
(USA / United Germany)

Director: Hugh Hudson; *Producers:* Stanley R Jaffe, Allyn Stewart; *Co-*

producer: John D Schofield; *Screenplay:*
Paula Milne, Susan Shilliday (based on
the autobiography of Kuki Gallmann);
Director of photography: Bernard Lutic;
Production design: Andrew Sanders;
Editing: Scott Thomas; *Music:* Maurice
Jarre.
Cast: Kim Basinger (Kuki Gallmann),
Vincent Perez (Paolo Gallmann), Eva
Marie Saint (Franca), Liam Aiken
(Emanuele aged seven), Garrett
Strommen (Emanuele aged 17),
Winston Ntshona (old Pokot chief),
Daniel Craig (Declan Fielding), Lance
Reddick (Simon), Connie Chiume
(Wanjiku), James Ngcobo (Luka), Joko
Scott (Mirimuk), Sabelo Ngobese
(young Mapengo), Zacharia Phali
(Mapengo, early teens), Nick Boraine
(Duncan Maitland), Susan Danford
(Esther Maitland), Ian Roberts (Mike
Donovan), Susan Monteregge (Karen
Donovan), Jessica Perritt (Lade Diana
Delemere), Steven Jennings (Vincenzo),
Patrick Lyster (Sven), John Carson
(Pembroke headmaster), Shannon
Esrechowitz (Siri), Michael Brosnihan
(Charlie aged 14), Theo Landey (Sam
aged 21), Nick Lorentz (Aiden
Whittaker), Valeria Cavalli (Marina),
Allison Daugherty (Luciana), Paolo
Lorimer (Carlo), Federico Scribani
(Roberto), Sophie Hayden (Gabriella),
Giselda Volodi (Rachel), Daniela Foà
(Maria), Nathi Khunene, Patrick Bokaba
& Dominic Dimba (bandits), Ernest
Ndlovu (man in boot), Patrick
Mofokeng (young police officer),
Kenneth Kambule & Rayburn Sengwayo
(Somali poachers), Emma Vaughan

Jones (Sveva aged three), Frances
Slabolepszy (Hannah Maitland), Frances
Nacman (nurse), Nadine Maharaj
(Ema's friend).
US release: 5 May 2000

SOME VOICES
101 minutes
FilmFour / Dragon Pictures
(Great Britain)
Director: Simon Cellan Jones; *Producers:*
Graham Broadbent, Damian Jones;
Screenplay: Joe Penhall (based on his
play); *Director of photography:* David
Odd; *Production design:* Zoe MacLeod;
Editing: Elen Pierce Lewis; *Music:* Adrian
Johnston.
Cast: **Daniel Craig (Ray)**, David
Morrissey (Pete), Kelly Macdonald
(Laura), Julie Graham (Mandy), Peter
McDonald (Dave), Nicholas Palliser
(Ray's friend), Huss Garbiya (man with
mobile), Edward Tudor Pole (lighter
seller), Ashley Walters (kitchen hand),
Gem Durham (cashier), Cate Fowler
(Benefits Agency woman).
UK release: 25 August 2000

HOTEL SPLENDIDE
98 minutes
FilmFour / Renegade Films / Canal+ /
Charles Gassot (Great Britain / France)
Director: Terence Gross; *Executive
producer:* Robert Buckler; *Co-executive
producer:* Charles Gassot; *Producer:* Ildiko
Kemeny; *Associate producers:* Mark Frith,
Amanda McKenzie Stuart; *Screenplay:*
Terence Gross; *Director of photography:*
Gyula Pados; *Production design:* Alison
Dominitz; *Editing:* Michael Ellis; *Music:*

Mark Tschanz.

Cast: Toni Colette (Kath), **Daniel Craig (Ronald Blanche)**, Katrin Cartlidge (Cora Blanche), Stephen Tompkinson (Dezmond Blanche), Hugh O'Conor (Stanley Smith), Helen McCrory (Lorna Bull), Peter Vaughan (Morton Blanche), Joerg Stadler (Sergei Gorgomov), Clare Cathcart (Lorraine Bell), John Boswall (bellboy), Toby Jones (kitchen boy), Dan Hildebrand (waiter), Nadine Leonard (chambermaid), Len Hibberd (fisherman), Imogen Claire (Mrs Blanche).

UK release: 22 September 2000

THE SOUTH BANK SHOW: MARC QUINN

Season 24, Episode 11

65 minutes

London Weekend Television

(Great Britain)

Director/Producer: Susan Shaw; *Film director:* Gerald Fox; *Film creator:* Marc Quinn; *Film music:* Massive Attack.

Cast: **Daniel Craig (the artist)**; Melvyn Bragg (presenter).

UK tx: 17 December 2000

SWORD OF HONOUR

191 minutes (shown in two parts)

Channel 4 / Talkback Productions

(Great Britain)

Director: Bill Anderson; *Executive producers:* John Chapman, Peter Fincham; *Producer:* Gillian McNeill; *Script:* William Boyd (based on the Evelyn Waugh novels *Men at Arms, Officers and Gentlemen* and *Unconditional Surrender*); *Director of photography:* Daf

Hobson; *Production design:* Ben Scott; *Editing:* Joe Walker; *Music:* Nina Humphreys.

Cast: **Daniel Craig (Guy Crouchback)**, Megan Dodds (Virginia Troy), Leslie Phillips (Gervaise Crouchback), Selina Cadell (Angela Crouchback), Edward Petherbridge (Perigrin Crouchback), Simon Williams (Major Sprat), Malcolm Storry (Major Tickeridge), Robert Pugh (Brigadier Ritchie-Hook), Stephen Mangan (Frank de Souza), Richard Coyle (Trimmer McTavish), Julian Rhind-Tutt (Ian Kilbannock), Tom Wisdom (Ivor Claire), Guy Henry (Ludovic), Nicholas Boulton (Bertie), James Weber-Brown (Tom Blackhouse), Geoffrey Streatfield (Eddie), Sean McKenzie (Sergeant Smiley), Abigail Cruttenden (Kerstie Kilbannock), Robert Daws (Major Hound), Katrin Cartlidge (Julia Stitch), Rupert Vansittart (Commander-in-Chief), Will Adamsdale (HOO headquarters officer), Nick Bartlett (Popforce officer), Christopher Benjamin (doctor), Peter Blythe (General Graves), Monica Brady (hotel receptionist), Rony Bridges (party guest), Tim Briggs (Sergeant Glass), Rebecca Cardinale (Italian woman), Simon Chandler (Major Irvine), Josh Cole (Sapper Captain Beech), Graham Crammond (Bellamy's barman), Christoph Dostal & Pier Gardini (blackshirts), Dan Fredenbirgh (radio operator), Adam Godley (Apthorpe), Peter Gunn (Sergeant Tozer), Patrick Hannaway (drill Sergeant), Harry Harrison (squad Sergeant), William Hope (General Clayton), Sidney Kean (Capo blackshirt), Chris Lennard (Dakar

Beach soldier), Joseph Long (Italian priest), Nick Lucas (Halberdier lecturer), Clunie Mackenzie (Mrs Tickeridge), Ivan Marevich (Bakic), Lloyd McGuire (mugging victim), Richard Norton (Australian sergeant), Robert Paterson (Stratton concierge), Serge Soric (Partisan General), Craig Stokes (Destroyer nurse), Mark Wakeling (Halberdier Sergeant), Damian Warren (Australian Sergeant). *UK tx:* 2 and 3 January 2001

LARA CROFT TOMB RAIDER

100 minutes
Lawrence Gordon Productions / Eidos Interactive / British Broadcasting Corporation / Tele-München / Marubeni/Toho-Towa / KFP Produktions (USA / United Germany / Great Britain / Japan)
Director: Simon West; *Executive producers:* Jeremy Heath-Smith, Stuart Baird; *Producers:* Lawrence Gordon, Lloyd Levin, Colin Wilson; *Co-producers:* Chris Kenny, Bobby Klein; *Associate producers:* Michael Levy, Jib Polhemus; *Screenplay:* Patrick Massett, John Zinman; *Story:* Sara B Cooper, Mike Werb, Michael Colleary; *Adaptation:* Simon West; *Director of photography:* Peter Menzies Jr.; *Production design:* Kirk M Petruccelli; *Editing:* Glen Scantlebury, Dallas S Puett, Eric Strand (uncredited), Mark Warner (uncredited) and Stuart Baird (uncredited); *Music:* Graeme Revell.
Cast: Angelina Jolie (Lara Croft), Jon Voight (Lord Richard Croft), Noah Taylor (Bryce), Iain Glen (Manfred Powell), **Daniel Craig (Alex West)**, Christopher Barrie (Hillary), Julian

Rhind-Tutt (Mr Pimms), Richard Johnson (distinguished gentleman), Leslie Phillips (Wilson), Robert Phillips (Assault Team Leader), Rachel Appleton (young Lara), Henry Wyndham (Boothby's auctioneer), David Y Cheung & David K S Tse (head laborers), Ayla Amiral (little Cambodian girl), Ozzie Yue (aged Buddhist monk), Wai-Keat Lau (young Buddhist monk), Stephanie Burns (little Inuit girl), Carl Chase (ancient high priest), Richenda Carey (imperious woman), Sylvano Clarke (UPS guy), Olegar Fedoro (Russian Commander), Anna Maria Everett (Maio) *US release:* 15 June 2001 *UK release:* 6 July 2001

ROAD TO PERDITION

117 minutes
Twentieth Century Fox / DreamWorks / Zanuck Company (USA)
Director: Sam Mendes; *Executive producers:* Joan Bradshaw, Walter F Parkes; *Producers:* Sam Mendes, Dean Zanuck, Richard D Zanuck; *Associate producers:* Tara B Cook, Cherylanne Martin; *Screenplay:* David Self (based on the graphic novel by Max Allan Collins and Richard Piers Rayner); *Director of photography:* Conrad Hall; *Production design:* Dennis Gassner; *Editing:* Jill Bilcock; *Music:* Thomas Newman.
Cast: Tom Hanks (Michael Sullivan), Paul Newman (John Rooney), Jude Law (Harlan Maguire), Jennifer Jason Leigh (Annie Sullivan), Stanley Tucci (Frank Nitti), **Daniel Craig (Connor Rooney)**, Tyler Hoechlin (Michael Sullivan Jr), Liam Aiken (Peter Sullivan), Dylan

Baker (Alexander Rance), Ciarán Hinds (Finn McGovern), Rob Maxey (drugstore owner), Craig Spidle & Ian Barford (Rooney's henchmen), Stephen Dunn, & Paul Turner (Finn McGovern's henchmen), Kathleen Keane, Brendan McKinney, Jackie Moran, Kieran O'Hare & John M Williams (Irish musicians), Nicholas Cade (boy Michael fights), John Sierros, Jon Sattler, Michael Brockman, John Judd, Christian Stolte & Jack Callahan (Rooney's business associates), Maureen Gallagher (Michael's teacher), Kevin Chamberlin (Frank the bouncer), Juanita Wilson (brothel maid), Doug Spinuzza (Calvino), Roderick Peeples & Keith Kupferer (Nitti's henchmen), Lee Roy Rogers (secretary), Kurt Naebig (tenement murderer), Lance Baker (crime scene policeman), Monte (living corpse), Duane Sharp (Father Callaway), Diane Dorsey (Aunt Sarah), Michael Sassone (motel manager), John Sterchi (cop at diner), Robert Jnes (farmer at diner), Lara Phillips (Ruby the waitress), Harry Groener (Mr McDougal), JoBe Cerny, Lawrence MacGowan, Timothy Hendrickson & Marty Higginbotham (bankers), Mina Badie (Betty the waitress), Ed Kross (young bank manager), Heidi Jayne Netzley (prostitute), Phil Ridarelli (hotel manager), Peggy Roder (Farmer Virginia), James Greene (Farmer Bill).
US release: 12 July 2002
UK release: 20 September 2002

COPENHAGEN

90 minutes
British Broadcasting Corporation / Fictionlab (Great Britain)
Director: Howard Davies; *Executive producers:* Simon Curtis, Eamon Fitzpatrick, Karen Robinson Hunte, Mary Mazur, Gordon Ronald; *Producers:* Megan Callaway, Richard Fell; *Script:* Howard Davies (based on the play by Michael Frayn); *Director of photography:* Ian Wilson; *Production design:* Candida Otton; *Editing:* Kevin Lester; *Music:* Dominic Muldowney.
Cast: Francesca Annis (Margrethe Bohr), **Daniel Craig (Werner Heisenberg)**, Stephen Rea (Niels Bohr).
UK tx: 27 September 2002 (BBC Four), 30 August 2003 (BBC2)

OCCASIONAL, STRONG

12 minutes
Rogue Films (Great Britain)
Director: Steve Green; *Executive producers:* Charlie Crompton, David van der Gaag; *Producer:* Colette Forbes; *Screenplay:* Steve Green, Jamie Kelsey; *Director of photography:* Peter Thwaites; *Art Director:* Rebecca Longcraine; *Editing:* Jon Harris; *Costume:* Kay Minter; *Music:* Anna del Ruby, Simon Davidson.
Cast: **Daniel Craig (Jim)**, Wayne Foskett (Jamie), Paul Angelis (Tony), Jonathon Kennedy (Dave), Jay Simpson (Steve), Dave Hill (Edwin), Mandana Jones (Cathy), Martin Griggin (Tom).
UK release: 12 December 2002
[filmed 1999]

SYLVIA

114 minutes

British Broadcasting Corporation / British Film Council / Capitol Films / Ruby Films (Great Britain / USA)

Director: Christine Jeffs; *Executive producers:* Jane Barclay, Sharon Harel, Robert Jones, Tracey Scoffield, David M Thompson; *Producer:* Alison Owen; *Co-producer:* Nerys Thomas; *Associate producer:* Phil Rymer; *Screenplay:* John Brownlow; *Director of photography:* John Toon; *Production design:* Maria Djurkovic; *Editing:* Tariq Anwar; *Music:* Gabriel Yared.

Cast: Gwyneth Paltrow (Sylvia Plath), **Daniel Craig (Ted Hughes)**, Jared Harris (Al Alvarez), Amira Casar (Assia Werill), Andrew Havill (David Werill), Sam Troughton (Tom Hadley-Clarke), Lucy Davenport (Doreen), Antony Strachan (Michael Boddy), Blythe Danner (Aurelia Plath), Michael Gambon (Professor Thomas), David Birkin (Morecambe), Alison Bruce (Elizabeth), Julian Firth (James Michie), Jeremy Fowlds (Mr Robinson), Sarah Guyler (Ted's Cambridge girlfriend), Theresa Healey (third woman at Ted Hughes' lecture), Liddy Holloway (Martha Bergstrom), Robyn Malcolm (first woman at Ted Hughes' lecture), Michael Mears (Charles Langridge), Siobhan Page (young American girl student), Derek Payne (vicar), Sonia Ritter (midwife), Billie Seymour (telegram boy), Katherine Tozer (Myra Norris), Eliza Wade (infant Frieda Hughes), Ben Want & Joel Want (baby Nicholas Hughes), Hannah Watkins (Tom's girlfriend), Tandi Wright (second woman at Ted Hughes' lecture).

US release: 17 October 2003 (limited)
UK release: 30 January 2004

THE MOTHER

112 minutes

BBC Films / Free Range Films / Renaissance Films (Great Britain)

Director: Roger Michell; *Executive producers:* Stephen Evans, Angus Finney, Tracey Scoffield, David M Thompson; *Producer:* Kevin Loader; *Screenplay:* Hanif Kureishi; *Director of photography:* Alwin Kuchler; *Production design:* Mark Tildesley; *Editing:* Nicolas Gaster; *Music:* Jeremy Sams.

Cast: Anne Reid (May), **Daniel Craig (Darren)**, Anna Wilson Jones (Helen), Peter Vaughan (Toots), Cathryn Bradshaw (Paula), Stephen Mackinotsh (Bobby), Oliver Ford Davies (Bruce), Danira Govich (au pair), Harry Michell (Harry), Rosie Michell (Rosie), Izabella Telezynska (Polish cleaner), Carlo Kureishi & Sachin Kureishi (Jack), Simon Mason (man in Tate Gallery), Jonah Coombes (estate agent).

UK release: 14 November 2003
US release: 28 May 2004

TEN MINUTES OLDER: THE CELLO

segment: 'Addicted to the Stars'

10 minutes

Odyssey Films / Matador Pictures / Road Movies Filmproduktion / Atom Films / Diablo Films / Filmforderungsanstalt / Why Not Productions
(United Germany / Great Britain / USA)

Director: Michael Radford; *Producer:* Soledad Gatti-Pascual; *Screenplay:* Michael Radford; *Director of photography:* Pascal Rabaud; *Production design:* Christina Moore; *Editing:* Lucia Zucchetti; *Music:* Jocelyn Pook.

Cast: **Daniel Craig (Cecil Thomas)**, Charles Simon (Martin), Roland Gift (co-pilot), Branka Katic (young woman), Claire Adamson (Hostess), Louis Mahoney (doctor), Daisy Beaumont (nun), Christian Paul Edwards Peck, Fergus Bell, Tim Skiffins, Daniel Oakes, Benjamin Schreiber, Adam Linolt, Elliott Lintott, Matthieu de Braconier & Karine Bedrossian (spacemen), Craig Winchcombe & Michael Radford (additional voice overs).

UK release: 12 December 2003

LAYER CAKE

105 minutes

Columbia Pictures / MARV Films (USA / Great Britain)

Director: Matthew Vaughn; *Executive producer:* Stephen Marks; *Producers:* Adam Bohling, David Reid, Matthew Vaughn; *Screenplay:* J J Connolly (based on his novel); *Director of photography:* Ben Davis; *Production design:* Kave Quinn; *Editing:* Jon Harris; *Music:* Lisa Gerrard, Ilan Eshkeri.

Cast: **Daniel Craig (XXXX)**, Colm Meaney (Gene), Kenneth Cranham (Jimmy Price), George Harris (Morty), Jamie Foreman (Duke), Marcel Iures (Slavo), Michael Gambon (Eddie Temple), Tom Hardy (Clarkie), Tamer Hassan (Terry), Ben Wishaw (Sidney), Burn Gorman (Gazza), Sally Hawkins

(Slasher), Sienna Miller (Tammy), Dexter Fletcher (Cody), Steve John Shepherd (Tiptoes), Brinley Green (Nobby), Francis Magee (Paul the Boatman), Dimitri Andreas (Angelo), Garry Tubbs (Brian), Natalie Lunghi (Charlie), Marvyn Benoit (Kinky), Rab Affleck (Mickey), Paul Orchard (Lucky), Stephen Walters (Shanks), Louis Emerick (Trevor), Darren Healy (Junkie 1), Matt Ryan (Junkie 2), Ivan Kaye (Freddie Hurst), Jason Flemyng (Larry [Crazy]), Ben Brasier (Jerry [Kilburn]), Neil Finnighan (Troop), Budgie Prewitt (golf host), Don McCorkindale (Albert Carter), Dragan Micanovic (Dragan).

UK release: 1 October 2004
US release: 13 May 2005

ENDURING LOVE

100 minutes

FilmFour / Free Range Films / Ingenious Film Partners / Inside Track Films / Pathe Pictures International / Ridgeway Productions / UK Film Council (Great Britain / USA)

Director: Roger Michell; *Executive producers:* Francois Ivernel, Cameron McCracken, Duncan Reid, Tessa Ross; *Producer:* Kevin Loader; *Associate producer:* Ian McEwan; *Screenplay:* Joe Penhall (based on the novel by Ian McEwan); *Director of photography:* Haris Zambarloukos; *Production design:* John-Paul Kelly; *Editing:* Nicolas Gaster; *Music:* Jeremy Sams.

Cast: **Daniel Craig (Joe Rose)**, Samantha Morton (Claire), Rhys Ifans (Jed Parry), Bill Nighy (Robin), Susan

Lynch (Rachel), Helen McCrory (Mrs Logan), Andrew Lincoln (TV producer), Corin Redgrave (Professor), Bill Weston (grandfather), Jeremy McCurdie (boy in balloon), Lee Sheward (John Logan), Nick Wilkinson (farmer), Aoife Carroll & Rory Carroll (Robin & Rachel's twins), Ben Whishaw (Spud), Justin Salinger (Frank), Rosanna Michell (Katie Logan), Ella Doyle (Katie Logan's friend), Félicité du Jeu (girl in Logan's car), Alexandra Aitken (Natasha), Anna Maxwell Martin (Penny), Algy (Logan's dog).

US release: 29 October 2004
UK release: 26 November 2004

SORSTALANSÁG

aka *Fateless*
140 minutes
Magyar Mozgókép Közalapítvány / Magic Media / EuroArts Entertainment / Renegade Films / Magyar Televízío / Mitteldeutscher Rundfunk / Israel Film Council (Hungary / United Germany / Great Britain / Israel)
Director: Lajos Koltai; *Executive producers:* Robert Buckler, Bernd Helthaler, László Vincze; *Producers:* Péter Barbalics, András Hámori, Ildikó Kemény, Jonathan Olsberg; *Screenplay:* Imre Kertész (based on his novel); *Director of photography:* Gyula Pados; *Production design:* Tibor Lázár; *Editing:* Hajnal Sellö; *Music:* Ennio Morricone.
Cast: Marcell Nagy (Gyura Köves), Áron Dimény (Bandi Citrom), András M Kecskés (Finn), József Gyabronka (unlucky man), Endre Harkányi (old Kollman), Béla Dóra (smoker), Bálint Péntek (pretty boy), Dániel Szabó

(Moskovich), Zsolt Dér (Rozi), János Bán (father), Judit Schell (stepmother), Ádám Rajhona (Mr Steiner), György Barkó (Mr Fleischmann), **Daniel Craig (US Army Sergeant)**, György Gazso (Mr Sütö), Sára Herrer (Annamária), Olga Koós (stepmother's mother), Piroska Molnár (Terka), Ildekó Kishonti (Uncle Vili's wife), Miklós Benedek (Uncle Vili), Péter Haumann (Uncle Lajos), László Baranyi (first relative), Vilmos Kun (grandfather), Márta Bakó (grandmother), István Komlós (male relative), Judit Meszléri (second relative), Andrea Szoták (third relative), Kati Lázár (Mrs Fleischmann), Ildikó Tóth (mother), Luca Seres (first girl), Juszti Balassa (second girl), Gáspár Mesés (Annamária's younger brother), József Szarvas (policeman), Jenö Nagy, Bence Behari, Patrick Holzmüller, Jakab Pilaszanovich, Zoltán Tóth, Dániel Lugosi, Péter Bryja, Krisztián Köles, Zsigmond Szilágyi & Lorand Ács (boys at custom house), Gergö Mészáros (cobbler), Gábor Nyiri (Hedge), Zoltán Bukovszky (boy), Ernö Fekete (foreman), István Göz (expert), Mildós B Székely (bitter faced man), Béla Spindler (seal faced man), Krisztián Kolovratnik (First Lieutenant), György Hunyadkürti (man at the window), István Uri (Csarni), György Bösze (Göz), István Mészáros (Zakariás), Géza Balkay (very drunk gendarme), András Szegö (knowledgeable man), Géza Schramek (Boda), Lászlo Joó (elderly man), Zoltán Dózsa (first genderme Sergeant), Áron Öze (second genderme Sergeant), Gábor Ferenczy (first man with armband), András Salamon (third man with armband), Ildikó Molnár (young girl's mother), Antal Cserna (respectable man), Zsolt Kovács (Bocskor), Péter Vallai (negotiating man), Zsolt László (Balogh), Attila Magyar (Gyulai), Péter Vida (Lénárt), András Surányi (second man with armband), Sándor Halmágyi (rabbi), Éva Vándor (delicate looking woman), Adrien Táncos (Erika), Zóltan Varga (Berei), Kriszta Biró (woman at the window), Ferenc Lengyel (geography teacher), József Kelemen (Szabó), Orsolya Tóth (young girl), Tibor Mertz (Fodor), Lajos Kovács (corrupt gendarme), Sándor Zsótér (SS selection officer), Géza Tóth (prisoner), Géza Laczkovich (old man), Zoltán Barabás Kiss (Sergeant), Attila Dolmány (capo), Zoltán Bezerédi (balding man), Péter Fancsikai (older Kollmann boy), Márton Brezina (younger Kollman boy), Mirkó Andrassew, Viktor Csúcs & Máté Papp (Kollmann choir), Péter Göth (pianist), Attila Besztercei (prisoner with armband), Károly Nemcsák (camp elder), Sándor Kömüves (Fazekas), Lajos Kulcsár (block VI elder), Szabolcs Thúróczy (first soldier), István Rimóczi (SS Sergeant), László Mehes (Sándor), József Lukács (Sergeant yelling), Jenö Kiss (SS soldier), Frank-Michael Köbe (second soldier), Péter Szokolay (works manager), Pál Oberfrank (Hungarian Doctor), Gergely Kocsis (nurse, Zeitz Rehmsdorf), Béla Paudits (protesting man), László Kövesdi & Richard Péter (bath attendants), Ciochki Maciej (Pjetkya), Ferenc Horváth (plump Hungarian patient), Gábor Máté (Uncle Miklós), Dávid Szanitter (Captain),

Csaba Gieler (interpreter), Máté Haumann (caught SS soldier), Anita Tóth (woman), Miklós Molnár (interrogating man), Ági Olasz (Bandi Citrom's sister), Mari Csomós (Bandi Citrom's mother), József Jámbor (ticket controller), Andor Lukács (intellectual), Anikó Gruíz (unfamiliar woman). *premiere:* 8 February 2005 (Hungarian Film Festival) *US release:* 6 January 2006 *UK release:* 5 May 2006

THE JACKET

103 minutes
VIP 2 Medienfonds /
VIP 3 Medienfonds / MP Pictures /
Section Eight Productions
(United Germany / USA / Scotland)
Director: John Maybury; *Executive producers:* Ben Cosgrove, Mark Cuban, Jennifer Fox, Andreas Grosch, Ori Marmur, Timothy J Nicholas, Chris Roberts, Peter E Strauss, Todd Wagner; *Producers:* Peter Guber, George Clooney, Steven Soderbergh; *Co-producers:* Marc Frydman, Kia Jans, Donald C McKeon, Philip McKeon, Marc Rocco, Andreas Schmid; *Screenplay:* Massy Tadjedin (based on a story by Tom Bleecker and Marc Rocco); *Director of photography:* Peter Deming; *Production design:* Alan Macdonald; *Editing:* Emma E Hickox; *Music:* Brian Eno.
Cast: Adrien Brody (Jack Starks), Keira Knightley (Jackie Price), Kris Kristofferson (Dr Thomas Becker), Jennifer Jason Leigh (Dr Beth Lorenson), Kelly Lynch (Jean Price), Brad Renfro (the stranger), **Daniel Craig (Rudy**

Mackenzie), Steven Mackintosh (Dr Hopkins), Brendan Coyle (Damon), Mackenzie Phillips (Nurse Harding), Laura Marano (young Jackie), Jason Lewis (Officer Harrison), Richard Dillane (Captain Medley), Jonah Lotan (first intern), Angel Coulby (second intern), Paul Birchard (doctor), Nigel Whitmey (Lieutenant), Ian Porter (Major), Antony Edridge (Dr Morgan), Kerry Shale (Prosecutor), Angus MacInnes (Judge), Richard Durden (Dr Hale), Tristan Gemmill (Officer Nash), Colin Stinton (jury foreman), Tara Summers (Nurse Nina), Angelo Andreou (Babak, Iraqi boy), Teresa Gallagher (Nurse Sally), Anne Kidd (state representative) Charneh Demir (Jamile, Iraqi mother), Francis Brady-Stewart (woman with dog), Lolly Susi (nurse), Garrick Hagon (defence lawyer), Fish (Jimmy Fleisher).

US release: 4 March 2005
UK release: 13 May 2005

ARCHANGEL

130 minutes (shown in two parts)
BBC Drama Group / Powercorp / Baltic Film Services (Great Britain)
Director: Jon Jones; *Executive producers:* Justin Bodle, Laura Mackie, Jessica Pope; *Producer:* Christopher Hall; *Script:* Dick Clement, Ian La Frenais (based on the novel by Robert Harris); *Director of photography:* Chris Seager; *Production design:* Michael Pickwoad; *Editing:* Sue Wyatt; *Music:* Rob Lane.
Cast: **Daniel Craig (Fluke Kelso)**, Ekaterina Rednikova (Zinaida), Gabriel Macht (R J O'Brian), Konstantin Lavronenko (Josef), Lev Prygunov (Mamantov), Alexey Diakov (Suvorin), Harry Ditson (Adelman), Tanya Moodie (Velma), Avtandil Makharadze (Stalin), Ludmilla Golubeva (Vavara), Igors Filipovs (Major Kretov), Anna Gerasimova (Anna), Juris Strenga (Tsarev), Claudia Harrison (Louise), Kaspars Zvigulis (young Papu), Valery Chernyak (old Papu), Aurelija Anuzhite (Olga), Igor Chernawsky (Yakov), Ervand Arzumanyan (Beria), Romualds Ancans (Arsenyev), Alexey Khardikov (Lev), Aris Rozentals (Gregor), Kristine Brize (young Zinaida), Ksenja Entelis (Yelena), Dmitrijs Palejes (Bunin), Rezija Kalnina (Valeshka), Imbi Strenga (Madame Mamantov).
UK tx: 19 and 20 March 2005

MUNICH

164 minutes
DreamWorks / Universal Studios / Amblin Entertainment / Kennedy-Marshall Company / Barry Mendel Productions / Alliance Atlantis Communications (USA / Canada)
Director: Steven Spielberg; *Producers:* Kathleen Kennedy, Barry Mendel, Steven Spielberg, Colin Wilson; *Screenplay:* Tony Kushner, Eric Roth (based on the book *Vengeance: The True Story of an Israeli Counter-Terrorist Team*, by George Jonas); *Director of photography:* Janusz Kaminski; *Production design:* Rick Carter; *Editing:* Michael Kahn; *Music:* John Williams.
Cast: Eric Bana (Avner), **Daniel Craig (Steve)**, Geoffrey Rush (Ephraim),

Mathieu Kassovitz (Robert), Hanns Zischler (Hans), Ciaran Hinds (Carl), Ayelet Zurer (Daphna), Gila Almagor (Avner's mother), Michael Lonsdale (Papa), Mathieu Amalric (Louis), Moritz Bleibtreu (Andreas), Valeria Bruni-Tedeschi (Sylvie), Meret Becker (Yvonne), Marie-Josée Croze (Jeanette), Yvan Attal (Tony, Andreas' friend), Ami Weinberg (General Zamir), Lynn Cohen (Golda Meir), Amos Lavie (General Yariv), Moshe Ivgy (Mike Harari), Michael Warshaviak (Attorney General Meir Shamgar), Ohad Shachar & Rafael Tabor (ministers), Sharon Cohen Alexander (General Nadev), Schmuel Calderon (General Hofi), Oded Teomi (Mossad accountant), Alon Abutul (Israeli soldier with Zamir), Makram Khoury (Wael Zwaiter), Igal Naor (Mahmoud Hamshari), Hiam Abbass (Marie Claude Hamshari), Mouna Soualmen (Amina Hamshari), Mostéfa Djadjam (Houssein Abad Al-Chir), Assi Cohen (newly-wed man), Lisa Werlinder (newley-wed bride), Djemal Barek (Zaid Muchassi), Derar Suleiman (Abu Youssef), Ziad Adwan (Kemel Adwan), Bijan Daneshmand (Kamal Nasser), Rim Turki (Adwan's wife), Jonathan Rozen (Ehud Barak), Charley H Gilleran, Jonathan Uziel, Guy Zu-Aretz, Yossi Sagie, Liron Levo & Ohad Knoller (commandos), Lyés Salem, Carim Messalti, Hichem Yacoubi & Omar Mostafa (Arab guards), Mahmoud Zemouri (older Lebanese man), Souad Amidou (Yussef's wife), Amrou Alkadhi (Yussef's son), Omar Metwally (Ali), Nasser Memarzia (older Palestinian),

Abdelhafid Metalsi (Palestinian in 30s), Karin Qayouh (young Palestinian), Mihalis Giannatos (Hotel Aristides porter), Faruk Pruti & Rad Lazar (KGB liaisons), Laurence Février (Papa's wife), Habir Yahya (girl with Papa), Mehdi Nebbou (Ali Hassan Salameh), Hicham Nazzal, Lemir Guerfa & Hisham Silman (Salameh guards), Brian Goodman, Richard Brake & Robert John Burke (belligerent Americans), Yehuda Levi & Danny Zahavi (Tel Aviv airport soldiers), Itay Barnea (Israeli deputy consul NY), Elyse Klaits (consulate secretary), Nabil Yajjou (young Tarifa guard), Karim Saleh (Issa), Merik Tadros (Tony 'The Cowboy'), Mousa Kraish (Mohammed Safed, 'Badran'), Karim Saidi (Adnan Al-Gashey, 'Kader'), Mohammed Khouas (Jamal Al-Gashey, 'Samir'), David Ali Hamade (Paulo), Ben Youcef (Saleh), Sami Samir (Abu Halla), Guri Weinberg (Moshe Weinberg), Sam Feuer (Yossef Romano), Sabi Dorr (Yossef Gutfreund), Wojciech Machinicki (Tuvia Sokolovsky), David Feldman (Kehat Shorr), Ori Pfeffer (Andre Spitzer), Shmuel Edleman (Jacov Springer), Joseph Sokolsky (Amitzir Shapira), Lior Perel (David Berger), Ossie Beck (Eliezer Halfin), Guy Amir (Mark Slavin), Haguy Wigdor (Zeev Friedman), Roei Avigdori (Gad Tsabari), Kevin Collins & Daniel Bess (American athletes), Baya Belal & Ula Tabari (Palestinian women watching TV), Saïda Bekkouche & Fettouma Bouamari (Aida refugee camp women), Alexander Beyer (German reporter in Munich underground), Amos Shoub, Geoffrey Dowell & Rana Werbin (Israeli news anchors), Jane Garda (Italian girl in car), Félicité du Jeu (young Swiss bank official), Gil Soriano (man in Haifa bar), Mordechai Ben Shachar (older man in Haifa bar), Amina Al-Aidroos & Leda Mansour (Palestinian teachers), Sasha Spielberg (young Israeli woman watching TV), Renana Raz & Hagit Dasberg-Shamul (Israeli women watching TV), Patrick Kennedy, Stéphane Freiss, Arturo Arribas, Yaron Josef Motolla & Jalil Naciri (foreign reporters in Munich underground), Martin Antroub & Joram Voelklein (camera crew at Munich), Michael Schenk (photographer at Munich), Andreas Lust & Tom Wlaschiha (news crew at Furstenfeldbrook).

US release: 23 December 2005 (limited), 6 January 2006 (general)
UK release: 27 January 2006

RENAISSANCE

105 minutes
Onyx Films / Millimages / Luxanimation / Timefirm / France 2 Cinéma
(France / Luxembourg / Great Britain)
Director: Christian Volckman; *Executive producers:* Jake Eberts, Lilian Eche, Ilann Girard, Louise Goodsill, Ralph Kamp, Ariane Payen; *Producers:* Roch Lener, Aton Soumache, Alexis Vonarb; *Co-producer:* Timothy Burrill; *Screenplay:* Alexandre de La Patelliere, Mathieu Delaporte; *Adaptation:* Jean-Bernard Pouy, Patrick Raynal; *Art direction:* Pascal Valdes; *Editing:* Pascal Tosi; *Music:* Nicholas Dodd.
Voice cast (English-language version):

Daniel Craig (Barthélémy Karas), Catherine McCormack (Brislane Tasuiev), Romola Garai (Ilona Tasuiev), Ian Holm (Dr Jonas Muller), Kevork Malikyan (Nusrat Farfella), Jonathan Pryce (Paul Dellenbach), Rick Warden (Amiel), Nina Sosanya (Reparaz), Lachele Carl (Nora), Sean Pertwee (Montoya), Sean Barrett (Naghib), Breffini McKenna (Dimitri), Christopher Parkinson (Karas boy), Pax Baldwin (Farfella boy), Wayne Forester (administrator), Julia Brahms (Avalon woman).
UK release: 28 July 2006
US release: 22 September 2006 (limited)

INFAMOUS

110 minutes
Warner Bros Entertainment / Killer Films-John Wells Productions / Jack and Henry Productions / Longfellow Pictures (USA)
Director/screenplay: Douglas McGrath (based on George Plimpton's book, *Truman Capote: In Which Various Friends, Enemies, Acquaintances and Detractors Recall His Turbulent Career*); *Executive producer:* John Wells; *Producers:* Jocelyn Hayes, Christine Vachon, Anne Walker-McBay; *Associate producers:* Charles Pugliese, Audrey Rosenberg; *Director of photography:* Bruno Delbonnel; *Production design:* Judy Becker; *Editing:* Camilla Toniolo; *Music:* Rachel Portman.
Cast: Toby Jones (Truman Capote), Sandra Bullock (Nelle Harper Lee), **Daniel Craig (Perry Smith)**, Peter Bogdanovich (Bennett Cerf), Jeff Daniels (Alvin Dewey), Hope Davis (Slim

Keith), Gwyneth Paltrow (Kitty Dean), Isabella Rossellini (Marella Agnelli), Juliet Stevenson (Diana Vreeland), Sigourney Weaver (Babe Paley), John Benjamin Hickey (Jack Dunphy), Lee Pace (Dick Hickcock), Mark Rubin, Steve Schwelling, Glover Johns Gill, Rey Arteaga, Justin Sherburn & Andrew Halbreich (El Morocco band), Michael Panes (Gore Vidal), Frank G Curcio (William Shawn), Terry Bennett (DA's secretary), Mitch Baker (first reporter), Grant James (second reporter), Sheila Bailey-Lucas (waitress), Richard Dillard (man on street), Glover Bennett Jamison (desk clerk), Marco Perella (Clifford Hope), Libby Villari (Delores Hope), Joey Basham (Paul Dewey), Marian Aleta Jones (Ellen Bechner), Terri Zee (Nancy Hickey), Richard Jones (Andy Erhart), Brian Shoop (Everett Ogburn), Brady Coleman (first prisoner), Turk Pipkin (second prisoner), Ray Gestaut (Lee Andews), Joe Cordi (piano player), Lee Ritchey (Bill Paley), Brett Brock (Tex Smith), Leticia Trejo (Flo Smith), Brady Hender (young Perry), Zachery Burnett (young Truman), Brent McCoy (Herb Clutter), Gail Cronauer (Bonnie Clutter), Austin Chittim (Kenyon Clutter), Morgan Farris (Nancy Clutter), Dennis Letts (Judge Tate), Gabriel Folse (foreman), Charles Mooneyhan (first prison guard), J.D. Young (second prison guard), Steve Flanagin (chaplain), Michael Conway (Doctor).

US release: 13 October 2006 (limited)
UK release: 19 January 2007

CASINO ROYALE

144 minutes
Danjaq / United Artists /
Columbia Pictures / Eon Productions /
Stillking Productions /
Casino Royale Productions /
Casino Royale US / Babelsberg Film
(Great Britain / USA / Czech Republic /
United Germany)
Director: Martin Campbell; *Executive producers:* Anthony Waye, Callum McDougall; *Producers:* Michael G Wilson, Barbara Broccoli; *Co-producers:* David Minkowski, Matthew Stillman; *Associate producer:* Andrew Noakes; *Assistant producer:* David G Wilson; *Screenplay:* Neal Purvis, Robert Wade, Paul Haggis (based on the novel by Ian Fleming); *Director of photography:* Phil Méheux; *Production design:* Peter Lamont; *Editing:* Stuart Baird; *Music:* David Arnold.

Cast: **Daniel Craig (James Bond)**, Eva Green (Vesper Lynd), Mads Mikkelsen (Le Chiffre), Judi Dench (M), Jeffrey Wright (Felix Leiter), Giancarlo Giannini (Rene Mathis), Caterina Murino (Solange), Simon Abkarian (Alex Dimitrios), Isaach De Bankole (Steven Obanno), Jesper Christensen (Mr White), Ivana Milicevic (Valenka), Tobias Menzies (Villiers), Claudio Santamaria (Carlos), Sébastien Foucan (Mollaka), Malcolm Sinclair (Dryden), Richard Sammel (Gettler), Ludger Pistor (Mendel), Joseph Millson (Carter), David Shah (Fisher), Clemens Shick (Kratt), Emmanuel Avena (Leo), Tom Chadbon (stockbroker), Ade (Infante), Urbano Barberini (Tomelli), Tsai Chin

(Madame Wu), Charlie Levi Leroy (Gallardo), Lazar Ristovski (Kaminofsky), Tom So (Fukutu), Veruschka (Gräfin von Wallenstein), Daniel Andreas (dealer), Carlos Leal (tournament director), Christina Cole (Ocean Club receptionist), Jürgen Tarrach (Schultz), John Gold, Jerry Inzerillo, Diane Hartford (Ocean Club card players), Jessica Miller (Ocean Club dealer), Leos Stránsky (tall man), Paul Battacharjee & Crispin Bonham-Carter (hot room doctors), Simon Cox & Rebecca Gethings (hot room technicians), Peter Notley (MI6 technician), John Chancer (police Commander), Peter Brooke & Jason Durran (airport policemen), Robert Jezek (arresting officer), Robert G Slade (pilot), Félicité du Jeu (French news reporter), Michaela Ochotska (shop assistant), Michael Offei (Obanno's Lieutenant), Makhoudia Diaw (Obanno's liaison), Michael G Wilson (Chief of Police), Martina Duralová & Marcela Martincáková (Police Chief's girlfriends), Vladimír Kulhavy (Croatian General), Valentine Nonyela (Nambutu Embassy official), Dusan Pelech (bartender), Phil Méheux (Treasury bureaucrat), Alessandra Ambrosio & Veronika Hladíková (tennis girls), Regina Gabajová (Hotel Splendide clerk), Olutunji Ebun-Cole (Cola kid), Martin Ucík (barman), Vlasta Svátková (waitress), Miroslav Simünek (disapproving man), Ivan G'Vera (Venice hotel concierge), Jiri Lenc (Hotel Splendide limo driver), Jaroslav Jankovsky (Hermitage waiter).
UK premiere: 14 November 2006
UK release: 16 November 2006

US release: 17 November 2006

THE CATHERINE TATE COMIC RELIEF SPECIAL

34 minutes
British Broadcasting Company / Tiger Aspect / Comic Relief (Great Britain)
Director: Gordon Anderson; *Producer:* Sophie-Clarke-Jervoise; *Script:* Catherine Tate, Aschlin Ditta, Gordon Henderson, Jonathan Harvey; *Directors of photography:* Pete Rowe, John Sorapure; *Production design:* Jo Sutherland; *Editing:* Chris Wadsworth; *Music:* Howard Goodall.

Cast: Catherine Tate (Lauren Cooper / Geordie Georgie / Elaine Figgis / Joannie 'Nan' Taylor), Aschlin Ditta (Alan), Richard Lumsden (Martin), Geraldine McNulty (Prime Minister's aide), Niky Wardley (Liese Jackson / Susan), **Daniel Craig (himself)**; Noel Edmonds (himself); Lenny Henry (himself); The Right Honourable Tony Blair, Prime Minister (himself); David Tennant (Lauren's new English teacher).
UK tx: 16 March 2007

THE INVASION

93 minutes
Oliver Pictures Incorporated / Village Roadshow Pictures / Vertigo Entertainment / Silver Pictures / Warner Bros Pictures (USA)
Directors: Oliver Hirschbiegel, James McTeigue (reshoots); *Executive producers:* Bruce Berman, Doug Davison, Susan Downey, Roy Lee, Steve Richards, Ronald G Smith; *Producer:* Joel Silver; *Associate*

producer: David Gambino; *Screenplay:* Dave Kajganich (based on the novel *The Body Snatchers* by Jack Finney); *Additional material:* Andy Wachowski, Larry Wachowski; *Director of photography:* Rainer Klausmann; *Production design:* Jack Fisk; *Editing:* Hans Funck, Joel Negron; *Music:* John Ottman.

Cast: Nicole Kidman (Carol Bennell), **Daniel Craig (Ben Driscoll)**, Jeremy Northam (Tucker Kaufman), Jackson Bond (Oliver Bennell), Jeffrey Wright (Dr Stephen Galeano), Veronica Cartwright (Wendy Lenk), Josef Sommer (Dr Henryk Belicec), Celia Weston (Ludmilla Belicec), Roger Rees (Yorish), Eric Benjamin (Gene), Susan Floyd (Pam), Stephanie Berry (Carly), Alexis Raben (Danila, Belicec's aide), Adam LeFevre (Richard Lenk), Joanna Merlin (Joan Kaufman), Field Blauvelt (census taker), Rhonda Overby (Dina Twain), Reid Sasser (NASA official), Brandon Price (John), Mia Arnice Chambers (Jan), Ava Lenet (Mrs Cunningham), Michael Andrew Kelly (dog owner), Jeremiah Hake (Andy), Luray Cooper (cop in tunnel), Nanna Ingvarsson (panicked woman in tunnel), Jeff Wincott (transit cop), Wes Johnson (news stand vendor), Parker Webb (man in rags), Cloie Wyatt Taylor (sobbing teen), John Colton (field reporter), John Leslie Wolfe (Tucker's colleague), Michael Stone Forrest (butler), Tim Scanlin (subway guy), Tara Garwood (subway girl), Genevieve Adell (sleep deprived driver), Derren Fuentest (helpful cop), Darla Mason Robinson (crying woman), Brian Augustus Parnell (street cop), Benjamin Bullard (boy in train station), Jean Miller (transition nurse), Jean Schertler (elderly lady), James Bouchet (security guard), Becky Woodley (Mrs Robinson).

US release: 17 August 2007
UK release: 12 October 2007

THE GOLDEN COMPASS

113 minutes
New Line Cinema /
Scholastic Productions / Depth of Field
/ Rhythm and Hues
(USA / Great Britain)

Director: Chris Weitz; *Executive producers:* Toby Emmerich, Michael Lynne, Ileen Maisel, Andrew Miano, Mark Ordesky, Bob Shaye, Paul Weitz; *Producers:* Bill Carraro, Deborah Forte; *Co-producer:* Bill Nikolas Korda; *Screenplay:* Chris Weitz (based on the novel *Northern Lights*, by Philip Pullman); *Director of photography:* Henry Braham; *Production design:* Dennis Gassner; *Editing:* Anne V Coates, Peter Honess, Kevin Tent; *Music:* Alexandre Desplat.

Cast: Nicole Kidman (Marisa Coulter), **Daniel Craig (Lord Asriel)**, Dakota Blue Richards (Lyra Belacqua), Roger (Ben Walker), Freddie Highmore (voice of Pantalaimon), Ian McKellan (voice of Iorek Byrnison), Eva Green (Serafina Pekkala), Jim Carter (Lord John Faa), Tom Courtenay (Farder Coram), Ian McShane (voice of Ragnar Sturlusson), Sam Elliott (Lee Scoresby), Christopher Lee (First High Councillor), Kristin Scott-Thomas (voice of Stelmaria), Edward de Souza (Second High Councillor), Kathy Bates (voice of

Hester), Simon McBurney (Fra Pavel), Jack Shepherd (Master), Magda Szubanski (Mrs Lonsdale), Derek Jacobi (Magisterial Emissary), Claire Higgins (Ma Costa), Charlie Rowe (Billy Costa), Steven Loton (Tony Costa), Michael Antoniou (Kerim Costa), Mark Mottram (Jaxer Costa), Paul Antony-Barber (Bolvangar Doctor), Jason Watkins (Bolvangar Official), Hattie Morahan (Sister Clara), John Bett (Thorold), John Franklyn-Robbins (librarian), Jonathan Laury (younger fellow), Tommy Luther (Jacob Huismans/Daemon puppeteer), James Rawlings (passing scholar), Joao de Sousa (Hunt), Habib Nasiib Nader (Ragnar), Theo Fraser Steele (Magisterial Officer), Bill Hurst (Police Captain), Elliot Cowan (Commanding Officer), Sam Hoare (Second-in-Command), Thomas Arnold, David Garrick, Brian Nickels & Gary Kane (Gobblers), Alfred Harmsworth (Gyptian kid), Charles Evanson, Patrick Cleary, Tarek Khalil, Madrios Ohannessian & Sandra Wolfe (Gyptian Chiefs), Hewson Osbourne, Albert Kendrick, John Cartier & Chris Abbott (fellows), Alex Terentyev (Tartar Officer), David Forman (Samoyed kidnapper).

UK premiere: 27 November 2007
UK release: 5 December 2007
US release: 7 December 2007

FLASHBACKS OF A FOOL

113 minutes
Left Turn Films /
Sherazade Film Development /
Ugly Duckling Films (Great Britain)
Director: Baillie Walsh; *Executive*
producers: Steffen Aumueller, Brian Avery, Susanne Bohnet, **Daniel Craig**, Sean Ellis, Marina Grasic, Jan Körbelin, Norman Merry, Glenn M. Stewart; *Producers:* Lene Bausager, Damon Bryant, Claus Clausen, Genevieve Hofmeyr; *Associate producer:* Winnie Li; *Screenplay:* Baillie Walsh; *Director of photography:* John Mathieson; *Production design:* Laurence Dorman; *Editing:* Struan Clay; *Music:* Richard Hartley.

Cast: **Daniel Craig (Joe Scot)**, Harry Eden (young Joe Scot), Eve (Ophelia Franklin), Miriam Karlin (Mrs Rogers), Jodhi May (Evelyn Adams), Helen McCrory (Peggy Tickell), Olivia Williams (Grace Scott), Felicity Jones (young Ruth Davies), Keeley Hawes (Jesse Scot), Sid Mitchell (Chillo), Alfie Allen (Kevin Hubble), Claire Forlani (Ruth Davies), Mark Strong (Mannie Miesel), James D'Arcy (Jack Adams), Annabel Linder (Dawn), Max Deacon (Boots McKay), Angie Ruiz (Priscilla), Emilia Fox (Sister Jean), Gina Athans (Apple), Julie Ordon (Carrie Ann), Erich Conrad (DJ), Sue Dall (maitre d'), Alwyn Kotze (Ritchie Smith), Pope Jerrod (waiter), Darron Meyer (valet), Mia Clifford (young Jesse Scot), Jodie Tomlinson (Jane Adams), Dexter Bryant (Diesel), Max Robson (Max), Jade Bryant (teenage girl).

UK premiere: 13 April 2008
UK release: 18 April 2008

QUANTUM OF SOLACE

106 minutes
Danjaq / Eon Productions / MGM /
Sony Columbia / United Artists

(Great Britain / USA)

Director: Marc Forster; *Executive producers:* Anthony Waye, Callum McDougall; *Producers:* Michael G. Wilson, Barbara Broccoli; *Screenplay:* Joshua Zetuma, Paul Haggis, Neal Purvis, Robert Wade; *Director of photography:* Roberto Schaefer; *Production design:* Dennis Gassner; *Editing:* Matt Chesse, Richard Pearson; *Music:* David Arnold.

Cast: **Daniel Craig (James Bond)**, Mathieu Amalric (Dominic Greene), Olga Kurylenko (Camille), Gemma Arterton (Agent Fields), Judi Dench (M), Jeffrey Wright (Felix Leiter), Anatole Taubman (Elvis), Giancarlo Giannini (Rene Mathis), Joachin Cosio (General Medrano), Jesper Christensen (Mr White), Rory Kinnear (Bill Tanner), Tim Piggott-Smith (British Foreign Secretary), Glenn Foster (Henry Mitchell), David Harbour (Gregg Beam), Fernando Guillén Cuervo (Bolivian Chief of Police), Jesús Ochoa (Lieutenant Orso), Neil Jackson (Mr Slate), Simon Kassianides (Yusef), Stana Katic (Corinne Veneau), Rachel McDowall (Anna), Tracy Redington (MI6 agent), Raffaello Degruttola (Alfa driver), Laurence Richardson (police officer), Kiera Chaplin (receptionist).
UK premiere: 29 October 2008
UK release: 31 October 2008
US release: 14 November 2008

DEFIANCE

120 minutes
Grosvenor Park Productions /
The Bedford Falls Company (USA)
Director/Producer: Edward Zwick;

Producer: Pieter Jan Brugge; *Co-producer:* Roland Tec; *Associate producer:* Troy Putney; *Screenplay:* Edward Zwick, Clay Frohman (from the book by Nechama Tec); *Director of photography:* Eduardo Serra; *Production design:* Dan Weil; *Editing:* Steven Rosenblum; *Music:* James Newton Howard.

Cast: **Daniel Craig (Tuvia Bielski)**, Liev Schreiber (Zus Bielski), Jamie Bell (Asael Bielski), George MacKay (Aron Bielski), Mia Wasikowska (Chaya), Alexa Davalos (Lilka), Jodhi May (Tamara Skedeksky), Mark Margolis (the Ghetto Elder), Mark Feuerstein (Malbin), Tomas Arana (Ben Zion), Iddo Goldbierg (Yitzchak Shulman), Jacek Koman (Koscik), Allan Corduner (Shamon), Sam Spruell (Arkady Lubezanski), Markus von Lingen (SS scout), Sakals Uzdavinys (Lova), Rolandas Boravskis (Gramov).
US release: 12 December 2008
UK release: 9 January 2009

I, LUCIFER

Bright Angel / Design Concepts /
Lucifer Rising / Shooting Stars
(Great Britain)
Director: Dan Harris; *Executive producer:* John Evangelides; *Co-executive producer:* David Logan; *Producers:* Michael Dougherty, Paige Simpson, Clark Westerman; *Screenplay:* Dan Harris, Michael Dougherty (based on the novel by Glen Duncan); *Adaptation:* David Logan.

Cast: **Daniel Craig (Lucifer)**, Ewan McGregor (Declan Gunn), Stephen Samson (Advocate).
2009

BIBLIOGRAPHY

Adams, Guy. 'A hunk in trunks: The image that was the making of a new Bond'.
  The Independent 18 November 2006.
Braun, Liz. 'Infamous kind of Bond-ing'. *Toronto Sun* October 13, 2006.
Clarke, Gerald. *Capote. A Biography.* Cardinal (London) 1989.
Donnelly, Claire and Webster, Nick. 'Exclusive: Potatohead Wasn't Cool'.
  The Mirror 15 October 2005.
Feeney Callan, Michael. *Sean Connery: His Life and Films.* W H Allen (London) 1982.
Hoggard, Liz. 'Agent provocateur'. *The Observer* December 31 2006.
Hoggard, Liz. 'Better safe than sorry'. *The Observer* July 31 2005.
Jeffries, Stuart. 'Seven's deadly sins'. *The Guardian* November 17 2006.
Kirkland, Bruce. 'Sienna Miller's one tough cookie'. *Toronto Sun* December 18, 2005.
Lawrence, Will. 'This is a Serious Gangster Movie'. *Empire* October 2004.
Lister, David. 'Daniel Craig should try a bit of method acting.'
  The Independent 11 March 2006.
Morris, Mark. 'Declaration of Waugh'. *The Guardian* January 2 2001.
Morris, Mark. 'Everyone's talking about ... Daniel Craig,
  Brit-hot co-star of Tomb Raider'. *The Observer* June 3 2001.
Murphy, Robert (ed). *Directors in British and Irish Cinema. A Reference Companion.*
  British Film Institute (London) 2006.
Parsons, Tony. 'View to a Will'. *The Mirror* 17 October 2005.
Pym, John (ed). *Time Out Film Guide 2006.* Penguin (London) 2005.
Rampton, James. 'History in the making'. *The Independent* 9 March 2005.
Rose, Steve. 'Gang related'. *The Guardian* September 14 2002.
Sweet, Matthew. 'Daniel Craig – Reluctant Star'.
  Independent on Sunday 22 September 2002.
Tucker, Ian. 'Box-office romance'. *The Observer* November 2 2003.
Wood, Gaby. 'Rhymes of Passion'. *The Observer* April 27 2003.
Yates, Charles. 'The Brit boy Dan good'. *The Sun* July 2002.

INTERNET

British Broadcasting Corporation *(www.bbc.co.uk)*
British Film Institute *(www.bfi.org.uk)*
FilmExposed Magazine *(www.filmexposed.com)*
The Internet Movie Database *(uk.imdb.com)*
Mirror.co.uk *(www.mirror.co.uk)*
The Cinema Source *(www.thecinemasource.com)*
Tiscali UK *(www.tiscali.co.uk)*
UnderGroundOnline *(www.ugo.com)*

PICTURE CREDITS

All film publicity pictures are copyright their respective distributors (see 'Television and Film Credits'). Other photos copyright as follows:

COVER
Front: Theo Kingma/Rex Features

COLOUR SECTION 1
PAGE 1: Rex Features; PAGE 2 & 3A: ITV/Rex Features; PAGE 3B: Dreamworks/Everett Collection/Rex Features; PAGE 4B: Focus/Everett Collection/Rex Features; PAGE 5A: Everett Collection/Rex Features; PAGES 6, 8: Sony Pictures/Everett Collection/Rex Features; PAGE 7: Paramount/Everett Collection/Rex Features.

COLOUR SECTION 2
PAGE 1: Rex Features; PAGE 2A: Thinkfilm/Everett Collection/Rex Features; PAGE 3A: Universal/Everett Collection/Rex Features; PAGE 5B: Buena Vista/Everett Collection/Rex Reatures; PAGE 6A: Paramount/Everett Collection/Rex Features; PAGE 6B & 7: MGM/Everett Collection/Rex Features.

ACKNOWLEDGMENTS

My thanks to Helen Coleman, Marcus Hearn, John Horne,
Ingrid von Hunnius, Gary Kramer, Mark Lonsdale, David O'Leary
and Richard Reynolds.